The Bad Infinity

PAJ Books

Bonnie Marranca and Gautam Dasgupta,
Series Editors

The Bad Infinity

EIGHT PLAYS BY MAC WELLMAN

The Johns Hopkins University Press
Baltimore and London

©1994 The Johns Hopkins University Press
All rights reserved
Printed in the United States of America on acid-free paper

The Johns Hopkins University Press
2715 North Charles Street
Baltimore, Maryland 21218–4319
The Johns Hopkins Press Ltd., London

Library of Congress Cataloging-in-Publication Data
Wellman, Mac.
    The bad infinity / by Mac Wellman.
        p.   cm.—(PAJ books)
    ISBN 0-8018-4687-0.— ISBN 0-8018-4688-9 (pbk.)
    I. Title.   II. Series.
PS3573.E46883   1994
812'.54—dc20   93-1911

A catalog record for this book is available from the British Library.

Page 278 constitutes a continuation of the copyright page.

Frontispiece: From a 1985 production of *The Bad Infinity* by the Brass Tacks Theatre of Minneapolis. The actors are Anne Devitt (*left*) and Karen Esbjornson (*right*).

Contents

Poisonous Tomatoes

A STATEMENT ON LOGIC AND THE THEATER

The logic of the world and the logic of the theater are the same, but the relation of these is not so simple, it seems to me. Things can happen on stage that do not happen in the "real" world and vice versa. But the logic of events vis-à-vis other events on stage is the same as that of the ordinary reality we inhabit. What is called drama is only the embodiment in gesture and language of this logic, this worldliness.

Why, you might ask, is the relation between these two logics a complex one? Kierkegaard said that a direct relation to the deity was the definition of paganism, and he meant by this that the attempt to grasp and seize divinity by the appropriation of a human definition was to create an idol, an unreal apparition that possessed no truth. If we take the world we know as an act of collective imagining, an idol of the modern mind, it becomes apparent that reality as such becomes subject to the same—or a similar—danger: decay of the perceptual process, enactment of an unreal idol reality. The banishment of the real world. In other terms, the thing itself is replaced by successive (repetitive) images of the thing.

In American theater this idolatry bears the name of naturalism. Its origin is the same as that of the paganism Kierkegaard wrote of: the desire to subsume all human experience under labels, definitions, and explanations and therefore to substitute rationalizations for experience.

The logic of *The Bad Infinity* is an attempt to suggest the logic of this decayed act of collective imagining. It is not *interesting* at this point in human time to portray the real world as it seems to be in its own terms; but it is interesting to unfold, in human terms, the logic of its illogic and so get at the nut of our contemporary human experience.

I am a pessimist, but a cheerful one. I believe, along with Beckett and Handke and Witkiewicz, that the depth is on the surface. The inside is on the outside. But we are not less human because our hopes and dreams and wishes are the stuff of advertising slogans and images; that would be to succumb to the repetitions—to the idols of ourselves. No, it is simply that our relation to the drama of our lives has become more complex, reflexive, recondite even. It matters who is behind the reassuring voice, the fine gesture, the eloquent phrase about freedom, liberty, and equality. Villains no longer look like villains (did they ever?), nor perhaps do heroes and heroines.

We live in a low and contemptible time, a time when ideals are mocked and scorned, when the merely human is expendable, when those in position of official trust have put aside any pretense to disinterestedness and practice openly the grossest kind of self-aggrandizement. Theater, as a minor province of journalism—and that is what the current theater establishment amounts to in my opinion—has accommodated itself to this state of affairs with nary a blush. I do not believe I can change the world much by writing plays, but I can provide a critique of reality—this collective act of imagining.

We need a dozen Mark Twains, a score of Bierces, a hundred Menckens to do justice to the times. Those of us involved in this critique of apparent reality cannot expect to convince many, much less can we expect our views to prevail (the time may be past for all that); all we can expect is to have some fun, share some laughter, and go out with a modicum of self-respect. We must love the truth not because it favors us but because it is the truth.

This statement was presented at the discussion "The Logic of the Stage," organized in conjunction with a production of *The Bad Infinity* by the Brass Tacks Theatre of Minneapolis in May 1985.

The Bad Infinity

Harm's Way   (1978)

CHARACTERS *(in order of appearance)*

    MOTHER
    CHILD
    FISHEYE
    SANTOUCHE
    ISLE OF MERCY
    BY WAY OF BEING HIDDEN
    CHORUS
    CROW'S-FOOT
    CROW'S-FOOT'S HELPER
    POP STAR
    A MAN
    COOK
    BLACKMANGE
    WIZARD

The CHORUS consists of three musicians, men or women, dressed like the rest. They are seated in low chairs on a small platform off to the right. This platform is not part of the scenery and should remain *as is* throughout the entire play. The instrumental ensemble should consist of a fiddle, a drum, and a flute or trumpet. Aside from providing incidental music for the play the members of the CHORUS speak and take part in the action as indicated in the notes to each scene.

All the characters drink from the same poisoned well that is recognizably American, and midwestern at that. The time might be any time in the last seventy years, or even—not impossibly—in the next.

Harm's Way was premiered November 14, 1985, at La Mama Annex in new York City. This play is for Yolanda Gerritsen.

Scene one. An alley between darkened tenements. The MOTHER *is
chasing her* CHILD *about in an attempt to get him to eat a sandwich
she is holding in one hand. She has a revolver in her pocket.*

MOTHER	Ugly kid. Eat!
CHILD	Witch. Go stuff it.
MOTHER	Watch your mouth.
CHILD	Don't want that crap. It's crap.
MOTHER	Good American cheese. Real baloney
	On Wonderbread. Eat it. Or else.
CHILD	Crap.
MOTHER	You don't eat it and I'll whip you good.
CHILD	Crap sandwich.
MOTHER	I'll show your ass.
CHILD	Stuff it up
	Your ass, witch.
MOTHER	You don't eat that sandwich
	And I'll kill you good.
CHILD	Suck my
	Dingus, witch.
MOTHER	Lemme at you, I'll bust your chops.
CHILD	Nyah! Nyah!
MOTHER	Kid don't talk to his mother like that.
	I'll teach you, little son of a bitch.

She shoots him.

No respect . . .

FISHEYE *enters.*

FISHEYE	What's going on?
MOTHER	Little shit-ass wouldn't eat his sandwich,
	And I showed him.

SANTOUCHE *enters.*

SANTOUCHE	Hey, you . . .
MOTHER	No goddamn respect . . .

SANTOUCHE	What's happening here? Who's the stiff?
MOTHER	Kid, that's all.
	None of your business.
SANTOUCHE	What happened, Fisheye?
FISHEYE	She and the kid were
	Fighting, and then she
	Pulls out the gun and
	Shoots him, Santouche.
	I never seen anything
	Like it.
SANTOUCHE	Fucking monster . . .
MOTHER	Guess I showed him.
FISHEYE	Hey, Santouche . . .
SANTOUCHE	Shut up.
MOTHER	No fucking respect.
SANTOUCHE	You really do that?
MOTHER	No fucking respect.
SANTOUCHE	Lady, I was talking
	To you.
MOTHER	HE DIDN'T HAVE NO FUCKING
	RESPECT.
SANTOUCHE	I asked you a question,
	Bitch.
FISHEYE	Santouche . . .
SANTOUCHE	Shut up . . .
MOTHER	Leave me alone, big shot.
	You got no respect either.
SANTOUCHE	I'll show you respect, bitch.
FISHEYE	Santouche!

SANTOUCHE *shoots her.*

SANTOUCHE	Fucking unnatural cunt. I can't stand 'em.
FISHEYE	Santouche, are you crazy?
SANTOUCHE	Killed her own flesh and blood.
	He won't eat his sandwich, my ass!
FISHEYE	Santouche, let's get the hell
	Out of here.
SANTOUCHE	All in good time.
CHORUS	What's going on? What's all
	The noise? Someone's been shot.

SANTOUCHE	Let's haul ass
	Out of here.
FISHEYE	Santouche . . .
SANTOUCHE	Move it, Fisheye, move it!

Scene two. The interior of a small, sparsely furnished house. ISLE OF MERCY *is seated at a table.* SANTOUCHE *is pacing back and forth.*

ISLE OF MERCY	What's wrong?
SANTOUCHE	I've got to go away for a while.
ISLE OF MERCY	Why?
SANTOUCHE	I killed somebody. Had to. Didn't
	Particularly want to, but I did. So
	I've got to go someplace where I'll
	Be safe. Quiet.
ISLE OF MERCY	How long?
SANTOUCHE	Don't know.
ISLE OF MERCY	What am I supposed to do?
SANTOUCHE	Not your problem, *Isle of Mercy.*
ISLE OF MERCY	Don't call me that.
SANTOUCHE	It's funny. *Isle of Mercy.*
	A pretty name for a pretty woman.
ISLE OF MERCY	It's not my name.
SANTOUCHE	It's your name, if I say it is.
	You got a better one?
ISLE OF MERCY	You know it.
SANTOUCHE	I need money. I'll have to sell
	My things. Need money quick.
ISLE OF MERCY	How long?
SANTOUCHE	Lay off! I'm hassled enough.
ISLE OF MERCY	I am simply trying to figure out
	What to do. That's all. How can
	I know what to do otherwise?
SANTOUCHE	Talk too much. I need money.
ISLE OF MERCY	We don't have it.
SANTOUCHE	Have to sell something.
	You have to sell something
	For me.
ISLE OF MERCY	What? But what?
SANTOUCHE	The watch.
ISLE OF MERCY	It's broken.

SANTOUCHE	It's a gold watch.
ISLE OF MERCY	It stopped working a long time ago.
SANTOUCHE	You never wound it. It runs. It's a Gold watch. A thing like that's got To be worth something. Where is it?
ISLE OF MERCY	Here. In the box.
SANTOUCHE	Let me see it, stupid.
ISLE OF MERCY	Watch what you say.
SANTOUCHE	Let me see the damn watch.
ISLE OF MERCY	It's broken.
SANTOUCHE	You never wound it right.
ISLE OF MERCY	How do you wind a watch wrong?
SANTOUCHE	You wound it backwards. I saw you.
ISLE OF MERCY	I never touched it.
SANTOUCHE	You did too.
ISLE OF MERCY	I never touched it. It's yours.
SANTOUCHE	I'll wind it up.
ISLE OF MERCY	Go ahead.
SANTOUCHE	Shut up.
ISLE OF MERCY	Leave me alone.
SANTOUCHE	It won't wind.
ISLE OF MERCY	I told you.
SANTOUCHE	You told me nothing. It's broken.
ISLE OF MERCY	I told you.
SANTOUCHE	I need money. What am I going to do . . .
ISLE OF MERCY	Sell it anyhow. It's gold, like you say.
SANTOUCHE	Not worth crap.
ISLE OF MERCY	Sure it is, even broken.
SANTOUCHE	Shut up.
ISLE OF MERCY	It's worth something. I'll sell it for you.
SANTOUCHE	I've got to get out of here.
ISLE OF MERCY	It'll be all right.
SANTOUCHE	Easy for you to say.
ISLE OF MERCY	I'm trying to help.
SANTOUCHE	Big help you are.
ISLE OF MERCY	I'll sell the watch and get the money To you.
SANTOUCHE	They'll throw me in the can. I won't go again. Had enough. It's too much. They'll have to Kill me first.

ISLE OF MERCY	Shut up.
SANTOUCHE	I won't go.
ISLE OF MERCY	Won't have to go if I sell the watch.
SANTOUCHE	I'll try it.
ISLE OF MERCY	Cheer up.
SANTOUCHE	How long will it take?
ISLE OF MERCY	A couple of days at most.
SANTOUCHE	Meet me at the fair. Take the boat across the river.
ISLE OF MERCY	How long?
SANTOUCHE	Two days. At sundown. By the fair.
ISLE OF MERCY	All right.
SANTOUCHE	Bring the money. I'll be hiding.
ISLE OF MERCY	How'll I find you?
SANTOUCHE	I'll find you. I'll look different.
ISLE OF MERCY	I'll be there with the money.
SANTOUCHE	I'm all packed.
ISLE OF MERCY	Santouche.
SANTOUCHE	That's all. Have to get the hell Out of here. Bring the money. Once The heat's off I'll be back. Maybe I'll be lucky.
ISLE OF MERCY	Santouche . . .
SANTOUCHE	Have to go now. Don't bother me . . .
ISLE OF MERCY	Who'd you kill?
SANTOUCHE	Don't give me any trouble. I can't Take it. Just bring me the money. And Don't you mess around while I'm gone Or there'll be trouble, real trouble.
ISLE OF MERCY	Santouche!
SANTOUCHE	Told you I have to go.

He exits.

ISLE OF MERCY	*(Playing with the watch.)* No wonder it's broken. There's some Kind of big, long hair in here. All Tangled and twisted up in here. Funny- Looking thing.

She pulls out the main spring.

> Now look what I've done. It's more
> Broken now than it was before.

Scene three. A nightmarish hillside. Dim fires and explosions in the distance. There are three tall poles, or posts, on top of which are mounted wagon wheels. By Way of Being Hidden *and two dummies are strapped respectively atop each of these.*

Santouche	What are you doing up there? Hey, you!
	They must be some apples in that tree!
By Way of	Sombitch, let me down
Being	Outa here, hey stupid!
Hidden	
Santouche	Who're you calling stupid?
By Way of	You, asshole. Let me down.
Santouche	And what if I don't want to?
By Way of	For Chrissakes, man!
Santouche	How come you got up there
	In the first place?
By Way of	It's all part of the show.
Santouche	What show?
By Way of	Never mind. Just let me down.
Santouche	Why should I bust my ass?
By Way of	Look, I'll do good by you, you'll see.
	You let me down and I'll even it up,
	Don't you worry about that, a man like me
	You can trust, I swear.
Santouche	Well, how do I get you down?
By Way of	I'll show you . . .
Santouche	What about them?
By Way of	Croaked. You numbskull.
Santouche	I don't know about this . . .
By Way of	Chickenshit, dumb chickenshit!
Santouche	What, who you calling
	Chickenshit, you!
By Way of	You, chickenshit, you're afraid
	To climb this pole.
Santouche	Hell if I am.
By Way of	You are.
Santouche	What's your name, anyhow?
By Way of	By Way of Being Hidden.
Santouche	No, I asked for your name.
By Way of	*By Way of Being Hidden.* That's my
	Name. Now get a move on, Chicken-

	Shit, or come dark and the rats'll Gnaw my eyes out.
SANTOUCHE	Shit if I care, what kind of a name Is that?
BY WAY OF	Son, what is your name?
SANTOUCHE	Santouche.
BY WAY OF	Santouche, my friend, much as I Enjoy the pleasures of conversation, And like yourself, no doubt, would never Presume upon the honorable disinterest Of a true friend . . .
SANTOUCHE	Cut the crap.
BY WAY OF	Are you going to let me down, Chickenshit?
SANTOUCHE	All in good time. You got money?
BY WAY OF	You think if I had money I'd've Got myself strapped up here, like a Goddamn human scarecrow?
SANTOUCHE	You said it was part of the show.
BY WAY OF	Santouche, I swear I will Richly repay your generosity if you Only shinny up this pole and cut these Straps, you'll see, I'm not bullshitting.
SANTOUCHE	Well, all right, just let me figure Out a safe way of getting up there.
BY WAY OF	For Jesus Christ's sake, there isn't Any safe way of getting up here! Don't think, Santouche, just do It. Don't you have no spirit of adventure?
SANTOUCHE	*By Way of Being Hidden,* my ass!
Pause.	
BY WAY OF	I'm a girl.
Pause.	
SANTOUCHE	Be right up.

Scene four. A small group of circus wagons and a tent in a clearing in the forest. The CHORUS *comes onstage and acts as an audience for* CROW'S-FOOT'S *exhortations.*

| CROW'S-FOOT | Ladies and gents! This is the final call! |

ISLE OF MERCY	What's going on here?
CHORUS	We're waiting for the Guyanousa.
	They've got one in that tent. . . .
CROW'S-FOOT	Ladies and gents! This is the final call
	For to get a glimpse at one of the most
	Astonishing marvels ever presented 'neath
	The blue of God's welkin: a creature so
	Rare it has never come across another
	Like it, a creature so fabulous it has
	Never even heard tell of itself, a creature
	So lopsided—with the feet longer on one
	Side than the t'other—that it can graze
	On the steepest mountain slope; *and*
	Ladies and gents, there is so much more
	To be gleaned about this creature: some of it
	Scandalous, some of it horrifying, and all
	Of it amazing, at the very least! And
	Two bits, a measly one-quarter of a dollar,
	Will buy you admission to the tent, where
	Even now the creature is snorting and
	Stamping and shaking his shaggy locks. So
	If there's anyone out there who'd still
	Like a ticket he'd better holler because,
	Ladies and gents, this is the last call. And
	Them that miss this shot to see the fabulous
	One time only legendary Guyanousa may have to
	Wait twenty, thirty, who knows how many years before
	Another such opportunity presents itself. So it's last
	call, ladies and gents, last call! Last call! Last call!
ISLE OF MERCY	Sir, I'd like a ticket. Me, I'd like a ticket.
CROW'S-FOOT'S HELPER	Mr. Crow's-foot . . .
CROW'S-FOOT	Yes, my dear, you come right over here,
	And I'll give you your ticket.
CROW'S-FOOT'S HELPER	Mr. Crow's-foot!
CROW'S-FOOT	Yes, Mr. Suggs?
CROW'S-FOOT'S HELPER	Hot damn, Mr. Crow's-foot! The Guyanousa am loose!

CROW'S-FOOT	Holy Jesus Mother of Mary I'm getting Out of here!
CROW'S-FOOT'S HELPER	AYEEEEE!
CROW'S-FOOT	Last time it got loose it ate up The whole town of Dead Snake Junction, Dogcatcher and all!
CROW'S-FOOT'S HELPER	The Guyanousa am loose!

Crowd flees screaming.

            The Guyanousa am loose!

CROW'S-FOOT'S HELPER *runs into the tent.* ISLE OF MERCY *doesn't budge.*

CROW'S-FOOT	The Guyanousa am loose!

Pause.

            Little lady, hadn't you better
            Run off, too? You don't want to get
            Eaten up, or God forbid, *molested* . . .

Pause.

            . . . by an ugly, evil-smelling,
            Hellfire-breathing, tree-uprooting
            Creature with no respect, that
            Ain't never been housebroken,
            Tamed, or otherwise civilized,
            Now do you?

ISLE OF MERCY	I paid my quarter. I want to see The Guyanousa.
CROW'S-FOOT	We can't hold it off forever, Can we Mr. Suggs? Mr. Suggs? The Lord Be praised, it must've already Ate up Mr. Suggs! You'd better haul ass out of here, Young lady. Creature's got a strange Hankering for the innards of young Girls. Terrible things happened In the last town, I assure you . . .
ISLE OF MERCY	I paid. I want to see.
CROW'S-FOOT	Young lady wants to see the Guyanousa, Mr. Suggs, ain't that rich!

The Guyanousa am loose!
Don't you understand, young lady?
You'll be killed; tore up; massacreed.
God, what a bloody mess there'll be:
Gore and blood and ruination a-
Hanging from the treetops.

ISLE OF MERCY   I won't go till I see the Guyanousa.

CROW'S-FOOT   She won't go, Mr. Suggs, do you
Hear me? Till she catches sight
Of the Guyanousa. Maybe we'd
Just better oblige her, do you
Hear me, Mr. Suggs? She wants
To see the flaming Guyanousa! Suggs!
Pardon me, young lady, I'll just
Tiptoe in the tent and see what awful
Fate has befallen my colleague.

ISLE OF MERCY   There ain't no Guyanousa. You're a liar.

CROW'S-FOOT   Oh, now, don't say that.

ISLE OF MERCY   That was my last quarter.
I want to see the Guyanousa.

CROW'S-FOOT   You'll be ate up. Scram.

ISLE OF MERCY   You're a cheat.

CROW'S-FOOT   Beat it, bitch.

ISLE OF MERCY   Give me my money back.

CROW'S-FOOT   Get lost.

ISLE OF MERCY   I need the quarter. Otherwise
I can't cross the river.

CROW'S-FOOT   What river?

ISLE OF MERCY   Chagrin River.

CROW'S-FOOT   There's no river. Someone's diddled you.

ISLE OF MERCY   Sure there is. Chagrin River.

CROW'S-FOOT   It's part of the show. The con.

ISLE OF MERCY   Give me my quarter back.

CROW'S-FOOT   Go whistle for it.

ISLE OF MERCY   I don't have any money left.

CROW'S-FOOT   No skin off my teeth.

ISLE OF MERCY   You're a liar.

CROW'S-FOOT   Sucker born every day.

ISLE OF MERCY   I'm no sucker.
Give me my money back.

CROW'S-FOOT   Get out of here.

ISLE OF MERCY	You're a crook.
CROW'S-FOOT	Honest as any man Can afford to be. A man's Got to live.
ISLE OF MERCY	Heard that before.
CROW'S-FOOT	Cynic. Beat it.
ISLE OF MERCY	Not till I get my money back. I've got to have that quarter.
CROW'S-FOOT	I told you: there ain't no Such thing as any Anger River. It's part of the show.
ISLE OF MERCY	Got to sell my watch and meet My man on the other side.
CROW'S-FOOT	He must be part of the con, too.
ISLE OF MERCY	If he was here you wouldn't Say that.
CROW'S-FOOT	You don't beat it and I'll turn The dogs loose on you.
ISLE OF MERCY	Why not the Guyanousa?
CROW'S-FOOT	What?
ISLE OF MERCY	You're a filthy liar.
CROW'S-FOOT	It's an honest day's work. That's all.
ISLE OF MERCY	I want my quarter back.
CROW'S-FOOT	There's other ways to get it.
ISLE OF MERCY	What do you mean?
CROW'S-FOOT	You're young yet. You can earn it On your back.
ISLE OF MERCY	You cheated me.
CROW'S-FOOT	Nothing special about you. Are you clean? Still, who'd Want to put it in you?
ISLE OF MERCY	I don't do things like that.
CROW'S-FOOT	Still, you're not much to look at. You could be a Gypsy and read Hands. Can you read hands?
ISLE OF MERCY	Give me my quarter.
CROW'S-FOOT	Look, bitch, I'm trying to help you.
ISLE OF MERCY	Won't do it.
CROW'S-FOOT	If you had a beard . . .
ISLE OF MERCY	Just give me my quarter.
CROW'S-FOOT	Can you walk on your hands?

ISLE OF MERCY	Bastard.
CROW'S-FOOT	Here's my card. I am *The Guyanousa.* Look, my dear, you'd better make up Your mind and make it up quick. If You're not part of the show, you're Part of them that takes it all in, And that's a fool. Think it over.
ISLE OF MERCY	What am I going to do?
CROW'S-FOOT	You're wasting my time.
ISLE OF MERCY	Bastard.
CROW'S-FOOT	Think it over.

Scene five. She sits down on the ground. The POP STAR *resembles a scarecrow tied to a stake. He holds an enormous guitar. As he sings he moves only his head and hands. There should be long pauses between stanzas. During these everyone on stage, including the* POP STAR, *should remain completely immobile. Again, the* CHORUS *acts, onstage, as an audience. All three members of the* CHORUS *are mounted on short stilts, and they lean together, forming a kind of human tripod. When the* POP STAR *sings they moan and sway gently back and forth.* SANTOUCHE *and* BY WAY OF BEING HIDDEN *sit on the ground listening to the music.*

POP STAR	You got to You got to You got to You got to You got to You got to You got to You got to You got to You got to You got to Fry your head, You got to Fuck the dead. You got to You got to You got to You got to

You got to
You got to
You got to
You got to
Be what you
Think you want
To be if you
Want to know
Who plays what
Part in the show.

You got to
Get out
My way,
You got to
Move away,
You got to
Do what I
Say when I
Say what
My way is,
You got to
Do what I say
'Cause my way's
Harm's way.

Repeat more softly the whole song till the end of the scene.

BY WAY OF	You like it?
SANTOUCHE	What say?
BY WAY OF	You deaf?
SANTOUCHE	What say?
BY WAY OF	You deaf?
SANTOUCHE	What say?
BY WAY OF	Dead head.
SANTOUCHE	After what I done for you,
	How come you're not more grateful?
BY WAY OF	Brought you to the show
	Didn't I? That's grateful.
SANTOUCHE	I am a man . . .
BY WAY OF	Bum lay.
SANTOUCHE	Find yourself another.
BY WAY OF	Hey, I didn't mean it.

SANTOUCHE	Fuck yourself. If this Is the show, it sucks.
BY WAY OF	Brought you to the show. What did you expect?
SANTOUCHE	Music.
BY WAY OF	This is music.
SANTOUCHE	I mean music Music. This sucks.
BY WAY OF	What the hell Do you expect From me?
SANTOUCHE	Nothing. I'm going. So long.
BY WAY OF	Hey, Santouche. Hey, man, You gonna walk Out on me?
SANTOUCHE	There's a place I've got to be at By tomorrow. Other side of the river.
BY WAY OF	Other side of the river? You're crazy.
SANTOUCHE	I'm going.
BY WAY OF	What for? What for?

He goes out.

SHADDUP!

Music stops. Pause.

Nobody runs out on me.

Pause.

Wonder what's so hot
On the other side of the river.

Scene six. Another hillside. This one has a small, mullioned window emplanted in it with a dim light shining through. Old gravestones are scattered about. The MAN *is standing in a waist-deep grave he has dug. His companion, a dummy, is propped against a nearby tree. The dummy's chest is pierced by several arrows, and there is a hatchet buried in his forehead.* SANTOUCHE, *walking on stilts, appears behind the hill. After greeting the* MAN, *he climbs down to earth.*

SANTOUCHE	All on a-fucking-count of that goddam watch That don't keep time, and that goddam woman That couldn't tell the fucking time if the

	Goddam watch kept it. Wonder where the hell
	She is.
MAN	Hey, you, shinbones.
SANTOUCHE	You talking to me, ground hog?
MAN	Yeah, you. Who'd you think I was talking to?
SANTOUCHE	What're you doing in that hole?
MAN	Well, I'm not here
	For my beauty sleep,
	That's for sure. Come here.
SANTOUCHE	What's wrong with him?
MAN	Stiff. Can't you see, a fucking stiff.
SANTOUCHE	That much I can tell.
MAN	He was being difficult.
SANTOUCHE	What did you say?
MAN	It's why I killed him.
SANTOUCHE	I don't understand your meaning.
MAN	How would you, if I haven't
	Explained my meaning to you?
SANTOUCHE	Got a point there.
MAN	This is . . .
SANTOUCHE	Well, good day, sir. I think I'll
	Just mosey on down to the road . . .
	It's been a real pleasure.
MAN	*(Pulls out a gun.)* Hold on, buddy.
SANTOUCHE	You meet such interesting
	People . . .
MAN	One step farther and I'll drill ya.
SANTOUCHE	Just a figure of speech.
	I wasn't really planning to walk off
	Like that. After all, we haven't even
	Been properly introduced. My name's
	Santouche.
MAN	Now listen, bud, and listen good . . .
	You listening?
SANTOUCHE	I'm listening. Real close . . .
MAN	This stiff is stiff 'cause he won't
	Bury me. He wouldn't do it. So I
	Off him, and he *still* won't do it.
	Seems simple enough to me. Shovel
	A few yards of dirt over me. I told
	Him I'd lie real still, and not to

Worry if I started to squirm around
Once he got to my face. I told him
He could have my stuff. Shoes. Pack.
Good hat. And a couple guns. That's
Not asking a whole lot, it seems
To me. Well, he had some kind of old-
Fashioned ethical-humanist compunctions
About burying a living man. We talked
It over a long time. He threatened
To take off without helping me out . . .

SANTOUCHE	I'll bury you, sure I will, no sweat.
MAN	Shut up. It's not polite to interrupt.
SANTOUCHE	Sorry. I was just trying to be neighborly.
MAN	I don't want you to bury me. I want him To.
SANTOUCHE	But he's dead . . .
MAN	That's where you come in.
SANTOUCHE	I'm afraid I don't get what you mean, Or maybe I'm just thick.
MAN	He won't listen to me.
SANTOUCHE	No, it doesn't look as though he'll do A whole lot of listening from here on in.
MAN	But you *are* listening to me.
SANTOUCHE	Oh yes, I certainly am, and it's a great Pleasure to do so.
MAN	Then you talk to him.
SANTOUCHE	What?
MAN	I say you talk to him, and convince him He ought to do as I say.
SANTOUCHE	But, he's a stiff . . .
MAN	And you better be pretty goddamn persuasive.
SANTOUCHE	You're pulling my leg.
MAN	Because if you don't talk that pigheaded Son of a bitch into burying me, I'm likely To get angry again, and I'll just have to Blow you away for sure, and, bud, you'll look As worse off as him. And that ain't good.
SANTOUCHE	No, indeed, sir, it ain't good at all.
MAN	Well, what say, my young man?
SANTOUCHE	I guess I see it your way.
MAN	I'm so glad you'll listen to reason.

SANTOUCHE	Well, it's no trouble, my friend. I mean
	I do like to be helpful, particularly to
	One like yourself, who is so . . .
MAN	Persuasive . . .
SANTOUCHE	All right . . . ah. You . . . ah . . . forgot one thing.
MAN	What's that?
SANTOUCHE	What's his name?
MAN	Cleveland. Mr. Grover Cleveland.
SANTOUCHE	Thanks.
MAN	You're welcome.
SANTOUCHE	Ah, Mr. Cleveland . . .
MAN	You don't need to be so formal.
	A friend of mine's a friend of his.
SANTOUCHE	Oh, I see. Ah, Grover, old man.
MAN	That's better . . .
SANTOUCHE	Ah yes, Grover, my friend. I hear
	You're unwilling to oblige our
	Common friend here, ah . . .
	Might I ask what your name is, sir?
MAN	Surely. I'm called William McKinley.
SANTOUCHE	Ah yes, Mr. McKinley here desires
	That I do my utmost to convince
	You of the folly of your ways, in so
	Willfully resisting his blandishments
	To the effect that you assist him in his
	Ardent wish to be—er—interred, at this
	Time, in this place . . .
MAN	That's very good.
SANTOUCHE	Thank you kindly, Mr. McKinley, I'll just
	Go on.
MAN	Don't let me interfere.
SANTOUCHE	Now, my dear Mr. Cleveland, much as I do not
	Wish to presume to offer unsolicited advice,
	Especially in the case of so recent a friendship . . .
MAN	Very tactful. I like that . . .

SANTOUCHE *kicks the gun away and grabs it.*

	Shit.
SANTOUCHE	Okay, stiff, get out of that hole, and get out of
	There quick.
MAN	It was only a joke.

SANTOUCHE	Joke, my ass. Move! Or I'll blow your Balls off one by one.
MAN	Don't. Don't. Don't . . .
SANTOUCHE	Now grab that stiff, stiff, and throw Him in the hole.
MAN	What're you so angry about? It was a Joke. It's all in good spirits, I assure You.
SANTOUCHE	Now you get in the hole, too.
MAN	What are you going to do?
SANTOUCHE	Just what you said you wanted.
MAN	You must be crazy.
SANTOUCHE	Shut up, Mr. McKinley.

SANTOUCHE *begins to shovel dirt over the* MAN.

MAN	It was a joke, just part of the show. I was bored. Have pity on me. The future Is boredom. I wouldn't have harmed you, I Swear! It was all part of the show.
SANTOUCHE	(*Shovels rapidly.*) Eat shit. Eat dirt. Eat shit. Dirt . . . shit . . . Dirt . . .
MAN	But I'll suffocate. You can't be serious.
SANTOUCHE	Mr. McKinley, sir, my name is Santouche. And I am very serious.
MAN	You're a monster.
SANTOUCHE	I'm doing you a favor. Get your head Down or I'll shoot your ears off. Get Down . . .
MAN	Help, a monster!

SANTOUCHE *kills him with the shovel.*

SANTOUCHE	You're part of nobody's show now, My friend.

Finishes burying the MAN.

Takes all kinds, my friend.
A man who fools with me hurts me,
And I'll be obliged to hate him.

Pause.

You started it, buster . . .
. . . won't go playing your tricks
On anyone else.

Pause.

> . . . guess I showed you.

Pause.

> . . . wonder who the hell he was.

Pause.

> . . . buried two presidents today!
> First time I ever did that.

Pause.

> . . . *didn't mean me no harm!* My ass!

Pause.

> . . . *all part of the show.* You are dead,
> Man, and I spit on your stiff, and,
> Man, you can't do one blessed thing
> About it!

Pause.

> . . . wonder who the hell he was.

Pause.

> . . . *part of the show!*

Scene seven. A starry night. Isle of Mercy *sits on a boulder looking at the moon. The* Two Children *are at first hidden in the shadows. The* Chorus *sings a song.*

Chorus   This is
Isle of Mercy's song.
It won't be long.
She is very
Very tough.
She got no inside,
Got no outside.
Whoever told you so,
They lied.

First Child   Hey, lady.
Pause.

Second Child   Hey, lady,
What are you doing?

Isle of Mercy   Looking at stars.
Pause.

Second Child   I said what are you
Doing?

Isle of Mercy   I said *looking*
At stars. Can't you hear?

Pause.

That light
Up there.
That's a star.

SECOND CHILD   Ain't you lonely
Sitting there?

ISLE OF MERCY   Nope . . . Sometimes.

Pause.

FIRST CHILD   I got a rock with a face
On it.

Pause.

FIRST CHILD   I got a rock with a face
On it.

ISLE OF MERCY   I heard you the first time.

Pause.

FIRST CHILD   You want to see it?

Pause.

You want to see it?

Pause.

ISLE OF MERCY   Okay. Show me the rock
With the face on it.

She examines the rock.

That ain't no face . . .

SECOND CHILD   I told you that wasn't no face.

FIRST CHILD   Sure looks like it to me.

Pause.

The Moon's got a face, see.

They all look up briefly.

Sometimes he turns his face
To one side. Sometimes it's
Straight on. I can't see
Too good. It's awful far.

SECOND CHILD   He can't see straight.

ISLE OF MERCY   I was talking to him.
You don't need to butt in.

FIRST CHILD   The moon's a rock with
A face on it.

ISLE OF MERCY   Pretty big rock, if it's just a rock.

Pause.

	Whose kids are you
	Anyhow? Crowsfoot's?
SECOND CHILD	Hell no . . .
FIRST CHILD	We borned ourselves
	Out of rocks.
ISLE OF MERCY	Kids don't come
	From rocks, stupid.
FIRST CHILD	Shit, I know that.
ISLE OF MERCY	Where do they come from?
FIRST CHILD	You know . . .

CROWSFOOT *enters.*

CROWSFOOT	Well my dear, are my little
	Self-begotten bastards bothering
	You? If they grieve you, take a
	Stone to 'em.
ISLE OF MERCY	Go back to the wagon, Crowsfoot.
CROWSFOOT	They's a customer. You come along.
ISLE OF MERCY	I am relaxing with my friends.
CROWSFOOT	The Wheel of Possibility don't slow down
	For nobody no how, that's for sure.
	You rattle your bones, and get a move
	On. Hup, hup!
ISLE OF MERCY	Scram, Crowsfoot.
CROWSFOOT	Pretty lady, you are pushing me
	To extreme acts of unkind coercion.

She stands up on tiptoe and peers offstage as though to catch a glimpse of the prospective customer. Then she sits back down. Pause.

ISLE OF MERCY	I won't do it.
CROWSFOOT	Yes you will.
ISLE OF MERCY	No I won't.
CROWSFOOT	Yes you will.
ISLE OF MERCY	Think you can tell me what to do!
CROWSFOOT	You'll do exactly what I tell you to.
	Pause.
ISLE OF MERCY	Shit on you.
CROWSFOOT	Watch your mouth.
ISLE OF MERCY	I won't do it.

CROWSFOOT	Yes you will.
ISLE OF MERCY	*You* fuck him then.
CROWSFOOT	Now Mercy, cool down . . .
ISLE OF MERCY	You know who that is?
CROWSFOOT	He's just like everybody else.
ISLE OF MERCY	That is the devil himself.
CROWSFOOT	So? I'm not particular.
ISLE OF MERCY	I am.
CROWSFOOT	You can't afford it.
ISLE OF MERCY	Oh yes I can. Like The man said *There is* *Some shit I do not* *Eat.*

> *Pause.*

CROWSFOOT	You want me to give You another one of my Speechifications?

> *Pause.*

ISLE OF MERCY	You win.
CROWSFOOT	Come along then.

> CROWSFOOT *leaves.* ISLE OF MERCY *gets up to go.*

ISLE OF MERCY.	So long.
BOTH CHILDREN	So long.

> *Pause. She sits back down.*

FIRST CHILD	Moon's where the ghosts Go.
ISLE OF MERCY	Why do they do that?
FIRST CHILD	So no one can hurt them.
SECOND CHILD	Who can hurt a ghost, Stupid? A ghost's a dead Thing. It don't have to Be protected.

> *Pause.*

ISLE OF MERCY	Maybe the moon's a ghost . . .
SECOND CHILD	You ever seen a ghost?
FIRST CHILD	What do you mean by that?
SECOND CHILD	I'm getting scared.

	Come on, let's go
	Back to the wagon.
CROWSFOOT	*(Off)* Isle of Mercy!
ISLE OF MERCY	They ain't no such thing
	As a ghost.
FIRST CHILD	Why'd you say that
	About the moon being
	A ghost?
SECOND CHILD	Let's go back, come on!
ISLE OF MERCY	I don't know.
FIRST CHILD	You talk funny. For a girl.
ISLE OF MERCY	You know what I'd do
	If I was a ghost?
CROWSFOOT	*(Off)* Isle of Mercy!
SECOND CHILD	I'm getting out of here!
FIRST CHILD	If I was a ghost I'd
	Fly away. Fly right smack
	Out of here. That's for damn
	Sure.
SECOND CHILD	You're both crazy.

SECOND CHILD *goes out. Pause.*

Scene eight. In front of an old saloon. Noise of conversation and merriment from within. As he attempts to enter the saloon, SAN-TOUCHE bumps into FISHEYE, who is leaving it. Later on in the scene, the COOK is played by a member of the CHORUS.

SANTOUCHE	Fisheye! What're you doing
	This side of the river?
FISHEYE	Lucky I found you. You can't
	Go in there. Blackmange's having
	A party. It's his birthday.
SANTOUCHE	Thought I smelled something
	That stunk.
FISHEYE	You gotta be real careful.
SANTOUCHE	How many men's he got
	With him?
FISHEYE	Only nine.
SANTOUCHE	Armed?
FISHEYE	Knives, side arms, grenades.

SANTOUCHE	Can you cover me
	From the kitchen?
FISHEYE	You can't be serious. He's armed!
SANTOUCHE	Fisheye, I'm going in there.
FISHEYE	They'll massacre ya . . .
SANTOUCHE	Not if you help.
FISHEYE	What's your plan?
SANTOUCHE	You cover me from the
	Kitchen.
FISHEYE	Won't be a party to this . . .

SANTOUCHE *pulls a gun on him.*

	Anything you say, Santouche.
SANTOUCHE	Remember all the good
	I done ya.
FISHEYE	You're right. I ought to be more
	Grateful. We'll get 'em in the
	Cross fire.
SANTOUCHE	Blackmange! I don't believe it!
FISHEYE	It's him all right.
SANTOUCHE	After all these years . . .
	He'll get his!
FISHEYE	I guess . . .
SANTOUCHE	Don't be scared, Fisheye.
FISHEYE	What happens if they decide
	To bust out the back way?
SANTOUCHE	I'll cut 'em down before
	They get to you.
FISHEYE	All right, then.
SANTOUCHE	I'll start after you fire the
	First shot, only lay off old
	Blackmange himself. I want him . . .

FISHEYE *exits as* BY WAY OF BEING HIDDEN *enters.*

BY WAY OF	Aren't you Santouche?
SANTOUCHE	You look familiar, but I don't have
	Any time. You clear out of here if you
	Want to stay alive.
BY WAY OF	It's a matter of some importance.
SANTOUCHE	Back off, bitch, or you're a dead
	Man.

BY WAY OF	You saved my life. Now you're gonna Take it for no reason? I mean, I was only trying to help. But Seeing as how you seem to mean Business . . .
SANTOUCHE	That's better. Now you just stay there Till me and my friend are finished.
BY WAY OF	Fine with me.
SANTOUCHE	Blackmange, you asshole!

FISHEYE *begins to fire. Yells and screams from within.* SANTOUCHE *begins to fire through windows and doors of the saloon.*

Blackmange!

BLACKMANGE *stumbles through the door. Slumps.* SANTOUCHE *shoots him several times.* BLACKMANGE *falls and lies motionless. Shooting subsides.*

Got him, Fisheye! I got him. Hey,
Fisheye, I got him. He's dead. Just
Look at him. Stinking, ugly stiff.
Whoopee! Hey, Fisheye . . .

COOK *enters.*

COOK	He's dead.
SANTOUCHE	Dead? Fisheye?
COOK	The whole gang went busting out the Back way. You kept plugging the stiff. They ripped him up good. He's dead. They're Gone. They'll come back for you, Santouche.
SANTOUCHE	Get lost.
COOK	They'll do a number on you.

COOK *exits.*

BY WAY OF	Santouche, my friend.
SANTOUCHE	What is it?
BY WAY OF	You remember me?
SANTOUCHE	Nope.
BY WAY OF	My name's By Way of Being Hidden.
SANTOUCHE	Oh, you. Beat it.
BY WAY OF	I still want to return the favor.
SANTOUCHE	Beat it.
BY WAY OF	You saved my life.

SANTOUCHE	My friend's croaked, can't you see? Beat it!
BY WAY OF	Your lady's been abducted.
SANTOUCHE	What!
BY WAY OF	That's right.
SANTOUCHE	Who? Where?
BY WAY OF	Don't know.
SANTOUCHE	Shit if you don't know. Some kind of Favor that is! You don't tell me who's Got her and I'll . . .
BY WAY OF	Easy now. I don't know who's got her, But I do know who does know . . .
SANTOUCHE	Who's that?
BY WAY OF	Him.
SANTOUCHE	The stiff.
BY WAY OF	Yep.
SANTOUCHE	Blackmange?
BY WAY OF	Him. The stiff.
SANTOUCHE	But. He's dead.
BY WAY OF	Yup. You killed him.
SANTOUCHE	Why didn't you tell me?
BY WAY OF	I tried.
SANTOUCHE	You didn't try hard enough.
BY WAY OF	What am I supposed to do?
SANTOUCHE	Shut up.
BY WAY OF	But fortunately I have An idea.
SANTOUCHE	Shut up. How do I know You're telling me the truth about Isle of Mercy?
BY WAY OF	Wasn't she supposed to show up About now?
SANTOUCHE	About now . . .
BY WAY OF	But she hasn't.
SANTOUCHE	She hasn't . . .
BY WAY OF	Now what do you suppose Might be holding her up?
SANTOUCHE	She was going to sell My watch.
BY WAY OF	She was going around With money on her?
SANTOUCHE	That's right.

BY WAY OF	All alone?
SANTOUCHE	That's right.
Pause.	
BY WAY OF	You want to hear my idea?
SANTOUCHE	No. Beat it.
BY WAY OF	All right, just trying to be of use,
	Didn't mean no harm.
SANTOUCHE	Get lost. Leave me alone. Beat it.
BY WAY OF	Be seeing you.
SANTOUCHE	What the hell am I going to do?
BY WAY OF	Want to hear my idea?
SANTOUCHE	Beat it, lady, or I'll lay you out
	For the buzzards.
BY WAY OF	Okay, okay, just trying to help . . .
SANTOUCHE	What am I going to do?
BY WAY OF	I got a friend who's got a friend as
	Can make that stiff talk. It's true.
SANTOUCHE	What'd you say?

Scene nine. A clearing in the forest. BY WAY OF BEING HIDDEN, SANTOUCHE, *and the corpse of* BLACKMANGE. *The* WIZARD *is dressed as the others except he sports a necklace of onions, garlic, and rattlesnake skins. In addition, his top hat is festooned with leafy twigs and switches. He carries a small black bag full of bottles and tins.* BY WAY OF BEING HIDDEN *carries a large black suitcase.*

All the WIZARD *does to revivify* BLACKMANGE *is knead a paste from the flour, water, and whiskey; roll the paste into a little ball; plant a garlic clove in the ball; and carefully place the ball under the dead man's tongue.*

WIZARD	That's the corpse?
BY WAY OF	Yup.
WIZARD	How'd he croak?
BY WAY OF	Well, it wasn't measles.
WIZARD	How'd he croak?
BY WAY OF	Shot. Ah. Several times.
WIZARD	Uhm. So you say.
BY WAY OF	Can you do it?
WIZARD	Maybe.
SANTOUCHE	Well? Can he do it?
BY WAY OF	Says maybe.

SANTOUCHE	Shit.
WIZARD	I'll need some
	Flour, water, and
	A bottle of whiskey.
BY WAY OF	Coming right up.

Rummages through the large suitcase for the desired articles.

SANTOUCHE	What you gonna do?
WIZARD	Like patching a tire.
BY WAY OF	Hear that, Santouche?
	Like patching a tire!
SANTOUCHE	I hear it.
WIZARD	Is that the killer?
BY WAY OF	That's the killer.
WIZARD	Was there bad blood
	Between?
BY WAY OF	You might say.
WIZARD	By Way of Being Hidden,
	I don't want none of your
	Horse crap. This is serious
	Business. And you get that
	Man outa sight, hear?
BY WAY OF	Santouche, you get
	Out of sight, you hear?
SANTOUCHE	Why? I stand where I please,
	As I please.
BY WAY OF	If the stiff sees you
	It won't work.
SANTOUCHE	Hell.
WIZARD	It's true, son.
SANTOUCHE	All right, all right. Shit, man!
	Can't get no peace from a man
	Even by killing him no more.
WIZARD	This world
	Is full of dark souls
	And wondrous things.
SANTOUCHE	What kind of sawbones
	Can bring a man back to life
	Anyhow?
WIZARD	Young man, you are disturbing
	Me. This is America. Therefore

Anything can happen. . . .
Aside from which, the object is
Not to restore the poor stiff
From across the murky deeps of
Styx, which is ridiculous;
But a more pragmatic and wholly
American one: namely, to bring
Him temporarily back from across
The shadowy waters of Lethe.

SANTOUCHE	Afraid I lost you,
	Bud.
BY WAY OF	A stiff's a stiff.
WIZARD	What I mean is that all we need
	Is his memory. He don't have to
	Be alive, you dig?
SANTOUCHE	Yeah . . . but.
WIZARD	All we got to do is trick him
	Into thinking he's alive.
SANTOUCHE	Is that all . . .
BY WAY OF	No shit.
WIZARD	That is the practical approach
	To the art of undoing death.
SANTOUCHE	I'm afraid I still don't understand,
	Doc, but I'll take your word for it.
	All I want is results.
WIZARD	My sentiments exactly . . .
SANTOUCHE	By Way, I have a feeling he's bullshit . . .
BY WAY OF	Shut up, Santouche.
SANTOUCHE	That stiff don't know beans.
WIZARD	Shut up, killer.
SANTOUCHE	Only ones end up getting killed
	Have had it coming. Like him.
WIZARD	Oh yeah? What'd he do?
SANTOUCHE	Spit in my eye. Told me off
	In front of people. Went and stooled
	On me good.
WIZARD	Concerning what?
SANTOUCHE	Never you mind. I spent some time
	Out of circulation on account of him.
WIZARD	So you killed him.

SANTOUCHE	Let's just say he got
	His comeuppance.
BY WAY OF	Let's just say . . .
SANTOUCHE	You're a wise one, you are.
WIZARD	Gentlemen, we are about
	Ready to begin *The Con.*
SANTOUCHE	What's he talking about? What con?
BY WAY OF	What con is that, Doc?
WIZARD	Friends, we are about to
	Fool death himself. It's
	All part of the show.
BY WAY OF	Hot damn! He's serious.
SANTOUCHE	The man is out of his mind!
WIZARD	What's his name?
SANTOUCHE	Who?
WIZARD	The stiff, imbecile!
SANTOUCHE	Blackmange.
WIZARD	Blackmange? What kind of a name's that?
SANTOUCHE	It's because he's so ugly.
WIZARD	Blackmange, my friend, are you awake?
SANTOUCHE	Nothing's happening.
BY WAY OF	Shut up.
WIZARD	Blackmange, sit up now, you've been
	Asleep for a long time, why it's past noon,
	The birds are a-singing, sun is a-shining away,
	Pretty girls are a-wiggling their asses out in the street,
	Ain't you ever going to get up? Ain't you hungry?
BLACKMANGE	Ahhhhhhhhhh.
WIZARD	Blackmange, I'm going to do right by you,
	I swear it, I'll kill 'em myself, whoever
	It was done this to you, you'll see, who was it?
	Tell me, Blackmange, and I'll nail 'em good,
	You'll see.
BLACKMANGE	Ahhhhhhhhhh.
SANTOUCHE	What's he up to? Is he going to stool . . .
BY WAY OF	Shut up.
WIZARD	Who done it, tell me, Blackmange?
BLACKMANGE	Dunno . . .
WIZARD	The girl, who's got the girl? Maybe
	He done it, I'll get him for you, you'll
	See, come on, Blackmange.

BLACKMANGE	Ahhhhhhhhhhhhh.
SANTOUCHE	Jesus fucking Christ.
WIZARD	Her name's Isle of Mercy.
BLACKMANGE	Santouche girl. He done it. He killed me.
WIZARD	What about the girl? Who's got her?
BLACKMANGE	He done it. Ahhhh.
WIZARD	I'll settle his apples, you bet I will,
	But that girl, who's got her? The guy that's
	Got her's in on it, I swear, he and Santouche,
	I swear, who was it?
BLACKMANGE	Santouche . . . and *him?*
WIZARD	Who was it? He's the real one, he set you up,
	I swear he did, he was laughing at you, come on,
	Who was it, old Blackmange, only way for me to get
	even,
	No, don't go back to sleep without telling me,
	Who's the man who's got Isle of Mercy?
BLACKMANGE	Guyanousa's got her.
WIZARD	What's that? What'd you say?
SANTOUCHE	Did you hear what he said?
BY WAY OF	I don't get it: *guy snoozing* . . .
	What's that? I don't get it.
SANTOUCHE	Can you make out what it is?
WIZARD	Who's got her? Who was it, Blackmange?
	He done you in, that one.
BLACKMANGE	Guyanousa's got her.
WIZARD	*Guyanousa's got her.* Now it clicks.
	The Guyanousa is a side-show con.
BY WAY OF	That's right. Now I remember.
BLACKMANGE	Ahhhhhhm . . . kill him.
WIZARD	Fuck you stiff! Go back to being
	Dead. We're going to feed you to pigs.
	Santouche's here, take a look at him.
SANTOUCHE	Fuck you, Blackmange.
BLACKMANGE	Ahhhhh . . .
BY WAY OF	He's dead again.
WIZARD	He always was. Now he knows it again.
SANTOUCHE	The Guyanousa.
WIZARD	Friends, I'll be going now. Please
	Don't hesitate to get in touch if
	You should ever require my services

	Again. I also raise storms, debase coin,
	Cause floods, stunt crops, induce a few
	Miscarriages, and on a good day I can
	Throw a close election.
SANTOUCHE	Here's your money, beat it.
WIZARD	Be seeing you, kind gentlefolk, be seeing you.

WIZARD *exits.*

SANTOUCHE	No one does that to me.
BY WAY OF	What are you talking about?
SANTOUCHE	The Guyanousa.
BY WAY OF	Aren't you glad for the favor
	I done you?
SANTOUCHE	I'll get him good.
BY WAY OF	You don't sound grateful.
SANTOUCHE	Shit on you. Beat it.
BY WAY OF	Last time I ever help you out.
SANTOUCHE	Leave me alone, understand?
BY WAY OF	All right, all right, I didn't mean
	Anything by it. I'm sorry, I'm going.
SANTOUCHE	Fucking side-show con man.

Scene ten. A circus wagon standing on an open plain. SANTOUCHE, *looking very exhausted, sits downstage to the left. He takes off his boots and rubs his feet. The members of the* CHORUS *speak their lines in turn from their usual position offstage to the right.*

CHORISTER 1	Guyanousa? I heard of it, but offhand
	I can't recall what it was I heard.
CHORISTER 2	Never heard of it. You must be crazy.
CHORISTER 3	I heard of it, but there ain't no
	Such thing, of that I'm sure.
CHORISTER 1	Nope.
CHORISTER 2	Search me.
CHORISTER 3	Never heard of it.
CHORISTER 1	*Guya-what?!* You must be stewed!
CHORISTER 2	A story that's told by folks
	Round here. Don't you pay it no
	Nevermind.
CHORISTER 3	It's against the laws of nature for such
	A creature to exist. Of that I am sure.

CHORISTER 1	Somebody pulling your leg, fella!
CHORISTER 2	But that was all part of the show,
	Bud, they ain't nobody takes such things
	Serious anymore.
CHORISTER 3	I hear there's wonderful strange creatures
	At the far end of the world. That's what I
	Hear.

CROW'S-FOOT *emerges from the wagon, walks downstage, and sits next to* SANTOUCHE.

CROW'S-FOOT	My friend, mind if I sit down beside you?
SANTOUCHE	Nope.
CROW'S-FOOT	Crow's-foot's the name. What's yours?
SANTOUCHE	Santouche.
CROW'S-FOOT	You look beat.
SANTOUCHE	Yup.
CROW'S-FOOT	I bear good news.

Pause.

SANTOUCHE	Go away.
CROW'S-FOOT	You're a fortunate man.
SANTOUCHE	Go away.
CROW'S-FOOT	I am the first ordained minister of the Church
	Of Christ Fornicator. No shit, it's true. And
	I got my license right here. Now, you, friend,
	What woe has been your lot, who can tell? You
	Look like a disaster. What you need's a nice
	Little piece. Now you can get it, and get saved
	At the same time. Ticket's only a quarter.
	You don't want to miss out on a good thing, do you?
SANTOUCHE	Don't have no quarter.
CROW'S-FOOT	Come on, don't feel shy. It'd be
	Good for you. Buy your ticket. Climb
	In my wagon there. My little madonna,
	She's got fine moves, and my friend, it's
	Not every day you can get saved and laid
	At the same time. Why, it's practically
	Miraculous. Only costs a quarter.
SANTOUCHE	Don't want no pussy.
CROW'S-FOOT	The Lord don't have much use for melancholia,
	My friend.

SANTOUCHE	Don't want it.
CROW'S-FOOT	How do you expect to get *it* if you don't Want *it*?
SANTOUCHE	Fed up.
CROW'S-FOOT	You look like a fine, strapping man of God. There is no point in all this down and out misery. I'll tell you because I know from my own experience. If you turn your heart to Christ Fornicator, you Will find untold bliss. Satisfaction guaranteed. Once you got enlightenment anything is possible. *No one ever gonna shove your face in shit, no one* *Ever gonna call you names!* If you got *it*, friend, and I mean *get it,* you're gonna get laid both in body and soul! With the Lord doing it in your heart, you're gonna Have a big edge on the next man, friend, and in this Evil son of a bitch's world, full of conniving wildcats, You need every bit of edge you can get. Ain't it so, Friend? Don't matter where it comes from. How about It?
SANTOUCHE	Had enough. Don't want nothing.
CROW'S-FOOT	Now I was as empty and bitter as you are once, before I got religion. Then I put down my quarter, and all of A sudden *I saw* that all my former life was spent in Folly. And that squaring the circle of desire and completion Was a cinch.

    Pause.

        What it comes down to, friend, is quite simply that
        YOU CAN HAVE WHAT YOU WANT. IT'S YOURS
            FOR THE TAKING.
        Before that I saw this world as a vast, gray country
        Full of liars, cheats, scoundrels, fools who all looked
        Alike. Monsters even. It was a nightmare lit up only by
        The fires of vengeance and hatred. I was even a con
            man
        Myself. It was part of the show, I am ashamed to say.
        You look like you know whereof I am speaking. I prac-
            ticed

	Deception on my fellow men. It was all like a vision
	Of some dark, grimy, sooty, barren, wind-swept
	country.
	Why the things I done! And you know, I never got laid.
SANTOUCHE	What was your con?
CROW'S-FOOT	I can see you're a child of darkness
	Still, my friend.
SANTOUCHE	Your con, what was it?
CROW'S-FOOT	Shameful, I cheated folk by pretending
	To be a fabulous beast.
SANTOUCHE	I've done things like that. *Are you for real?*
CROW'S-FOOT	Do I not radiate gladness and
	The joy of fulsome success?
SANTOUCHE	You smell like a bank of roses.
CROW'S-FOOT	My friend, why not let me enlist you right this
	Minute in our double-indemnified and wholly tax-
	Deductible Church of Christ Fornicator, and lead
	You to a consummation devoutly to be wished?
SANTOUCHE	(*Gives* CROW'S-FOOT *a quarter*)
	What kind of a beast were you?
CROW'S-FOOT	What did you say?
CROW'S-FOOT	Let us not dwell on the antediluvian,
	My friend, let me lead you instead up . . .
SANTOUCHE	Just curious, that's all.
	I was a killer.
CROW'S-FOOT	I see. Well, if I can't interest you, young
	Man, I guess I'll be seeing you. Aha! Yes,

He looks at the watch, which is still sprung.

	It's getting late. Nevertheless, I wish you well.
	Our paths may be different, but our hearts . . .
SANTOUCHE	Where did you get that watch?
CROW'S-FOOT	What! Why? This watch?
SANTOUCHE	The watch. Where did you get it?
CROW'S-FOOT	You *do* ask questions.
SANTOUCHE	Where?
CROW'S-FOOT	Ah . . .
SANTOUCHE	I think we have some matters to discuss, my
	friend.

CROW'S-FOOT	Oh, I wouldn't want to detain you any Further.
SANTOUCHE	No trouble, I'm sure. Your little presentation Has stirred up quite a commotion in my cynic breast, And I am eager to learn more.
CROW'S-FOOT	I can tell by your bearing that you're a man Of eminence. My poor insignificant surmises could Be of no possible interest to one of your erudition, And mental prowess. Therefore . . .
SANTOUCHE	On the contrary . . .

Pulls out his gun.

CROW'S-FOOT	You want your quarter back?

Scene eleven. The same as in the previous scene. The circus wagon is turned upside down, and one wheel is spinning. It is nearly dark. The FIRST CHILD *and* SECOND CHILD, *who cry out at* SANTOUCHE, *are hiding in some bushes. They dart from one place to another as he tries to catch them.* SANTOUCHE *and* ISLE OF MERCY *stand facing each other.*

The CHORUS *sings a song.*

>Spiderman
>Give me your hand,
>What I see
>Frightens me.
>rock sucks
>trash is art
>art is trash
>pray
>for those
>who don't believe
>I am a killer.

>There was a man
>Called Santouche.
>What's he done?
>Killed a man
>Then he run.
>Prey read bile.
>>rock sucks, etc.

Where's he now?
Same old story,
Same old line,
Same day service.
Where's he now,
Old Santouche?
Ask his lady,
Ask his lady,
Isle of Mercy.
He's gone crazy.
Killed someone
and then he run.
Anyone, anyone.
And he run,
And he run.
       rock sucks, etc.

Spiderman
Give me your hand.
What I see
Frightens me.
Go to crutch.
Poor Santouch.
War ship bog.
Burma shave.
       rock sucks, etc.

SANTOUCHE	You, look at you, fucking whore.
ISLE OF MERCY	Got the money. Had to get the money.
SANTOUCHE	You, look at you.
ISLE OF MERCY	Couldn't sell the watch.
	It was busted. Lost my quarter.
SANTOUCHE	Shut up.
ISLE OF MERCY	Here's the money.
SANTOUCHE	How come you stayed
	With him then?
ISLE OF MERCY	You didn't have to kill him.
SANTOUCHE	After what he done?
ISLE OF MERCY	None of your business.
SANTOUCHE	You and him in on it
	Together?

ISLE OF MERCY	Things don't always
	Work out right.
SANTOUCHE	Shut up.
ISLE OF MERCY	You shut up. I got my pride.
SANTOUCHE	You got nothing. Except me,
	And I don't know if I want you
	Anymore.

Pause.

ISLE OF MERCY	Here's the money. I'm leaving.
SANTOUCHE	What?
ISLE OF MERCY	Going.
SANTOUCHE	Sit down.
ISLE OF MERCY	I'm leaving. Going. I'm finished
	With people mad all the time. Sick of it.
	Like you.
SANTOUCHE	Who'd take you in?
ISLE OF MERCY	Don't bother me.
	Who'd treat me worse? I used to love
	You, Santouche, but you're a killer,
	And I'm sick of that.
SANTOUCHE	Bitch. Sit down. I told you.
ISLE OF MERCY	You eat shit, Santouche.
SANTOUCHE	Don't talk to me that way.
ISLE OF MERCY	Now I'm getting mad, Jesus!
SANTOUCHE	None of them got killed, but
	Had it coming, I assure you.
ISLE OF MERCY	World's a bad place, I know.
SANTOUCHE	So leave me be. And sit down.
ISLE OF MERCY	No, I don't want to. Too much
	Too soon. You know, I can't stand
	The sight of you, Santouche.
SANTOUCHE	Isle of Mercy!
ISLE OF MERCY	That's not my name. You're a pig.
SANTOUCHE	You're not going anyplace
	Without my say-so.
ISLE OF MERCY	Here's your stink money.

She throws it at him.

SANTOUCHE	Where would you go
	Anyhow? Stay.

ISLE OF MERCY	And do what?
SANTOUCHE	I got a reputation to maintain.
ISLE OF MERCY	Look at you. You been taking drugs.
	You don't even look right.
SANTOUCHE	I won't let you go.
ISLE OF MERCY	Santouche, I won't stay.
SANTOUCHE	You can't let me down.
ISLE OF MERCY	I'm going. Good-by.
SANTOUCHE	I won't let you.
ISLE OF MERCY	You gonna kill me?
SANTOUCHE	I can't let it happen.
ISLE OF MERCY	Why don't you kill me, too,
	Santouche? You'd better, because
	That's the only way I'm going
	To stay here.
SANTOUCHE	You shut up.
ISLE OF MERCY	Yeah. I'll shut up. So long, Santouche.
SANTOUCHE	You stay.
ISLE OF MERCY	What you going to do, Santouche,
	Shoot me in the back? Well, go right
	Ahead, if you want to. I don't give a crap
	About you. I just feel sick.
SANTOUCHE	Hold on, Isle of Mercy.
ISLE OF MERCY	So long.

He shoots her in the back.

SANTOUCHE	I told you.

Pause.

Dumb thing to do.

Pause.

Everybody telling me what to do.
Got my pride. People won't leave you
Alone.

Pause.

Got no respect. That's the trouble.

Pause.

You don't treat me right.

Pause.

Who the hell you think you are,
Fancy lady?

Pause.

Busted my watch, you did.

Pause.

People get what they deserve.

Pause.

FIRST CHILD	Going to kill everybody, mister?
SANTOUCHE	Who's that?
FIRST CHILD	Going to kill everybody, mister?
SANTOUCHE	Who're you talking to?
SECOND CHILD	You gonna kill me, mister?
SANTOUCHE	Who're you, kid? Hey!
	You! Where're you hiding?
FIRST CHILD	You gonna kill both of us, mister?
SANTOUCHE	You better shut your mouth,
	Kid . . .
SECOND CHILD	You gonna kill everybody, mister?
SANTOUCHE	Little son of a bitch . . .
FIRST CHILD	You going to kill everybody, mister?
SANTOUCHE	SHUT UP, YOU LITTLE SHITHEAD!
SECOND CHILD	You gonna kill me, mister?
SANTOUCHE	Leave me alone, or I will!
FIRST CHILD	You going to kill me, mister?
SANTOUCHE	Fuck, how many of you are there?
SECOND CHILD	You gonna kill everybody, mister?
SANTOUCHE	Stop it!
FIRST CHILD	You gonna kill everybody, mister?
SANTOUCHE	LEAVE ME ALONE!
SECOND CHILD	You gonna kill everyone, mister?
SANTOUCHE	GODDAMN, COCK-SUCKING,
	MOTHERFUCKING, SHITHEADED . . .
FIRST CHILD	You gonna kill everybody, mister?
SANTOUCHE	Leave me alone, goddamn it . . .
SECOND CHILD	You gonna kill everybody, mister?
SANTOUCHE	Hell . . . what's the use?

He sits down.

CHORUS   You gonna kill everyone, mister?
              You gonna kill everyone, mister?
              You gonna kill everyone, mister?
              You gonna kill everyone, mister?
              You gonna kill everyone, mister?

Blackout.

The Self-begotten (1982)

The Self-begotten is the fourth in a series of five plays that develop, through overlapping and complementary themes and anecdotal material, the fictional story of certain individuals in contemporary Washington, D.C., and other capitals of the free world.

The other plays are, in order of composition: *Energumen, Diseases of the Well-dressed,* and *The Professional Frenchman.* A fifth play remains to be written.

The MAN IN ARABIAN HEADDRESS is attired in a conventional business suit. He is about thirty-five years old.

The GIRL WITH MOUSE EARS is scantily clad. She is in her twenties.

SENATOR ARMITRAGE is a robust fifty or so. He, too, wears a conventional business suit, but has removed his trousers (which are neatly folded over the back of a chair). His undershorts are colorful and billowy. Of course, before he departs he does put his trousers back on.

The fugitive senatorial boot, like the soul, remains quite lost.

The Self-begotten was premiered May 14, 1982, at Ensemble Studio Theatre in New York City. It is cheerfully dedicated to Yolanda.

Scene begins with dim light coming up on the naked figure of SENATOR ARMITRAGE'S DREAM SELF *scurrying about on the floor. This is downstage of the darkened living-room ensemble, where the* SENATOR *himself is seated, talking to the* MAN IN ARABIAN HEADDRESS. *Sound of wind is faintly audible.*

SENATOR ARMITRAGE	I had a dream I was Scrambling around, Confused, in a strange Place; I had lost Something, lost Something precious . . .
SENATOR'S DREAM SELF	I've lost my soul.

gaining the world,
losing the soul

He points to an OLD MAN *in an aviator suit with a long, white, flowing beard who appears in a ball of light atop a rickety stepladder. The* OLD MAN *has a pair of wings that he slowly flaps as though preparing hesitantly to fly.*

But there it is!

OLD MAN *keeps trying to fly.*

Same old soul!

SENATOR ARMITRAGE	Same old soul.

Blackout. Lights come up on the living room, where SENATOR ARMITRAGE *and the* MAN IN ARABIAN HEADDRESS *are seated in easy chairs, facing each other. The* MAN *has his back to the audience throughout.*

My dreams always end up
Happy.

He takes a big slug from his drink, which has been resting on a coffee table between the two.

Well, I guess I live right.
Like I was saying
Before we got onto dreams,
Back in Mad Wolf,
That's the county seat,
Back in Mad Wolf.

The MAN *mumbles something we do not hear.*

Sure, I can help out you boys.
Why, everything above board,
Of course, no sleight of hand.
One thing you can say about America: it works.

Pause.

You ever heard of John Sleight?

The MAN *mumbles something.*

Well, look what happened to him.
Messed around with the
Wrong people. Microchips.
A comfortable living, now, that's
All he really wanted . . .
Say, what's her name, the young lady?

The MAN *mumbles something. The* SENATOR *nods. Pause.*

A man must be careful.
The exercise of power demands
A kind of muscle. She's cute . . .
So anyhoo . . .
John Sleight sets himself up in
Old Shintar, among the Patzinaks.
Old name was Patzinakstan.
New name's something else.
Shintar's the capital, see?
Kinda like the Mad Wolf of
Patzinakstan, if you follow.
Rose of Isphahan, see? All that.
Microchip plant courtesy of

He burps.

Intertop. Skilled local population
Willing to work hard. Cheap.
Not like American labor, *nosirreebob!*
Work hard. Little itty-bitty chips.

John Sleight oversees the local P.R.
And operations. Intertop's man.
I was liaison with the director
Because the Agency burrowed in there
Good. A slew of moles digging up
Useful factoids. Anticommunism.
To back up the prince, our friend.
Intertop and the Agency close on
Police matters and management stuff.
But it's about the prince, see?
Our man, but no principles, gosh no.
Riots in Shintar, bad.
Mind if I go to the head?
In there?
Which one? Talkative cuss . . .

The MAN *mumbles something. The* SENATOR *exits. The* GIRL *enters and empties the ashtray. After exchanging glances with the* MAN, *she exits. Pause. The* SENATOR *enters, minus one boot. From this point he is subject to fits of daydreamlike musing.*

You can make yourself into any
Damn thing you want to. Whatever
It is you want to make yourself
Into, you can. People are so much mud
Ready to be made into human mud pies.
Lost my boot.
You seen my boot? Shit!

The MAN *mumbles something.*

Oh, is that so?

The SENATOR *seats himself. Pause.*

So when
All these hellish disorders burst out
The prince turned into a royal pumpkin.
John Sleight vanished into thin air.
Rumor had it he was blowed up.

He burps.

No fucking way.

Musing.

Right and wrong and the limits of the American
Theater of influence, why it all

Don't mean moose dick.
Everybody thought so, though.
Me? I was in the dark, too. Serious dark.
Pardon, are those Arab shoes?
You know what happened to John Sleight?

Pause.

Beats me . . .
But what was I telling you all this for?
I got a mouth like the Mad Wolf River!
The most gosh-darn things
Ever, why they do tumble out.
I do what I can for Intertop.
I like being what I am.
Helping people. Like you.

GIRL *brings him another huge drink. Pause. She exits.*

Ah, what else in the way of, ah,
Poontang you got back there?
You don't drink, I see . . .

Musing.

Back in Mad Wolf people hung about in knots.
Waiting for the returns to come in, loyal.
I was the "reform" candidate!
Family don't speak to me now.

Pause.

Sometimes I hear this noise, machine noises, like,
Like huge pistons and crankshafts, the clanking
Of huge wheels and God-awfulest machinery, down
There, in the ground. First heard it back in Mad Wolf.

The MAN *mumbles something.*

The director? You know the director.
I have this theory about the director,
A patriotic American and a loyal
Friend of mine going back to the
Old days in Mad Wolf. Real estate.
You can turn night into day
With zoning, he used to say.
But roundabout five years ago
I began to notice something
Funny about him. Hard to put

Your finger on. His eyes looked glassy.
Like this . . .

He demonstrates.

And then it got to be so difficult
Even to get near the man.
I felt for a while I was
Being systematically excluded from the
Circle of power and resented it bitterly,
I did. But I bit the bullet . . .
But his eyes was funny, and
He creaked. Like this . . .

He demonstrates.

One day I noticed, we was at
A press conference, there were these
Little wheels under his shoes
And I wondered what in hell, my!
But it was the necktie finally
Tipped me off.
I was looking at some pictures
In my office. Group portraits
At christenings, conferences, state
Dinners, and such like. And the director
ALWAYS HAD ON THE SAME DAMN NECKTIE!
This ratty old black and green rep
With a couple of squirts of red, always.
You get what I mean? ALWAYS.
He had quite a way with the fair sex.
I am reading this book
Intimate Pages from the Sex Lives of Rich and
Famous Personages.

Musing.

In the middle of a wheat field in midsummer.
Blackbirds wheeling about in the awfulest blue. Bluest
. . .
I ever . . .
You ever.
You can do wonders
With zoning.
So like I say I KEEP MY EAR TO THE GROUND,
close

To the silent ground swell that is the voice of the . . .
Of the people. The only voice they do possess
And a damn hard one to hear.
Even harder to ignore once it has
Collected its thoughts together and put
Those thoughts into comprehensible language
Because.

Musing.

By God. It works at you. Like a foot
In a trap. Sometimes I have compared
The legislative process to a hay bailer
Gone crazy . . .

Pause.

I saw a fox chew off its own leg once.
To get out of a trap. My head hurts.

Musing.

I have stepped in too many puddles to keep
My feet dry. It's the sky reflected in those rain
Puddles. You seem to see through to infinity . . .
I like you.
I consider you my equal.
Without friends, a man is nothing.

GIRL *brings on another huge drink.*

I am not nothing and I guess I've
Proved that. Life goes on. I need money
Badly. Little honey on the side. She's
Got expensive tastes. Furs. Jewelry. Theater.
God, how a man needs it.
If I got it straight what you want
From me is. All above board. Straight.
And on the level. You see because I am
A public servant. Is. Go to the director.
See if the Agency. Can go in there. All on
The up and up. Put the screws to those.
Goddamn. Fucking. Hottentot. Cocksucker.
Reds that did the expropriating, right?
Suggest a trade-off with Intertop. Et cetera.
Okay. Fine with me.
But the most-favored-nation clause.
That's more difficult. I'm afraid.

For that I've got to hustle.
Can't promise you anything.
I surely can't.
Goddamn cocksuckers
Got a fucking steam-roller lobbying machine.
It's rough.
For that I don't know.
Now seeing as how
The generalissimo
Your brother wants
A microchip plant
For his country
Just like the prince.
I like self-made men.
Like the generalissimo.
A real doer.
Back in Mad Wolf
When we were kids
We used to thumb-fuck
Each other. You'd
Ram your thumb up
Your own ass, too,
Sometimes, when it got
Lonely.

Pause.

Times ago.
I've always gone
Pretty much by
Myself. I guess.
Fought hard for what-
Ever it was I believed
In at the time. Hard
To tell.
That little lady of yours,
She's all right, but.
Seems almost to
Me crazy how like
I was born myself.
Begot myself.
Carried myself
Around like a

Gosh-darn
Watermelon,
Then when the time
Came round at last
Dropped myself.
Borned myself into
This world. Fully grown.
Complete. Perfect. A
Whole.
Unity, I mean.
It's a sense of my
Own destiny I've
Always had.
People can tell.
They like it.
That I'm this way.
Second term now.
Seems like yesterday.
Oh me, oh my.
I'd like to turn
Myself inside out
To see what it feels like.
You Arabs do a lot of butt-
Fucking?
You ever butt-fuck someone?
Skip it.

Pause.

Where were we?

Musing.

So I told 'em: if you make 'em
Bigger I can sell 'em. Sure.
Pound a nail clean through
Its heart. That's how you
Kill a vampire. Only it's
Got to be a silver nail.
Or is it brass?
Don't get me wrong.
I am a pro.
I used to listen to myself speak.
I used to listen to myself speak

In front of mirrors.
I'd like to try it with a boy.

He lets out with a long moan.

Out on the sidewalk, in the rain,
Sitting on a wagon, selling pencils.
Outside on the sidewalk, in the rain,
Wondering what in the name
Of heaven has happened to me.
Always knew it would come to
This. It's all messed up. No way
Ever to make it right again, nope.
I knew in my heart it'd end
Like this. All those high ideals.
Principles. A moral order. A
Sense of civic responsibility and
Public cleanliness. I always knew
Somewhere down in the pit of my belly
I'd end up like this. Stewed.
Totally bombed. Talking to a
Fucking Arab, who wants to buy
My legislative ass. Hell, you ain't
Even an Arab.
If you ask me. Looks more like
A Jew. Think I'm dumb. Hell, man,
We are talking
United States fucking Senate.
Land of the home of the free.
And furthermore you have got
Somewhere one of my boots. I have
Said repeatedly I want it back, you hear!
My boot.
We are talking
United States senatorial boots.

Pause.

I will not be moved.

Musing.

Lost in the
Tussle. That girl, she's a wild one.
Maybe she's got my boot. Oh my God.

He moans again.

The Self-begotten

Oh my God! What has it all come to?
How come you just sit there and don't
Talk normal?

Pause.

I want my boot.

Pause.

My price is fifty thousand
In small unmarked bills.
And don't you play tricks.
I'll slam the whole weight
Of the goddamn republic
Come crashing down on you.
You'll be a grease smear
On the shifting sands, you will.
Come crashing down on you.
DON'T FUCK WITH THE LEGISLATIVE BRANCH!

On all fours now.

My boot. My boot.
Party caucus won't stand for this.
Never. Never. Mooncalf, I am.
I'll swear on a.
Justice demands the.
I know what justice is.
By God, in this case. Supposing it do
Like a little

Getting up abruptly.

Weird?

Girl appears at the door. The Man makes a sign to her. She disappears.

So what? AM I
TO ANSWER TO A MOB BECAUSE
THERE'S A LITTLE SWAGGER TO MY STRIDE?
BECAUSE I AM ON OCCASION A HIGH-STEPPER?
I'll swear my innocence. No confession.
I'll stonewall it all the way till doomsday.

The Girl enters with a briefcase, which she hands to the Man, who hands it to the Senator. The Senator opens the briefcase, looks in, and closes it. Pause.

Now how about the boot? The truth, damn it,
Is not what it fucking looks like.

Both men sit down. The GIRL *exits.*

Oh me, oh my.

Pause.

Fucking Arab.

Pause.

Did I ever tell you
The story of the drunken sailor?
Once upon a time there's this drunken
Sailor, see.
In a terrible state.
Gets worse and worse.
Lost his ship and another ship.
All his family and reputation shot.
Such reputation as a drunken sailor
Might conceivably possess. Anyway.
Ends up in the hospital.
At the hospital there's this young
Whore dying, and she's giving birth,
See? So after she's dead
They take the baby, as a joke, see,
And give it to the drunken sailor
And say: *Look what was inside you.*
Well, the drunken sailor looks
At the kid and he looks at the doctors
And he sobers up, and when he gets
Out of the hospital he signs on to
A ship and does okay and pretty soon
He buys a share in the ship and then
The ship and pretty soon a whole fleet
And the kid's going to school and
Pretty soon the kid's in college, see?
Studying to be an architect and the
Drunken sailor takes sick,
An old man now, and he's on his deathbed.
Son comes to his father's side, says:
Father, father . . .
And the old sailor says: *Boy, I am
Sorry about this . . .*

Father, father, it's you . . .
Don't call me that, son.
I ain't your father but your mother.
Your father was a rich lawyer
In San Francisco.
You get it?
See the old sailor
Was butt-fucked
By a rich lawyer in San Francisco . . .

Pause.

Took me a while to get it, too.

The GIRL *enters with his hat and coat. He puts on his trousers and prepares to go.*

Thing about the director is
He's dead. He's been dead
For five, six years now.
That's what I figure.
They just wheel him out
For public occasions. Saves
On wear and tear to use
The same tie. I guess. Now
What I don't know is
Who's behind it all.
Oh, he talks all right.
Pretty much the same as
Always, only the voice's
Gone all gravelly, harsh.
I'll talk to him for you
Best as I can. The way
I figure it, it don't make
No difference:
Someone's in there, listening.

Shakes hands with the MAN.

Thank you kindly, sir.

Pause. To the GIRL.

When you find that boot . . .
Wonder what they'd say back in
Mad Wolf could they see me now!

He chuckles. Exits.

The Bad Infinity   (1983)

CHARACTERS *(in order of appearance)*

CAT BURGLAR, the legendary BLAISE?

MEGAN, an appearance variously modulated

DEBORAH, an apparent appearance, more substantial than apparitional—much to her chagrin

DOG, the victim of chronic depression

JOHN SLEIGHT, alias SAM, a master of many identities

RAMON GUZMAN, an international entrepreneur and a real man trapped among phantoms

SENATOR ARMITRAGE, a person fallen from a great height, a political Humpty Dumpty

three WAITERS, at the Alibi Club

CHEF, of a sensitive and artistic nature, in apparent exile

SAM, alias himself, a rank amateur of many identities

MAN WITH WINGS, a dead SANTA, and an ANIMAL of Unknown Species

The Bad Infinity was premiered May 3, 1985, at Brass Tacks Theatre in Minneapolis, Minnesota. This play follows *Energumen, Diseases of the Well-dressed, The Professional Frenchman,* and *The Self-begotten,* and concludes the gestural—often highly elliptical—antic progress of these across the hollow land of Modern Empty Time.

The Bad Infinity is dedicated to the proposition that the theatrical body and soul of the world are not to be found in propositions per se, but in the subtle dialectic of gesture and spirit, parable and pratfall, dialogue and dance.

The play is for Yolanda, with love.

Scene one. A lavish penthouse apartment somewhere in northern Virginia. Fireplace. Door to bedroom. Door to hallway. A staircase leading to the roof garden. A large sofa with matching end tables. An upright piano. All these furnishings are of the most exquisite kind, and arranged with a decorator's eye. The immense window looks out on several other high rises. The cat burglar, BLAISE, *enters in near darkness through an air-conditioning vent, which he knocks out. He is dressed in black, wears a black mask and black gloves. He looks around at various objects, including candlesticks, a stereo, some small bronzes and porcelains arranged on shelves, but seems pleased with nothing. This continues for several minutes, but his search is in vain. There's simply nothing here worth the trouble. He looks in the liquor cabinet and finds a bottle of bourbon. With bottle in hand, he ambles over to the piano and sits down. Drinks. Bangs out a few notes. Takes another drink, and begins to play a rag. Stops suddenly, as if listening for a noise. Another drink. Now he launches into the main rag, playing with great enthusiasm, and even vocalizing with the music. Suddenly he slams the piano closed, wipes off his fingerprints, and bolts behind the sofa. Pause. He peers over the sofa, rushes over to the piano, grabs the bottle, and wiggles out the air-conditioning vent. Pause. Blackout.*

Scene two. The penthouse. MEGAN *and* DEBORAH *talk in an animated fashion. Windows of other apartments are visible. A piece of twilight sky.*

MEGAN	He's coming. Really, he's coming.
DEBORAH	Again?
MEGAN	No, silly girl, not *him*. Don.
DEBORAH	Don who?
MEGAN	Ramon's friend. After all, with Sam gone we need someone to cheer you up.
DEBORAH	I expect you've heard the good news.

MEGAN	Isn't it wonderful?
DEBORAH	An idea like that.
	After all this time.
	After all our doubts.
MEGAN	Oh, we shall all
	have such a wonderful
	time when it's begun.
DEBORAH	I'll say.
	Can pack up my books and stuff it.
MEGAN	Pardon me, Debby.

She picks up phone and dials.

Hello. Everything all right?

DOG *barks. She goes to the window.* DOG *appears in the window opposite, phone in hand, and waves.* MEGAN *waves back and hangs up.*

`	Would you like a drink?
DEBORAH	Sure, a scotch would be nice.
MEGAN	A neighbor in the next building.
	Going through a rough time. Family
	trouble. A bit depressed. So I call
	up every now and then.

Hands the drink to DEBORAH.

DEBORAH	Aren't you sweet.
MEGAN	People have to help out.
	It'll be different, soon.
DEBORAH	I expect we'll get used to the light.
MEGAN	When the statues come to life . . .
DEBORAH	When the statues come to life
	you know what I'm going to do?
MEGAN	Throw away your glasses and buy a
	boutique . . .
DEBORAH	Throw away my law books is more like it.
MEGAN	What a waste that would be,
	with your mind.
DEBORAH	Not really, Megan.
MEGAN	I've been grinning from ear to ear.
	Inside. Since I've heard the news.
	I've grown so fond of you, Deborah.

	Do you know how the world was created?
	Seriously, do you?
DEBORAH	Just like it is now, I would imagine.
MEGAN	No, it was created, according to
	an Egyptian myth, by an enormous
	dung beetle—scarab, it's called—
	who went about rolling, and kneading,
	and rolling this gigantic ball of shit,
	until it got bigger and bigger and bigger.
	Then it got quite out of hand. And so on.

While MEGAN *talks,* DEBORAH *spies a pair of woman's gloves and picks them up.*

DEBORAH	I didn't know you had invited her.
MEGAN	I didn't. She invited herself. Rude creature.
DEBORAH	In that case.

Gets up to go.

MEGAN	No, please stay.
DEBORAH	You should know better than to pull
	this on me. On a day like this.
	With all our good fortune.
	Where is she?
MEGAN	In the bedroom. Passed out. Really,
	it wasn't my doing.

Musing.

	Times being what they are.
DEBORAH	Not to mention our exceeding good fortune.

Looks out the window.

	What are they doing down there?
MEGAN	Expect a little commotion
	of some kind. A celebration,
	perhaps in honor of the coming.
	The light is thrilling isn't it?
	After all these years, just
	as I was beginning to doubt.
DEBORAH	I can't imagine you doubting, Megan.
MEGAN	Oh yes, I've had my moments.
	Never talk much about them.
	Don't see much point
	in complaining.

DEBORAH	And now it's not necessary.
MEGAN	So now the future shall be just like the past.

Musing.

	A happy throng of carefree peasantry . . . Or something like a pageant.
DEBORAH	I hardly have the language for what I feel. Not that I'm worried, mind you.
MEGAN	You always were so gloomy, dear.
DEBORAH	But I promise to change.
MEGAN	I always change. Change is my avocation. That's why I'm so . . .

An awkward pause.

DEBORAH	Articulate. I understand.
MEGAN	The sky is wonderful, isn't it?
DEBORAH	Looks so real it almost looks fake.
MEGAN	A remarkable effect . . .
DEBORAH	Whatever are they doing down there?
MEGAN	Playing stickball with a human head, ah, here she comes. She's awake.

Tidies up.

DEBORAH	I promise to be good.
MEGAN	Oh, you have changed, Debby.

Both look expectantly to the bedroom door. Pause. Blackout.

Scene three. The same. JOHN SLEIGHT *has joined* DEBORAH *and* MEGAN. *All three walk about casually, drinking and smoking.*

SLEIGHT	The big change came later when the banks began to understand my work.

Pause.

	They found that by simply making nothing happen they could advance their own interests as well as mine. All things come to those who wait. Money is time, and empty time is

the most valuable because it
costs nothing, involves no risky
transactions with leftist regimes
or desperate small entrepreneurs.
It can all be done by computer tie-in.
If you plug into the system you survive,
if you don't, you don't.

Pause.

It was this, in essence, I was trying
to tell Sam all along, but he was too
stubborn. Committed to an outworn
creed. A spiritual aborigine, so to speak.

DEBORAH   Must you mention his name?
MEGAN   I was just going to say the same thing.

Something strange happens. SLEIGHT *looks puzzled. They go back
to where they were at the beginning of the scene.*

SLEIGHT   The big change came later when the banks
began to understand my work.

Pause.

They found that by simply making
nothing happen they could advance
their own interests as well as mine.
All things come to those who wait.
Money is time, and empty time is
the most valuable because it
costs nothing, involves no risky
transactions with leftist regimes
or desperate small entrepreneurs.
It can all be done by computer tie-in.
If you plug into the system you survive,
if you don't, you don't.

Pause.

It was this, in essence, I was trying
to tell Sam all along, but he was too
stubborn. Committed to an outworn
creed. A spiritual aborigine, so to speak.

MEGAN   Must you mention his name?
DEBORAH   I was just going to say the same thing.
SLEIGHT   That was nearly perfect.

The Bad Infinity   65

He looks at his watch and screams. He does a pratfall and lies motionless. A bluish fluid pours down one wall, changing its color. A red carpet rolls out from the bedroom. GUZMAN *appears in the fireplace and enters.*

MEGAN	Oh, Ramon, it's so good of you.
RAMON	(*To* DEBORAH.) Charmed.
MEGAN	This is Deborah.
RAMON	I am delighted to make your acquaintance.

She spits in his face and sits with her back to the audience.

MEGAN	Ramon, this is John Sleight.
DEBORAH	(*Mimicking her.*) I'm not sure you've met.

She giggles.

MEGAN	This is an exercise of Mr. Sleight's.
	It's called "playing dead." Quite
	good for body and soul, really.
	May I get you a drink?

SLEIGHT *remains motionless on the floor.*

GUZMAN	Yes, Megan, I would like that.
MEGAN	John, won't you say hello to Mr. Guzman?
GUZMAN	Do not disturb him on my account.
MEGAN	We were just discussing the good news.
GUZMAN	You mean the
	chiasmus in the time-fabric potentiated
	by the isochronometric instigator?
DEBORAH	Of course, idiot.
RAMON	Where shall we be dining?
MEGAN	The club, of course.
RAMON	It might be fun to get out and go
	to the theater for a change.

DEBORAH *tries to stifle wild laughter.*

Do something different.

Awkward pause. SLEIGHT *is recovering.*

They're all these warm-hearted revivals
going on nowadays. Quite reassuring.

DEBORAH *breaks up again.*

I am particularly fond of this play about
the mountain of styrofoam I am reading
about. This fantastic pile of ice and

stone and prehistoric *merds* is inhabited
by some people who are lost.
They discover meaning in their
lostness and are reminiscing
on how sweet life has been
when this monstrous avalanche
smash them to tiny fragments.
Quite moving theater.

MEGAN	Not on an empty stomach, Ramon.
RAMON	Will Hilary be arriving soon?
SLEIGHT	(*Getting up.*) Soon enough, Mr. Guzman.
RAMON	Ah, you are recovered.
SLEIGHT	A taste of death is a fine tonic, sir.
RAMON	A medicine to be administered in small doses, John.
MEGAN	Mr. Guzman is such a wit.
Pause.	
	Can I get you something, John?
Pause.	
	Debby, what about you?
	Why don't you join us?
DEBORAH	Hilary won't be coming.
MEGAN	What a strange thing to say.
	Of course she will.
DEBORAH	Because she doesn't exist.
MEGAN	What nonsense, Ramon. Ignore her.
DEBORAH	Ignore me when I speak like that.
MEGAN	Would you like to see John's latest?
DEBORAH	Oh, I'd love to.
MEGAN	Not you, silly. I was asking Ramon.

DEBORAH *knocks herself on the forehead in mock astonishment
and collapses on the sofa and is motionless.*

RAMON	No, Megan, I have no interest in such toys.
MEGAN	Then perhaps I shall go myself.
SLEIGHT	*(Pouring himself a drink.)*
	I was just about to explain, Ramon,
	how the future can be controlled only
	by changing it into the past.
	Traditionally this has been
	the function of life, but now
	that mere life has become a

	far too chancy enterprise
	for those of us whose cat tracks
	the pavement singing old Beatles'
	dung beetle. One requires a thorn.
	I assure you, if you look out this
	window you can hear shapes of your
	eyesight drilling holes to China.
	Rearing up dead heaps of
	dollar bills. Banks going at it, bang-bang!
	And cropped photos of famous
	politicians turned into living turds.
	My work is called *The Bad Infinity!*
RAMON	It sounds fascinating.

Pause. SLEIGHT *finishes his drink.*

	You talk as if life were redundant.
SLEIGHT	When it works right and the switches
	mesh, I can conjure up a whole fear
	picture of picture's bungo. Some like a
	boy and girl dreaming of a play upon
	a bird's perch where they are dreaming
	of a television set that can turn itself
	off. All this reduced to a digital
	diorama of a video game in which
	the object of the game is to win points
	by drinking blood. Or a theater piece
	based on a video game in which a
	pair of TVs make love in the mind of a
	young lady whose lives are recounting in a
	miniseries as described in an unproduced
	treatment recycled for TV by video people
	for a talk show that is aired in the dark.
	You get me? It's safe because it's blank.
RAMON	It sounds quite mad to me, but if you
	can make money doing it, why not?
	What do you think, Deborah?
DEBORAH	For blank read *dead*.
SLEIGHT	You haven't lost your harsh, judging side,
	have you?
DEBORAH	You see this lampshade?

Holds it up.

RAMON	Whatever are you driving at?
DEBORAH	Why don't you wear it like a hat?
RAMON	A very good idea.

He does so.

MEGAN	I'm going to see the "Work."
	Then we'll go out to the theater.
SLEIGHT	Really, I think dinner would be
	a more appropriate idea.
DEBORAH	If we don't go to the theater I'll hang myself.
RAMON	Women, these northern women.
DEBORAH	I'll hang myself from the rafters
	and swing back and forth in the wind
	like a big old beach towel, and the
	rope will squeal like window hinges.

She demonstrates.

> I'll hang till the birds pick me clean
> and then I'll fly and fly and career
> over the city like a mad banshee and
> I'll shriek till I deafen all the
> fine people like you with your wars
> and money and fine clothes and endless
> boring technological bullcrap. I will.

She grabs a bottle of wine, takes a terrific swig, and pours the rest in a flowerpot. Climbs up on an end table. She places the bottle on her head and begins a malefic jig.

> A moment of pure jade.
> Glass between the sun and the moon.
> Death on a stick, life on the run.
> America.
> Ameria.
> Meria.
> Mericanica.
> Mercanicamera.
> Bodiless ordinaria.

She freezes.

> Photograph the photograph of the moon.

Pause.

> You polite asses.

Pause.

A sea of perpendictables.
Perpendictable paper dolls.

Pause.

See. Look, man. Open your head.

She gets no response. She quiets.

It's so like something no one ever saw
before. It's like the sudden appearance
and disappearance of a leopard in a
snake's dream. It's like cooking up a
really spectacular meal of raw food
starting with garbage.

Pause.

Oh, the energy that goes into a thing.
Horrid. Horrd. Horrd. Hord. Hord.
Hrd. Hrd. Hd. Hd. Hd. D. D. D. D.

Pause.

Take off that lampshade, you fucking cliché.

He puts it back on the lamp. DEBORAH *freezes as a Greek Nike.*

SLEIGHT	Care for a refill, Ramon?
RAMON	In the jungle, Sam, we practiced
	the most unspeakable atrocities on the
	natives, we did this not out of guilt.
	As you *norteamericanos* do. Or to improve
	ourselves and the world. Bah, you liberals.
	No, we do this for the hell of it.
	Yes, for the hell of it. To give us pleasure.
	Your blood has become thin.
	You are weak. Simple human joys
	as, for instance, of torture and slaughter
	and rapine no longer appeal to your
	delicate appetites. Amigo, I pity you.
SLEIGHT	You underestimate me, Ramon.
	"Feed the fires of paranoia," I always say.
MEGAN	A toast to Intertop.
RAMON	I rather toast the devil.
MEGAN	Poor sport.
SLEIGHT	By the way, how did you know I was Sam?
RAMON	It says so in the program.

SLEIGHT	YOU CAN GET OFF THE FUCKING TABLE NOW.
DEBORAH	I was wondering when you were going to notice me.

She gets down. Blackout. Pause. Lights back up. DEBORAH *and* MEGAN *prepare to go see* SLEIGHT's *"Work."*

SLEIGHT	Actually. I'm the Pseudo Sam. The Real Sam ran off to live in the forest.
RAMON	How original.
DEBORAH	"How original."

She spits in his face on her way out. Blackout.

Scene four. Darkness. Voices of ROMEO *and* JULIET *from act three, scene five. After a time, silence. Lights come up on two tape recorders on the floor with speakers facing each other, maybe fifteen feet apart. Just behind are two chairs facing each other, with mirrors propped up in both. Otherwise the room is empty.* MEGAN *and* DEBORAH *admire from one side, where the former has her finger on the light switch. They are a little drunk by now, and both giggle a lot.*

MEGAN	Quite remarkable, isn't it?
DEBORAH	A gas.

She burps. Pause.

MEGAN	Almost a perfect "bad infinity."
DEBORAH	Almost?
MEGAN	You can't really perceive the total effect. You see? If you stand here, for instance,

She stands in between the mirrors.

	your own image blocks out a small portion of infinity. You are left with a taint of finitude, which, despite the claims of proud Mr. John Sleight, occludes the unending accordion effect. It only works when no one's looking at it.
DEBORAH	That's pretty much as it should be.

MEGAN	"Should," Debby?
DEBORAH	Sorry.
MEGAN	The nicest thing about Shakespeare is that his works are a club to beat down our contemporaries. A cudgel.
DEBORAH	Never thought about it like that.
MEGAN	My innocence must be rubbing off on you.

Scratches herself.

	I like it here.
DEBORAH	Shall we rejoin the gentlemen?
MEGAN	It's wonderful, just for a short time, not to see the sky, not to hope or dream. Or wish. Or want. Or know. Or think. Or feel anything. To be entirely vacuous in the presence of the Master, Shakespeare. To be empty and to allow the pure water of his meaningless old-hat dead language to wash over us and make us clean. I want so to be clean.
DEBORAH	You sound like me.
MEGAN	Shall we go up?

Pause.

DEBORAH	You sound like me.
MEGAN	Shall we go up? I didn't use "should," you notice.
DEBORAH	It's going to be such an extravagantly wonderful evening.

They start out. Blackout. DEBORAH *giggles in the dark.*

Scene five. The penthouse. The four seated randomly throughout the room. Motionless. Long pause. RAMON *whistles a few bars from "Knickknack, Paddywhack, Give Your Dog a Bone." Pause.*

DEBORAH   What do you suppose ever happened to Blaise?

All are shocked at the mere idea. The MEN *hunker down in their seats.*

SLEIGHT   What do you suppose ever happened to Sam?

Sky turns purple; a MAN *appears on the wall of the building opposite, scampering like a lizard; the* DOG *appears in the window, howling and whining; on the edge of the roof garden above him a* MAN *appears with a pair of wings, which he flaps gingerly; a crowd of people begin leaping from windows and over the edge of the roof garden; the* MAN WITH WINGS *leaps, flapping furiously, and falls; lastly, the* DOG *flings himself out of the window; in each case the fall is followed, after a short interval, by a terrible thud. The sky changes to a deep purple. A score or so of plastic WallWalkers appear on the wall opposite, where the first* MAN *had been scampering. They creep down the wall in typical WallWalker fashion;* MEGAN *yawns.*

MEGAN   Shall we go?

They get up and prepare to go out. Blackout.

Scene six. Before the club. The four stand, holding overcoats, backs to the audience, looking at something in the sky. Former SENATOR ARMITRAGE *appears, kneeling on a low dolly, with a handful of pencils, which he is selling. A placard of some kind hangs around his neck. He addresses the audience as the others gaze off into the distance.*

ARMITRAGE   Fine people, seekers, all of you,
             lovers of truth, art, and journalism,
             tell me, truthfully, what have you found?
             What knowledge? Lord knows! The madness
             of pure lust and impure ways! Suppose
             you all mean to go in there?

Points to the club.

             The old club.

He cackles.

             The Alibi Club, it used to be called.
             Go in at your own risk. Things
             have changed. They serve

The Bad Infinity   73

human flesh nowadays,
and they're not real particular
where it comes from. Be warned.
I know: I, too, have flown.
I, too, have skimmed the cloud tops.

He muses.

Simple pleasures and
no apology, simple
murders,
the joy
blasted
or blasting through solid bedrock
to become a firefly.
Tipped over.
Like a foot scratching another foot.
Because our American appetite
the happy voice of all the
empty land, empty
heart, making it full. What
the gods were
meaningless
meaningless . . .

He looks around furtively.

I am walking up a gradual in-
cline that becomes steep. I
am all wind and silence and . . .

Pause.

Bright, healthy!

Pause.

Thunder and hats . . .

Pause.

The whole hay heap be damned!
Must go on. The bright doom . . .

Collecting himself.

I, too, have landed in the mire,
burnt out, a relic. A proud man
reduced to abject debasement . . .
Machination of lawyers, the press.
Vile, unsubstantiated charges.

Totally unproven. All of 'em. I was
betrayed, and a million billion
bumblebees are forever singing
in my dreams and daydreams.

He buzzes.

Buzzing me back to Mad Wolf. But
I'm a proud man, unbended. I work
for my daily blood, *bread.* I can
see the future better than any man,
having helped instigate it, by gosh.
And I'm telling you:
Don't go in this place.
It's not safe. It's crawling
with demons, devils, foreigners and
monstrosities. The Chef has quit.
He's fled to the forest.
He's fled to the forest to get away.
AND DON'T TOUCH THE FOOD, bah . . .

Scornfully.

You're not listening.

Pause.

You go in there and you'll pull the
trip wire on the most incredible
series of bad infinities known to
man.

Pause.

THE HORIZONTAL AVALANCHE!

Pause.

The Chef has quit, I tell you.

In despair.

Oh, my God.

Pause.

What it does to you.

He rolls himself off. DEBORAH *turns around.*

DEBORAH   What did that man say?
MEGAN   Shall we go in?

Blackout.

Scene seven. Total darkness. A squeaking sound, very quiet. Over this, a magisterial VOICE.

VOICE   Ladies and gentlemen. The sound you hear
                 is the sound of forty-nine million
                 bats. These vicious, feral
                 little monsters are in flight.
                 Perpetual flight. In
                 a space which contains all
                 of you, and all the visible
                 and invisible matter, imaginable
                 or unimaginable. Known
                 or unknown. In the entire
                 universe. This space is
                 roughly ten centimeters
                 on a side and weighs
                 approximately ten and a half
                 sestillion solar masses.
                 You will observe that no light emanates from this
                 space.

Pause.

                 Only the cries of forty-nine million bats.

Pause.

                 Creatures that have been in flight
                 since the beginning of time and not one
                 full collision has been recorded.

Pause.

                 Only the occasional brushing of a wing against
                 a furred ear, or a whisker against a claw.

Pause.

                 A bat infinity.

Pause.

                 Perhaps you can feel the occasional, slight,
                 barely perceptible brushing of their wings.

Silence.

Scene eight. In the dining room at the club. The four are preparing to order the main course. The FIRST WAITER *is in blackface.* DEBORAH *is lost in reverie, which is noticed only by* SLEIGHT.

SLEIGHT   Are you all right, Deb?

MEGAN	Waiter, the lumpfish roe is alive.
FIRST WAITER	Well, fuck my ass. I done beat on it till I thought I kilt it, but I guess I'll jus' beat on it some mo'.

FIRST WAITER *exits with dish.* SECOND WAITER *brings on bottles of wine.*

MEGAN	(*Getting up.*) We're going to see the pit. Aren't we, Ramon?
RAMON	(*Getting up.*) Quite, yes.
SECOND WAITER	French wine . . .

He exits.

SLEIGHT	There is a thing we aspire to, which is being continually lost, because we don't see we *already* possess it. So when we lose it, we don't even know we had it once, assuming we did. What is it?
DEBORAH	Cut the crap. Sam.
SLEIGHT	How did you recognize me?
DEBORAH	You don't look like him in the least.
SLEIGHT	Do you believe all this "statues-coming-to-life" bullcrap?
DEBORAH	Hell no. Intertop's bankrupt.
SLEIGHT	Bullshit.
DEBORAH	It's true. I can feel it.
SLEIGHT	You're psychic, I suppose.
DEBORAH	It's in the numbers. Actuarial tables.
SLEIGHT	I don't believe it. Look, Deb.

He reaches for her.

DEBORAH	Don't touch me.

Pause.

I don't want to feel anything.
It's too painful. I don't want
to be loved. I want to be feared.
I want to destroy everything human
in me. I want to become a monument
to my own incredulity, and to the
vileness and stupidity of the world.

Pause.

> And if you
> so much as lay a finger on me
> I'll scream. So help me I will.

He touches her with one finger. Pause.

> I've seen the world.
> I know what it is.
> I can't be fooled.

SLEIGHT There's still a chance.

DEBORAH How do you mean?

SLEIGHT Shush. They're coming back.

MEGAN *and* RAMON *return.*

RAMON It is very interesting, Mr. Sleight.
You see a big hole with flames
licking about in the bottom, and
thunders animating the surrounding
miasmus. Very extensive, I assure
you. Large serpents are writhing in
and around large flowerpots and
on the parquet. The members of the
staff throw live animals, which are
torn apart by the creatures of the bottom.
The wailing of the voices of the damned
is quite something to behold.

SLEIGHT A remarkable feat of engineering.

RAMON An amusing display, to say the least.

MEGAN I thought Ramon might be intrigued
by the new installation.

SLEIGHT Of course the illusion is quite
realistic.

DEBORAH You know better than me
about illusions.

MEGAN Shall we order? I'm famished.

THIRD WAITER *rushes out of the kitchen with a knife in his back.*
FIRST *and* SECOND WAITERS *follow in hot pursuit. Despite them, he*
makes it to the table.

THIRD WAITER Don't eat . . . the blood . . . sausage.

Collapses and is dragged off by FIRST WAITER. SECOND WAITER
comes up to the table.

MEGAN	My word.
SECOND WAITER	Ignore this man. Is new on staff. Have not learned how to behave. Sorry.

He exits.

MEGAN	Don't you find the question of behavior quite neglected, Ramon?

The latter becomes immediately agitated.

RAMON	Ah, yes. But in my opinion the question of behavior is reducible by a process of covert inspissitude to the more profound question of decorum, which is itself a three-dimensional graphic explosion of the two dimensional crystallization of the essential problem, which is the matter of PENMANSHIP. As you know, elegant handwriting has fallen into a state of neglect and disrepair, like the nation's bridges and highways and viaduct system. This must be remedied by a strict return

Rapping his spoon.

to fundamentals, as, for instance, the famous curve and the perfect line, straight line, not to be confused with the waving, wavering, twisted line, and the oblate, hyperbolic curve, which is abominated by the divinities and is, in fact, the Work of the Devil.

Pause.

"Demons inhabit the intersections of circles," as the poet tells us.

Pause.

But, *au fond,* what is required is discipline.

Pause.

Otherwise the handwriting becomes personalized, unscrutable, inscrupulous, unreadable, inane, evil. And if the hand come to delight in

Portentous pause.

                eccentricity for eccentricity's sake . . .

Another pause.

                who knows where next it may find
                pleasure?

He relaxes.

                I know my views are old hat, so to say,
                but they come from the heart.

He bows, banging head on the table.

MEGAN *(To* SECOND WAITER.*)* Sir, we shall order now.

    WAITER *bows, stalks off without taking their order.*

MEGAN	What do you suppose is wrong with him?
SLEIGHT	Head-wedged syndrome. Quite common.

    Begins doing push-ups. SECOND WAITER *reappears, very nonchalant.*

MEGAN	*Pardonne,* sir. We wish to order.
SECOND WAITER	I have already taken order.
MEGAN	But that is quite impossible.
SECOND WAITER	No, is truth. *Le Vrai semblance.*

    MEGAN *stands up, enraged. She belts him.*

MEGAN	My friends and I have not ordered yet, and I find this behavior on your part extraordinarily quadruped. Not to mention Negroid and beyond the pale. Skid mump. Poleax the hyperborean tomato plant chop up the telephone cancer monster boredom and wretching dry heaves with a needle stitching all their hearts together on a clothesline beneath the oilous ombulations of the sea swollen beyond its border to eat. Melted . . .
DEBORAH	The man is trying to speak, Megan. Two wrongs don't

	make a right. Remember the golden rule. For Christ's sake.
SLEIGHT	*(Gets up from the floor.)* You're right, Deborah.
SECOND WAITER	I am learning to take order by telepathic mysterium. It is an outcome of acupuncture for lower back syndrome. I go to Wu Chen Few. One needle go in wrong place. KA-BOOM. I am a genius of TABLE WAITING.
Pause.	
	I know WHAT YOU ALL WANT. IN THE DARK- NESS OF YOUR ABYSSAL CRAVING. I give you what you need instead.
SLEIGHT	My God, I believe the man.
RAMON	John, is true. I had noticed before his genius halo.
A weird light appears.	
MEGAN	And what is it we need, my good man?
SECOND WAITER	French wine. Eggs up the stream. Chicken smashed pot. Blight. Roasted plate. Bowel of lamb. Verbatim all around.
MEGAN	A genius!
SECOND WAITER	Of a minor sort.
He bows.	
	I go now.
Blackout.	

Scene nine. The dining room. After dinner. At the next table a customer is slumped over his meal. The room is filled with smoke. The SECOND WAITER is going about his business. The MEN look stunned.

MEGAN	Bet you've never seen the revolving Sky Room.
DEBORAH	Nope.
MEGAN	Would you like to?
DEBORAH	Not really. Might get seasick.
SECOND WAITER	Are we finished with dinner?

They nod. The WAITER *snaps his fingers. All the trays, plates, bottles, and covered dishes get up, hop on the floor, and scurry off into the kitchen.*

MEGAN   Ah, but the sky, with its infinite spaces, its
               unimaginable prospects, beckons.

DEBORAH   Oh, all right.

They exit. Pause.

RAMON   Sam, do you remember
               Havana?

SLEIGHT *puts on sunglasses and stares at* RAMON. *Pause.*

SLEIGHT   Never been to Havana.
     Pause.
               And the name is John.

RAMON   Intractable son of a bitch,
               aren't you?

     Pause.
               So
               you don't remember the flamingo
               garden at the Hotel Palacio?

     Pause.
               How we saw Hemingway get drunk.

     Pause.
               All those good times, laughter and
               dancing and hopes, yes, *hopes,*
               before we learned
               what the world is
               made of and what
               must be done to
               survive.

SLEIGHT   Escapes me totally, all of it.
               Never seen you before in my life.

RAMON   I tried to have you killed, don't
               you remember?

SLEIGHT   How interesting.

RAMON   Even that you don't recall.

SLEIGHT   It must have been someone else,
               I'm afraid.

RAMON   No, it was you. Only your name was
               Ralph Graytree.

SLEIGHT   Impossible.

Pause. Takes off glasses.

RAMON   What a magnificent liar you are.

SLEIGHT   Just an ordinary S.O.B. One of the guys.

RAMON   There are fractures in the Egg of Time
that lead us down winding corridors
of consciousness into realms covered
with sawdust and spiderwebs.

He stands up.

Basements . . .

He sits down.

basements of intellect, vestigial hiding
places where lurk phantasmal creatures
whose understanding of the secret
laws governing the inner clockwork
of human destiny is nonpareil.

Pause.

You understand?

SLEIGHT   You're mad.

RAMON *stands up and falls down. His shoelaces have been tied together.*

RAMON   Your agents have tied my shoelaces
together.

SLEIGHT   My agents have tied your shoelaces
together.

RAMON   It's all the same.

Pause.

Untie my shoelaces.

Pause. SLEIGHT *does so.*

SLEIGHT   Just a practical joke.

RAMON   Odd sense of humor you have.

Recovering his dignity.

So: you will not admit
your true identity. You
will not take on your
true destiny and act like a man.

SLEIGHT	Absolutely not.
Pause.	
	And besides, you have it all wrong,
	as well you know. It was I
	who tried to kill you.
RAMON	IT IS YOU.

He stands. Pause. SLEIGHT *stands.*

SLEIGHT	Never saw you before in my life.
RAMON	BUT IT IS YOU.
	YOU SENT SARPICON.
	WITH THE THROWING KNIVES.
	At last . . .

They both sit.

SLEIGHT	The truth is, it doesn't matter.
	The mask I wear is a true mask.
	Underneath is another mask,
	and underneath that one is
	another and another and so on.
	There is nothing else underneath.
	Do you understand that?
RAMON	Ah, but why not be friends?
	We have shared the most
	intimate of secrets, the secret
	of life and death. Sam . . .
Pause.	
	or whatever your name is . . .
SLEIGHT	It doesn't matter . . .
RAMON	We have both hired killers to
	murder each other. What
	stronger bond can there be?
	We are lovers in an infinite pas de deux
	of murder and . . .
SLEIGHT	It doesn't matter.
	You damn fool.
	Don't you see?

RAMON *weeps.*

	Money. Money is the only thing
	that's left. Money.
Pause.	

I'm not joking. The only thing.
Money is a God. The only God.
Don't waste my time
with this wretched disquisition
on murder and guilt. And the rest.

Pause.

It all belongs with fascinations,
curses, the mystery of love, the
romance of the rose.

Pause.

The old Egyptian soft-shoe . . .

RAMON   Fool.

SLEIGHT   Even Marxism is a dead mask.

RAMON   Intertop is finished.

SLEIGHT   What.

RAMON   House of cards. The banks
have begun to collapse.
Mexico. Poland. Brazil.
The Congo. Et cetera. Et cetera.
You've climbed on the wagon
too late. It is you, Sam, isn't it?
All the portfolios have begun to
detumesce;
our friends in the stabilized regimes
can't even pay the interest
on the interest on the interest.
The Mexicans.
Couldn't meet the scheduled payment
of a hundred thousand certified virgins.
We are on the verge of a
bad infinity of bank collapses.
The Holy City of Byzantium
is an apparition built on the shifting
mists hovering over another yet more
apparitional chunk of chimaera and mirage
floating over the lake . . .

He gestures grandly.

of oblivion. Nonentity. Unreal.
A bad infinity of bank collapses
such as the world has never seen.

We are all going to be swept
down the mouth of hell.
You, me along with the rest.

SLEIGHT   Aw, shit.
    Pause.

Just when I get ahead of the game.
Just when some things are beginning
to happen for me. They close the show.
All these years.
Face to the grindstone.
Hustling. Chiseling. Always
being undone by the remnant
of my good intentions. And now.
Finally. When I have at last
stamped down. Crushed. And murdered
all that's decent in me. Even my goddamn
curiosity. The whole show shuts down. Self-
destructs. Shit. Weasel shit. Just my luck!

    Pause.

WHY SHOULD I BELIEVE YOU? WHY,
YOU TRIED TO HAVE ME MURDERED.
I tried to have you murdered.
We don't even speak the same
ontological language.

    Rising.

Waiter, would you say this looks
like a human being?

SECOND   Looks like one. To be sure.
WAITER

RAMON   What about him?
WHAT DOES HE LOOK LIKE?

SECOND   Unconvincing replica of a thing. Mannequin.
WAITER

RAMON   You see. The disease is catching.
You must conceal your unreality.
Hope for good weather.
A house of cards is better than
no house at all. Only must tiptoe.
Whatever your name is, you.

SLEIGHT   *(Seats himself wearily.)* Shut up. Leave me be. You,

	say something.
SECOND WAITER	Have confession to make. Food is done with mirrors. Cork on string and papier-mâché. Food color and bottled smell. Chef have run off to the forest in pay dispute.
RAMON	Difficult to find good person for service industry.
SECOND WAITER	Everyone want to be computer genius.

He shrugs.

	Me, I can count to two.
SLEIGHT	That's all you need.
RAMON	Ah, the ladies return.
SLEIGHT	You have any real champagne

Pause.

back there?

Blackout.

Scene ten. The Rotating Sky Terrace. MEGAN *and* DEBORAH *behold the starry night. The latter carries a bottle. Scene begins with a pause.*

MEGAN	Everything will be revealed.
DEBORAH	Apparently.

Pause.

MEGAN	I don't know.

She takes the bottle from DEBORAH *and drinks. Then hands it back. Wipes her mouth. Pause.*

Life has been good to me.

Pause.

DEBORAH.	To me also.
	Except for the metaphysical snare.
	And braces, early on.

She takes a long slug.

Got what I wanted. Sort of. Puke.

Pause.

The sky opens to you as you open

	to it. What do you suppose
	ever happened to Blaise. Megan?
MEGAN	Oh, he comes around every now and then.
	He's a full-time burglar now. Enjoys
	his work immensely. Far more happy
	than he was at the Embassy. Not
	every man can make his hobby his
	life's work, and still make a living.
	He comes around every now and then.
	Looks around and messes things up a bit.
	Rarely takes anything. It's the danger
	he likes. The thrill. A man with purpose.
	I like to see that. Even if in terms of
	gestural language he's a bit deranged.
DEBORAH	But he is coming.
MEGAN	Never can be sure.
DEBORAH	Look at the sky. It grows and grows.
	Seems like the more you look at it,
	the more of it there is. I love the sky.
	Because it's so vast and dead and empty.

Pause.

	There's a way out. I know there is.
MEGAN	There's something wrong with you.

Pause.

	Everything will STILL be revealed.
	Despite the cynics.
	The statues will come to life.
	The wind will carry our messages
	across the emptiness. Our mortgaged
	fantasies will come to life. As
	predicted. No error. Perfect
	management. And optimum level of
	profit realization according to a
	norm established by reference to
	the sine-wave function of money,
	need, chance, and the entropic
	function of these. All this
	is perfectly clear because there
	is no possible error. Machines,
	Deborah, are the true innocents of our time.
DEBORAH	Our witches?

MEGAN	You might say.
DEBORAH	So there is, in your view, no way out.
MEGAN	None I would want to risk.

Pause.

DEBORAH	Don't you ever reach dead end?
MEGAN	The series is infinite.

Pause.

DEBORAH	Don't you ever reach dead end?
MEGAN	The series is infinite.

A star falls, then another.

DEBORAH	Look.

More stars fall.

MEGAN	Perhaps we should rejoin the men.
DEBORAH	To save appearances?
MEGAN	What appearances?

They laugh. Exit. Stars fall. Blackout.

Scene eleven. After dinner at the club. The four are drinking brandy, smoking and talking in an animated fashion. Everyone is a little drunk.

RAMON	A toast to Chaos!
MEGAN	I won't drink to that.
RAMON	To Divine Necessity, then.
DEBORAH	It's the same thing.
	I won't drink to that.

Pause. RAMON *becomes a touch distracted.*

RAMON	How can you not . . . a source of inspiration . . . Life wells up . . . in the heavens. Everything comes from chaos, and to chaos it returns. What you see when you look at the heavens is God's eye.
SLEIGHT	It is what God sees, I would say.
DEBORAH	God is blind.
MEGAN	Rubbish.
RAMON	God may play at dice, but he is

	certainly able to read what he throw.
SLEIGHT	Nonsense. If he were able to see he would hardly have made such a phenomenal spectacle.
RAMON	Anthropomorphist!

Pause.

MEGAN	Let's talk about something else.
SLEIGHT	Such as.
DEBORAH	Money.
SLEIGHT	Very good. You see, money is the paradox because money is happiness, and yet. Nothing destroys a society quicker than large sums of money in the hands of the unscrupulous, which is to say, the happy.
MEGAN	I am on the side of the happy. Personally.

Pause.

SLEIGHT	(*To* DEBORAH.) Lovely ring you have.
RAMON	Happiness is only a mask for the bourgeoisie.
DEBORAH	It is, isn't it?
RAMON	Without his happiness, the bourgeois does not exist.
DEBORAH	Star sapphire. Plutonium setting by Omensetter.
MEGAN	Something about the sky tonight, it reminds me.

She sighs.

Deeply, passionately, convincingly,
of all the things I've never done,
of all the feelings I've never felt,
of all the thoughts I've never thought.
But then the rewards of being an American
are very great, aren't they? Boxed in
is safer, in the long run. We wouldn't
want to run amok, would we?
It would be so easy.

FIRST *and* SECOND WAITERS *carry a dead* SANTA *from the kitchen.*
Pause.

SLEIGHT	You are assuming that the sky is what can be seen, but there is far, far more, that *cannot* be seen, and that *far more* is what interests me.
MEGAN	If you got close enough to it, you could see it, too.
SLEIGHT	I don't mean that.
DEBORAH	Then what do you mean?
MEGAN	Don't argue. Don't argue. Everything will turn out fine. It always does. Is that your ring on the floor, Deborah?
DEBORAH	I was just thinking of how, when I was a little kid, I used to lie on my back in the soft grass and look up at the night sky, the Milky Way, the planets, and all the summer constellations, and it felt as if I were adrift, or falling endlessly and forever, on and on. Somehow it was a very safe feeling. I discovered better things to do with my summer nights before long.
SLEIGHT	But that's the point: you assume the universe is coterminous with what you can see.
RAMON	Coterminous: quite a big word, John.
SLEIGHT	Means "has the same boundaries as."
DEBORAH	Where's my ring? Oh, dear.

She looks around on the table.

RAMON	The sure progress of modern science has eliminated all such phantasms as you talk of, John, besides. If we can't trust what we see with our own eyes, what can we trust? A banker cannot run a bank without money. It's absurd.
SLEIGHT	Unless it's Intertop.
MEGAN	What does he mean by that?
SLEIGHT	A bad joke. Sorry.
DEBORAH	Where the hell is my goddamn ring?

She looks under the table.

MEGAN	(*Helps her.*) I'll help you look for it, dear.

	Under here? Ramon, please.
	Lift your boot.
RAMON	The sure progress of modern science has
	made all such speculations useless.

While SLEIGHT *and* RAMON *argue,* MEGAN *and* DEBORAH *search all over the floor for the fugitive ring, occasionally cursing.*

SLEIGHT	I'm not sure of that. Modern science
	and all we know are based on a set of
	assumptions, assumptions that are as
	problematic as those of . . . illusion itself.
	Did it ever occur to you that the
	process of perception is TWOFOLD?
	Not only do we look at the things
	of the world. They LOOK right back.
	The world looks different, depending
	where you stand.
	It's as simple as that.
RAMON	Now you are talking relativism.
	Which is cultural rottenness.
DEBORAH	(*To* RAMON.) Watch it! With the feet!
SLEIGHT	What are you doing down there?
DEBORAH	Looking for the goddamn ring.
RAMON	Infinity is an idea without blemish.
	Let's drink to that.
DEBORAH	I know it's down here.
SLEIGHT	Would you get up so I can finish
	my goddamn story?
MEGAN	We can hear you, believe me.
DEBORAH	Go on. Please. It's fascinating.

MEGAN *and* DEBORAH *touch. Then embrace. Then kiss.*

SLEIGHT	In order to perceive you become NOTHING,
	that way the images before you can
	approach and occupy your space.
	In order to be whole, one must be
	empty. If the universe is truly a
	universe, there must be more than
	we can see, than we could ever see.

MEGAN *and* DEBORAH *resume the search for the ring.*

> If the world we know: with its wars

	of mercenary faction, its Intertops and Trilateral Commissions, its webs and tracery of memory vaults and electronic global political hijinks, is on the verge of catastrophic collapse. And it must be because its ugly visage fills every inch of the monitors of mind and heart and imagination. Then I say it must be a PHANTASM . . .
RAMON	You sound just like Sam. Ha!
SLEIGHT	An illusion. A mere appearance. I do sound a little like Sam.

Pause.

	. . . and the new world must be concealed underneath somehow, so close we can't perceive it, so near we could touch it, but we can't because we couldn't tell the new world if it came up and BIT US ON THE ASS.
RAMON	Very strange reasonings, Sam.
SLEIGHT	John's the name.
DEBORAH	Found it.

She gets up. Brushes herself off. So does MEGAN.

SLEIGHT	(*To* DEBORAH.) You don't understand.
MEGAN	What's there to understand?

She lights an exploding cigar. The cigar explodes.

	And besides, it's about to happen. The great apparition . . . the pouring forth of light, from the divine beaker of infinitude. The statues will come to life . . .
DEBORAH	And we will seem exactly as we are.

She laughs.

SLEIGHT	You're mad.
DEBORAH	I'm getting out of here.

She gets up. SLEIGHT *tries to stop her. She pulls away from him.* RAMON *tries to restrain* SLEIGHT. *She stops a few paces away. Turns.*

RAMON	Let her go, John.

DEBORAH	(*To* SLEIGHT.) I wouldn't fuck you if you were dipped in light and rolled in stardust . . .

She strides rapidly out. MEGAN *weeps.*

RAMON	Let her go, John. She doesn't belong with us.

Blackout.

Scene twelve. In the forest, SAM *and* CHEF *are fishing.* SAM *wears a dunce hat.* CHEF *wears a cook's hat and carries a large drum strapped around his neck, which he beats now and again with a large soup spoon. The sky boils overhead.*

CHEF	Do you hear drums, Sam? I think I hear drums.
SAM	Nope.
CHEF	I must be imagining things. Perhaps from a previous existence, in which I was scalped or eaten by bears.
SAM	You know the story of Rip Van Winkle? Well, the true story of Rip Van Winkle runs as follows: there's this old fart who went to sleep for twenty years and woke up to find everything THE SAME. Except him. He was twenty years older. Was he ever surprised. And horrified. EXACTLY THE SAME.

Opens a door in a nearby tree and pulls out a can of beer, which he opens and drinks. Pause. CHEF *looks skeptically at the stream. Gets up disgustedly.*

CHEF	*Sacre bleu!* What one must do. The President Reagan has even poisoned the waters of these remote purlieus so that are no fishes.

SAM	All you think about is food.
CHEF	At least we are FREE.

Walks around beating on his drum.

SAM	Stop that. It scares the fish.
CHEF	And the bears.
	Have you thought about the bears?
SAM	Bears are extinct.
CHEF	Don't believe it. I have seen pairs
	of fiendish eyes out there at night.
	Bears' eyes.
SAM	We're safer here than back there. Shit!
CHEF	You are a pessimist.
SAM	I am a realist.
CHEF	It does not matter. The words.
	I have decided I will not go back.
	You may go back, but I will not.
	I will live among the natives and
	eat nuts and berries. I will
	become pure in body and in mind.

Takes a deep breath. Exhales.

SAM	You're kidding yourself.
CHEF	How you mean?
SAM	We're exiles, damn you, don't you see?

Crushes the beer can and tosses it away.

	Slowly we'll degenerate. Become
	slovenly, misshapen, feral.
	Crouched over in our weeds
	and rags. Stinking from filth,
	disease, and unimaginable lecheries.
	We'll slowly become deranged. Mad.
	Our resilience will go first, then
	spirit, then health, and finally
	life. Bugs and vermin will feast on
	our unremembered bones. A true pity.
CHEF	You have a black way of looking at
	things, Sam.
SAM	I am a realist.
CHEF	I think you bear a deep grudge.
SAM	ME!? A DEEP GRUDGE!? Ha!

CHEF	A deep, festooning wound.
SAM	The word is *festering*. You ignorant frog.
	I do not.
CHEF	You may correct my words, but
	still, I am right.
SAM	I left because it was futile to
	oppose a world so involved in
	madness that it mirrors madness
	in every pair of eyes I see. Every
	pair. In every head. Business-
	men's. Artists'. Wise old men
	and women's. Pretty girls'. Even
	the little kids' on their way to
	school. Madness. Murder. Blood
	lust to blow the world apart
	and howl at the pieces while
	the dead in their graves roast
	in whirlwind fires of the holocaust
	to rise, like mandrakes, shrieking,
	I see it.

Knocks on the door of the tree. It opens.

Humanity disgusts me.

Takes out another beer. Opens it.

	Fuck it all.
	But I don't delude myself. Like you.
CHEF	I am an artist.
	An artist, he have an
	elevated view of things.
	Otherwise he die. Like
	a butterfly in the mud.

Pause.

SAM	I would go back, if
	I thought it would make
	any difference, But I've
	cashed in my chips.
	Burned my bridges.
	Only reason I'd go back
	now is to raise hell.
	It would do no good.

CHEF	I would go back, but no one can tell me how to cook. In my own kitchen I am God. I do not do these adulterations of the cuisine which are now required by the bottom-line philosophy. *La nouvelle cuisine!* That disgusts me. I am an artist.

A phone rings. An ANIMAL *walks up with the phone in its mouth.*
It looks expectantly at CHEF. *He takes the phone and listens.*

SAM	There is no God, no love, nothing of value, only perspectival and perceptual obliquities, great distance, and repetition upon repetition . . . a nightmare.
CHEF	(*Into the phone.*) HALLO! NO! *Absolute non.* I am not a yo-yo. I have come here to the wilder- ness in order to communicate with the vast celestial still- nesses, not in order to enhance my bargaining position. I do not want to be Maître d' at the Savoy. Tell Alphonse that. I am a proud man. My sense of honor forbid me to plan these kind of calculation.

Pause.

I know.

Pause.

I know.

Pause.

You have your thought police

in the wind, but this instant
they are telling mistruths.

Hangs up. ANIMAL *carries away the phone.*

SAM	You're an idealist, Pierre.
CHEF	What idiocy! They want an artist, but they pay for an un- skilled hammerer of wood boards. Impossible. In America only lawyers make the money. Artists is shit here.

Walks around beating on his drum.

SAM	Art is meaningless without a socialist state, Pierre.
CHEF	You and your Socialist state. I have seen your Socialist. In the true Socialist state the first one they put up to the stake is you and me. Bang-bang. We are gone. You think. Big mistake, if you ask me. You should learn to make a soufflé.

Phone rings. ANIMAL *returns.*

I am not here.

SAM *takes the phone.*

I am indisposed.

Walks around beating on his drum.

SAM	He's indisposed. *(To phone. Pause.)* It's the president. He wants to ask you a question.

CHEF *turns his back and crosses his arms.*

C'mon, Pierre.

He waits.

He won't come, Mr. President.
He's making a soufflé.

But if you give me your
number I'll have him
call you back. How's that?

Pause.

Hung up.
The bastard.

ANIMAL *takes phone away.*

CHEF

You see! You are a grand
fool. You have your president
and you do not speak out
your objections to his policy.
Your wild anarchist shit.
Because you have watch
so much television your head
is rubberized. Like a football.

He laughs.

I am a man of principle.
Fucked up, it is true.
If I have an opportunity
to confront your friend Jacques
I tell him to his face: *Scum,
you are not an artist. You
are only a lawyer disguised
as an owner of restaurant.
It is a repulsive spectacle
to work for such a man.*

Pause. SAM *laughs and snaps his fingers.*

SAM   I've decided.

He gets up.

CHEF   What are you doing?
SAM   Going back.
          Pause.
CHEF   Why? What for?

Laughs. Pounds his drum.

The hater of humanity is going back
to the city. Ho! Ho! A mystery!

SAM *begins to collect his things, which he stuffs into a duffle bag.*

They will not welcome you
with open arms. They will
say your hair is looking most
peculiar with vines and twigs.
They will say you are mad.
And they will be right.
I prefer exile.
Penury.

Pause.

Troglodytes are free. You,
you cannot be serious.
How am I to maintain
my sanity in this howling
uncivilized place without a
friend to share the fire with?
Sam! Listen! You must not!

SAM *finishes packing.*

Go on. I need no one.

Pause.

Man is born free but everywhere
is in chains.
It is a loathsome prospect,
humanity.
One could do worse than stay.

Scornful.

What will you find? Will you
find love in the city? Bah!
Love is for children.
For idiots.
A beautiful woman is a false
beautiful woman.

SAM   But she's still a beautiful woman.
CHEF   True.
SAM   I'm going now.
CHEF   Clown!

Pause.

Compromisist!

Pause.

Tool of the bourgeoisie!

Pause.

	Fascist!
Pause.	
	Pessimist!
Pause.	
	Gourmand!
SAM	I've got to get out of this place.
He exits.	
CHEF	So much for Intertop.
	Alone with the fish.
	And the sky.
Pause.	
	And the bears.

He looks around.

I shall beat myself to death
with my own fist.

He batters himself, then stops.

Pain is boring.

Pause.

I shall dream and live out
my days as a dreamer.

He shuts his eyes.

And I shall forget.
And forget. And forget.

Pause. He opens his eyes. Pause. He recites.

O saisons, ô châteaux!
Quelle âme est sans défauts?

J'ai fait la magique étude
Du bonheur, qu'aucun n'élude.

Salut à lui, chaque fois
Que chante le coq gaulois.

Ah! je n'aurais plus d'envie:
Il s'est chargé de ma vie.

Ce charme a pris âme et corps
Et disperse les efforts.

O saisons, ô châteaux!

L'heure de sa fuite, hélas!
Sera l'heure du trépas.

O saisons, ô châteaux!

Pause. He scratches his head.

"Feed the fires of paranoia,"
he told me.

Pause.

I shall keep off the beasts
by making faces.

He makes faces. A giant scarab rolls the sun across the sky. Slow blackout.

Dracula (1987)

CHARACTERS *(in order of appearance)*

MINA
three VAMPIRETTES
LUCY
JONATHAN HARKER
COACHMAN (DRACULA)
OLD WOMAN
PEASANTS
DRACULA
NUN
DR. SEWARD
VAN HELSING
SIMMONS
QUINCEY MORRIS
DOG

This version of *Dracula* (adapted from the novel by Bram Stoker) was commissioned by River Arts Repertory, Lawrence Sacharow, Artistic Director. It was premiered in Woodstock during the summer of 1987 under the direction of Len Jenkin. Music was composed by Melissa Shiflett.

Note: The occasional appearance of an asterisk in the middle of a speech indicates that the next speech begins to overlap at that point. A double asterisk indicates that a later speech (not the one immediately following) begins to overlap at that point. The overlapping speeches are all clearly marked in the text.

A view of Whitby. A moonlit night.

MINA The room was dark. The bed was empty. I lit a match
and found she was not there. The door was shut but
not locked as I had left it. "Thank God," I said to myself, "She cannot be far, as she is only in her night-
dress." I ran downstairs and looked in the sitting room.
Finally I came to the hall door and found it open. It
was not wide open, but the catch of the lock had not
caught. Lucy must have gone out as she was. I took a
big, heavy shawl and ran after. There was a bright, full
moon, with dense, black, driving clouds; and the clock
was striking one as I arrived at the Crescent. Not a soul
was in sight. I ran along the North Terrace, but could
see no sign of the white figure I expected. The entire
harbor of Whitby lay beneath me, and the glistening
sea beyond. At the edge of the West Cliff above the
pier, I looked across the harbor to the East Cliff, in
hope or fear—I don't know which—of seeing Lucy at
our favorite seat overlooking the town. For a moment
or two I could see nothing, as the shadow of a cloud ob-
scured Saint Mary's Church and all around it. Then, as
the cloud passed, I could see, there, just as I had expected, the silver light of the moon strike a half-
reclining figure, snowy white. But it seemed to me as
though something dark stood behind the seat and bent
over it.

What it was, whether man or beast, I could not tell; I
did not wait to catch another glance, but flew down the
steep steps to the pier and along by Gin Lane and the
fish market to the bridge, which was the only way to
reach the East Cliff. The town seemed dead, for not a
soul did I see. That was good. For Lucy's reputation
was at stake. My knees trembled, and my breath la-
bored as I toiled up the endless steps. When I got to the

105

top I could see the seat and the white figure. There was undoubtedly something long and black bending over her. Lucy! Lucy! Something raised its head.

Offstage, VAMPIRETTES *begin their vowel chant: "o, a, u.*

For a minute or so I lost sight of her. When I came into view again the cloud had passed, and the moonlight struck so brilliantly that I could see Lucy, quite distinctly, her head lying over the back of the seat. She was quite alone. Lucy is sleeping soundly now; and the reflex of dawn is high and far over the sea.

A bright light.

LUCY
It all seemed quite real, for I knew I was not dreaming. I only wanted to be at this particular spot—I don't know why, for I was afraid of something—I don't know what. I do know I wanted to do something; something very, very bad. I remember, though I suppose I was asleep, passing through the streets and over the bridge. A fish leaped as I passed by. And I heard a lot of dogs barking and howling, all barking at once, as I went up the steps. Then I had a vague memory of something long and dark with red eyes; and something very sweet and very bitter all around me at once; and then I seemed to be sinking into deep green water, and there was a singing in my ears, as I have heard there is to drowning men. My soul seemed to go out from my body and float about in the air. I seem to remember that, for a time, the West Lighthouse was underneath; as if I had been thrown into the air. All I wanted was to be with you and Jack and Quincey and dear Professor Van Helsing. And then I came back and found you shaking my body. I saw you do it before I felt you.

LUCY AND
MINA
(*Singing.*)The land beyond the forest;
Where night is red wine, and day
    an empty cup;
There my love is sleeping, sleeping.

She hears the dog bark;
She hears the water lapping;
She hears the ravings of the mad
    and understands.

                    In the land beyond the forest
                    My true love lies so still.
                    She sees the fish leap;
                    She sees the moon slide upon the water.

                    And she awakens; and she is thirsty.

MINA   Strange. This peculiar night has put me in mind of poor
                    Jonathan, and the journal of his last, sad, strange, busi-
                    ness trip. To the land beyond the forest . . .

LUCY   To the land beyond the forest? Whatever land beyond
                    the forest* do you mean?

MINA   You know which land,* Lucy.

LUCY   Why don't you simply say "Transylvania" and be done
                    with it?

MINA   Lucy, you are so fractious since we arrived in Whitby,
                    and your behavior in general has caused me no little
                    vexation.

LUCY   Mina, must you dwell on morbid matters? I am tired of
                    hearing about poor Jonathan and his journal. Whitby
                    is such a pleasant seaside town, if only you would let
                    yourself enjoy it. The harbor is quite colorful, full of cu-
                    rious folk and quaint pleasures. It is our holiday,
                    after all.

MINA   Lucy, how can you be so tactless?

LUCY   Forgive me, Mina. I don't wish to hurt you, really. It is
                    only that I worry about you. Why must we be forever
                    retelling the same old tale, as if the retelling of it might
                    ease your torment?

Transylvania. JONATHAN *appears, seated. A strange* COACHMAN
(DRACULA) *right. A stream of servants bring strange food. Bad
Gypsy music.*

JONATHAN   *(Reading from his journal.)*
                    . . . we were leaving the West and entering the East . . .

COACHMAN   Budapesth.

JONATHAN   Budapesth seems a wonderful place. We viewed the
                    ruins of . . .

COACHMAN   Klausenburgh.

JONATHAN   The Hotel Royale. I had for supper a chicken done up
                    some way with red pepper, which was very good, but
                    thirsty. Memo. Get recipe for Mina.

OLD WOMAN	(*Rushing in*). It is now the Eve of Saint George's Day. Do you not know that tonight, when the clock strikes midnight, all evil things in the world have full sway? Do you know where you are going, and what you are going to?

She puts a crucifix around his neck and exits, crossing herself. Turns back.

For your mother's sake.

Enter PEASANTS *with puppet box and musical instruments. They present a thumbnail "Dracula" as more strange food appears. See Appendix.*

JONATHAN	I have read that every known superstition is gathered up in the horseshoe of the Carpathians. Memo. Must ask the count about these.
	I had for breakfast more paprika and a sort of porridge of maize flour which they said was mamaliga . . .
COACHMAN	(*Correcting pronunciation.*) Mamaliga . . .
JONATHAN	. . . and eggplant stuffed with forcemeat, which they call implemata . . .
COACHMAN	Implemata . . .
JONATHAN	Memo. Get recipe for this also. Hhhquulptu.
COACHMAN	Bukovina.
JONATHAN	At Bukovina bit of a tumble with a pretty *fille de chambre* at the Golden Krone Hotel . . .
COACHMAN	Bistritz.
JONATHAN	At Bistritz I dined on what they call robber's steak, chunks of bacon, onion, and beef, seasoned with red pepper, and strung on sticks and roasted over the fire, in the simple style of London's cat's meat. The wine was golden Mediasch, which produces a queer sting on the tongue, which is, however, not disagreeable. I had only a couple of glasses of this, and nothing else.

We hear PEASANTS *muttering.*

JONATHAN	I could hear a lot of words, repeated. Queer words. I quietly got my polyglot dictionary from my bag and looked them out. I must say they were not cheering to me. Ordog (Satan), Pokol (hell), Stregoica (witch), Vrolok, vlkoslak, both of which mean the same thing; one being Slovak and the other Servian for something that is either werewolf or vampire.

COACHMAN	Borgo Pass.
JONATHAN	Memo. Must ask the count why these superstitions persist.

PEASANTS *exit hurriedly, leaving their musical instruments.*
DRACULA *appears wearing an apron and carrying a roast chicken
on a platter.*

DRACULA	Because your peasant is at heart a coward and a fool. It is said, for instance, that blue flames, the fire of Saint George's Eve, appear on one night, and on that night no man of this land will, if he can help it, leave his house. This and other idiotic legend. Harmless.
JONATHAN	I agree.
DRACULA	Possible to find much red gold where the blue flame dances. Treasure of olden days. We are in Transylvania, and Transylvania is not London.
JONATHAN	There you are right.
DRACULA	I am *boyar*, the common people know me, and I am master.
JONATHAN	There you are most certainly right.
DRACULA	I have studied all our correspondence. Come, tell me of England and of the house you have procured for me there.
JONATHAN	A bottle of old Tokay! How wonderful!
DRACULA	The house.
JONATHAN	The estate is called Carfax. Surrounded by a big wall. Built of heavy stones. The gates are of oak and iron. Massive. All eaten by rust, however. It has not been re-paired for years. Solid, Gothic, solemn. There is a deep, dark-looking pond which makes it gloomy. Third mort-gage. Easy terms. Next door is a private lunatic asy-lum. Run by an old acquaintance, a friend of my wife, Mina. His name is Jack Seward. In fact, he courted her before I, the dog. Unsuccessfully, of course.
DRACULA	I am glad that is old and big. We Transylvanian nobles love not to think our bones may lie among the com-mon lot. I seek not gaiety, or mirth, or the bright volup-tuousness of much sunshine and sparkling waters, which please the young and gay. I am no longer young; and my heart, through weary years of mourning over the dead, is not attuned to mirth. I love the shadow

and the shade and would be alone with my thoughts
when I may.

He begins to leave.

JONATHAN	Somehow his words and looks did not seem in accord.
DRACULA	By the by, I advise you not to leave your room at night, otherwise I cannot vouch for your safety.

Blackout. A convent near the Borgo Pass. JONATHAN *is now a raving lunatic.* MINA *and a* NUN *regard him with horror. As* JONATHAN *raves, the* NUN *discusses the case.*

JONATHAN   But I escaped before he could do his wicked thing to
me. Xxlld. Fpfptssc. So lovely there, we and the deadly.
I love Lucy. Kcm. Kcm. Bats. Bats. Interference from
the future. Red dogs. Nuns. Goop. Magic lanterns.
They warned me, they did. Can't say I wasn't warned.
All in the diaries, all of it. He's going to England. Fresh
blood. Needs it. Carfax. Large old stones. Easy terms.
Qqqmc. Mina must learn to keep a proper diary. It's a
horror. Like the movies. What's a movie? Moving
world. Yes, desperation. Bonka Bonka Bonka Bonk.
And oh, the terrible twitching bag. The poor mother
torn to pieces by hundreds of wolves in the awful court-
yard. Unspeakable. Xxxuumnoa. Fancy *him* at the British Museum, as a sort of tourist! Looking at the Ro-
setta stone! Bat. Baseball bat. What in the name of
heaven's that? Ah, the precious flask of slivovitz. I am a
radio. What's a radio?

Insane laughter.

The milk that is spilt cries out not afterwards. A dog-
eared diary, with real dog ears. I'd as soon eat mole-
cules with chopsticks as dine with Count Deville.
Dvlmnoa. Oao. Truly, the mad cause one to doubt the
plan of God. Ha ha. He shall enter, yes, like those horrid bulls. Bonka bonk. Judge Moneybag will solve this.
Beware the puppet show. The Black Dog shall land at
Whitby by the North Sea. With his dirt. In big boxes.
Oh. Then to downtown Whitby. Kkfffxxo. Get ye ham-
mers and a spike. Oh, the diaries are so important!
"What took it out?" What bloody well took it out indeed! Aye, there's the crux. O, a, u. O, a, u. X all the

way to X′ and half the alcohol. X all the way to the walking fruit stand that is the Lord Mayor of Popinjay. X all the way to Kfx. Peppercorn in my pocket, and, oh, my mind's on fire. Flies, spiders, sparrows, cats. Peach Bottom reactor full of sleepers, o, a, u. He shall slide under the sash and stand before me, as the moon does, in all her glory.

NUN   Madam, he has been like this since he was found by Gypsies wandering about in the Borgo Pass, leaping from tussock to tussock, raving about blood and wolves and the Lord knows what. He has suffered from a terrible brain seizure. It appears now he will survive, but unfortunately his wits may be a trifle impaired. Permanently. Unless heavily sedated, he goes on in this fashion interminably. He calls himself "Scardanelli" and remembers nothing of his former life. Which is why it took us so long, with the aid of merciful God, to locate his loved ones. He was very thins and pale when we found him. Truly, the torments of the mad almost make one doubt the plan of God.

Tears off her habit, throws it down, and tramples it. She sobs.

MINA   What could have produced such a violent effect on poor Jonathan?

Flashback to Castle Dracula. Foolish JONATHAN *has gone to sleep in the wrong part of the castle. It is night, and three* VAMPIRETTES *appear in the dim light. They sing the song "Do you know where you are going, and what you are going to?" (repeat). They approach and whisper and laugh lightly. Pause. Approach closer. It is very still.*

VAMPIRETTE 1   Who is to be the first?
VAMPIRETTE 2   Hush, silly, there are kisses for all.
DRACULA   (*Entering.*) How dare you disobey me? I warned you, he is mine. You shall have him only when I am done. He is a vital link in the plan which I have explained to you.
VAMPIRETTE 2   Just as at Kossovo! Why should we believe him? He will betray one of us to our enemies. Or all.* Just as before.
VAMPIRETTE 1   You, you never loved.
DRACULA   You know how well I have loved.

VAMPIRETTE 2	You said you loved Theodora, then you gave her to the Turks.
DRACULA	For the head of the Woiwode Stephen.
VAMPIRETTE 3	He was dead. What did it matter?
VAMPIRETTE 1	She was not yet* *vlkoslak.*
VAMPIRETTE 2	She was not yet one of us.
VAMPIRETTE 3	And she loved you so.
DRACULA	Be quiet, fools. Remember, the Woiwode Stephen was my brother.
VAMPIRETTE 3	All these centuries, and you still treat the fine ladies who serve you with contempt.
DRACULA	Be gone. Or you shall feel my wrath.
VAMPIRETTE 1	Are we to have nothing?

He throws a bag on the floor. As it twitches we hear a baby cry. They pause and seize it. Exit. DRACULA *turns to* JONATHAN. *Blackout. Lights up on the raving* JONATHAN/SCARDANELLI *as before. Now* SEWARD *has joined* MINA. *The* NUN *is gone.*

MINA	Dear Jack, what kind of sickness is this? Sucked dry as a prune, with his poor wits wandering like the fabled antipodes of Saint Viar. Oh, Jonathan, poor Jonathan. Why doesn't he recognize me?
SEWARD	Mina, it was wise of you to bring him here. Especially in view of our longstanding association. My asylum is the most up-to-date in this part of the country. My, your perfume makes me heady. I always was susceptible to odors, particularly female odors. No, this resembles some kind of absolute, bestial possession. As if—my God—the poor fellow had been terrified out of his right mind by some apparitional, but nevertheless fully convincing, monstrosity. It happens, especially when there is a congenital weakness of the personality structure.* As I recall being the case with Jonathan.
MINA	What on earth do you mean by a "congenital weakness of the personality structure"?
SEWARD	Let us be frank with each other, Mina. Jonathan always was an odd duck.
MINA	But what can be done?
SEWARD	I know of only one man who can help us. He is an alienist and specialist of obscure maladies. My professor at Leiden, in fact. Van Helsing is his name. He re-

	sides at Amsterdam and, owing to a peculiar and private disability of an unmentionable sort, is reluctant to travel.
MINA	Oh, dear.
SEWARD	But that's another matter. Without my assistance his renowned *Atlas of the Rat's Brain* simply would not've been possible.* But, perhaps, in this case, I may be able to prevail upon him.**

She exits. He doesn't notice.

	My, your perfume has the queerest effect on me. I do think I had better sit down.
MINA	Science is making truly remarkable advances these days.
VAN HELSING	Let me tell you, my friend, that are things done today in electrical science which would have been deemed unholy by the very men who discovered electricity.

He enters.

	There are mysteries in life. Why was it Methusalah lived nine hundred years? Can you tell why, when other spiders die small and soon, that one great spider lived centuries in the tower of the old Spanish church and grew and grew till, on descending, he drink the oil out of all the church lamps?
SEWARD	Whatever are you driving at?
VAN HELSING	From your letter, I surmise this may be a special case. May I become level with you, John? I have partially overcome my old fear of strange beds to come here. Who knows? Maybe I can decipher ancient mystery. Show me the poor man.

VAN HELSING *examines* JONATHAN.

SEWARD	Professor, let me be your student again. I feel like a madman lumbering through a bog in a mist, jumping from one tussock to another, in the mere blind effort to move without knowing where I am going.
VAN HELSING	Good image. My thesis is that I want you to believe.
SEWARD	To believe what?
VAN HELSING	To believe things that cannot.
SEWARD	Then you want me not to let some previous conviction injure the receptivity of my mind regarding some strange matter. Do I read your lesson right?

VAN HELSING	John, my friend. I am glad you call. This is not, I fear, normal mad. But unnatural one. Possession by dark forces of the forest. A virus of the undead. All signs indicate such. Vacant eye, like an empty wallet. Preposterous talk of wolf. Loss of memory of previous life: name, wife, solicitor's trade. A complete big blank. Instead, ridiculous new name, Scardanelli. Sudden abomination of garlic and spicy food. Insectivore habit. Have been bitten. Chewed about the throat. Mosquito bite? No, no, John. Is wampyr.* But not chewed enough to become undead self. No, but is work of wampyr.
SEWARD	What's that, in God's name?
VAN HELSING	(*Singing.*) He is brute.

He is devil and cruel.
And the heart of him
is not.

> My friends, this is much.

Appear at will,
when and where.
Direct the elements,
the storm, the fog, the thunder.

> My friends, this is much.

All meaner things
he can command:
the owl, the moth, the rat, the
fox, the wolf, the bat.

> My friends, this is much.

Can grow small,
become unknown . . .
How we find his where?
And having found it,
how can we destroy?

> My friends, this is much.

Brief DRACULA *cameo.*

VAN HELSING	Wampyr. Is undead. Bloodsucking mysterium. Inexplicable hocus-hocus. An abomination. Have read big, old tomes on such. In black mountains of Transylvania drunk Gypsies dance around the wooden red dog and shout horrible. *Ordog ordog ordog ordog vlkoslak!*

	Rage in blood. Tell tale of aristocrat *boyar* warrior clan who fight Turk with strange mud pies, flying door-jambs, bloiling slime from wizard pot. Something go wrong in alchemical concoction. Instead of normal necromancy, a change happen to this certain nobleman. He become an effigy of marble smooth—white, blood-eating, invulnerable to storm, crossbow, or musket. Undead be born. Virus cannot be traced to rotten meat, obscene sexual rite of autumnal haystack, nor the French itch. Maybe the devil have made this devil thing.
SEWARD	What must we do?
VAN HELSING	I am not prepare to say. Employ scientific method and hope for best. I have brought bottle of *oude genever*. Care for nightcap? Wampyr can wait.

He exits and SEWARD *summons* SIMMONS, *who brings chloral.*
SEWARD *takes some and leans back in drugged reverie.*

SEWARD	Chloral, the modern Morpheus! I must be careful not to let it be a habit. But I am weary and low in spirits tonight. Perhaps all my research into the human brain has been for nothing. The expeditions to Peru, Tangiers, Mbululand. I am tired of everyone. This damnable itch to reason it all out, and be impartial. To judge what is sane, and what is not. When all I want to do is leap from the top of Saint Mary's and flap to my death shrieking my hatred for all of them. Lucy, who would not have me, and Mina, who would not have me. And who both tempt me. As for the secret to mortal reason and mortal desire, how many brain smears have I examined and not found it? And our poor damned "Scardanelli" says his God is near, but difficult to grasp. When everyone knows that God is far away and lives in the sky. There is no limit to mortal aggravation.

As he slumbers, the VAMPIRETTES *sing. A floral cameo duo of*
LUCY *and* MINA *à la Fragonard.*

MINA	When Jonathan recovers the use of his faculties I shall be able to be very useful to him, and if I can stenograph well enough I can take down what he wants to say in this way and write it out for him on the typewriter, at which I am also practicing very hard.

LUCY	Mina, we have told all our secrets to each other since we were children. We have slept together and eaten together and laughed and cried together. And so now, Mina. Can't you guess? Oh, Mina, I love him. And him. And him.

Triple proposal cameo of SEWARD, VAN HELSING, *and* QUINCEY MORRIS.

	Well, my dear, number one came before lunch. Dr. Jack Seward, with the strong jaw and the good forehead. You know him, I believe. He was very cool outwardly . . .
SEWARD	Lucy, will you marry me?
LUCY	But he kept playing with a scalpel in a way that nearly made me scream! Just fancy! He is only nine and twenty and he has an immense lunatic asylum all under his care.* Number two is Quincey Morris. He is an American with such a sweet accent, who has become frightfully rich importing scrap metal to Japan and Winchesters to Latin America.
QUINCEY	Lucy, will you marry me?
LUCY	And sweet old Professor Van Helsing, who has been consulting with Jack on some strange matter. So stable and strong . . .
VAN HELSING	Lucy, will you marry me?
LUCY	Poor man, his wife lies in a coma near Amsterdam, a complete vegetable, due to a faulty innoculation during the recent outbreak of cholera in the Low Countries. Does that make his courting of me bigamy?
MINA	Yes, he always did play with a scalpel. Oh, go on.

Pause.

	It seems so important to keep a record of things. There is so little to hold on to otherwise. It all flies up the chimney. And what with Jonathan in the queer state he is in. I don't know what else to do. You might as well know, it is Jack's hospital where Jonathan is sequestered. And what with my weak stomach and all, Jack has* absolutely forbade me from seeing him.
LUCY	You know what I did? I told Dr. Seward I would not have him, but would have Quincey Morris instead. It was a fib, for I am very fond of Jack. But I was curious

to see what he would do. He blushed, and his ears moved up and down ever so slightly. Then he gave out with the most curious moan. I know what you're thinking, Mina: Why are men so noble when women are so little worthy of them?

Cross-fade to SEWARD *and* JONATHAN *seated, facing each other. They smoke cigars, take notes, and mirror each other.*

JONATHAN   I know what you're thinking, Dr. Seward. "A strange and sudden change in Scardanelli last night." You have noticed, haven't you? I began to get excited and sniff about like a dog. Your man Simmons, the lecher, was struck by my manner and, knowing your interest in me, encouraged me to talk. I am usually respectful to servants. Even to him. Sometimes I am positively obsequious. But last night all I would say was: "I don't want to talk to you. The master is at hand."

SEWARD   *(In a sudden rage).* What!? You don't mean to tell me you don't care about spiders anymore!?

JONATHAN   Bother them all! I don't care a pin about them.

SEWARD   You are too dangerous to be roaming about. Up to now your hobby has been catching flies. You have had such a number I have had myself to expostulate. Then you turn your mind to spiders. You have got several big fellows in a box. You feed them with your flies, I know. Soon your spiders are as great a nuisance as your flies. I say you must clear out some of these. You apparently acquiesce, cheerfully. Then a horrid blowfly, bloated with some carrion food, buzzes into the room. You catch it, hold it exultantly for a few minutes between thumb and forefinger, then, before I know what to do, you put it into your mouth and eat it.

JONATHAN   It was very good and wholesome. It was life, strong life. Life gives life.

SEWARD   Then the tame sparrow incident.

JONATHAN   I tamed the sparrow by feeding it with spiders. And flies.

SEWARD   Quite. That is the crux.

JONATHAN   My flies are considerably diminished, as you yourself requested, Dr. Seward.

SEWARD   Quite so. Indeed, you grow more interesting every day.

JONATHAN	But my sparrow is gone. It's flown away. But a kitten! A nice, little sleek, playful kitten. That is what I want. That I can play with, and teach, and feed and feed and feed and feed.
SEWARD	The thought that has been buzzing about in my mind lately is complete, and the theory proved. My maniac is of a peculiar kind. I shall have to invent a new classification for you. You are a zoophagous maniac.
JONATHAN	What the devil does "zoophagous" mean?
SEWARD	It means *life-eating,* you fiend. And what you desire is to absorb as many lives as you can, and you are scheming a plan to achieve this in a cumulative way. You give many flies to one spider, and many spiders to one sparrow, and now you want a cat to feed the sparrow to. BUT YOU YOURSELF HAVE EATEN THE SPARROW!

Slaps JONATHAN *on the back: feathers fly.*

	Men sneered at vivisection, yet look at its results today! Why not develop science in its most difficult and vital aspect—the knowledge of the brains?
JONATHAN	Shut up, Doctor. The master is coming.
SEWARD	Had I the secret of even one such mind—the key to the fancy of one such lunatic—I might advance my own branch of science to a pitch compared with which Burdon-Sanderson's physiology of Ferrier's brain knowledge would be as nothing.
JONATHAN	Envy is a crippling affliction, Dr. Seward, and your obsession with brain matter smacks of rank determinism.
SEWARD	What would you know of these higher things? I do believe one day I shall locate the spot, the very lobe, governing sexual license, which may, by application of the galvanic charge, be rendered inoperable, giving us some peace at night.
JONATHAN	I only asked for a kitten.
SEWARD	Ah, Lucy, how I wish you had forgiven me, for that day I spilled myself on your pretty pink skirt. It was beyond nature to control myself. Oh, Lucy, Lucy, though I have sat upon and crushed my hat I cannot be angry with you, nor can I be angry with my friend Quincey Morris, that American ape, whose happiness is yours; but I

	must only wait on, hopeless. And work. And try not to think of you and him. In a little room at that inn. By the Aerated Bread Company. Your favorite satins. Lilac and the odor of your . . . And you and him, like beasts, at it. Work! And work!
JONATHAN	What about my kitten?
SEWARD	You shall not have a cat, you shall have an opiate. Simmons, prepare an opiate for Scardanelli, a powerful opiate. We must get to the bottom of this "wampyr" business.

SIMMONS *administers the opiate.* JONATHAN *becomes strange.*

JONATHAN.	I am here to do your bidding, master. I am your slave, and you will reward me, for I shall be faithful. I have worshipped you long and afar off. Now that you are near, I await your commands, and you will not pass me by, will you dear master, in your distribution of good things?

They close in on him like tigers. Cross-fade to LUCY's *seat on the East Cliff. Sound of wind.* SIMMONS *entertains* LUCY *with a song.*

| SIMMONS | We all go down to the sea,
and do there secretly
What we crave in the dark.
Bonka, bonka, bonka, bonk. |
|---|---|
| | Mad Sally has me in her mouth.
Bonka, bonka, bonka, bonk. |
| | Mad Sally has me in her mouth.
Mad Sally, never a complaint.
Mad Sally, up against the wall.
Mad Sally, hanging from her knees.
Bonka, bonka, bonka, bonk. |
| | We all go down to the sea, etc. |
| | Mad Sally, never a complaint.
Mad Sally, humping on a grave.
Mad Sally, and the Royal Navy.
Bonka, bonka, bonka, bonk. |
| | We all go down to the sea, etc. |
| SIMMONS | That's the song old man Swales used to sing. The oldest loony in the place. Face like the arsehole of that rhinos- |

teros I seen at the carny near the Black Dog. A bloomin' bewhiskered pineapple. Banished from the Royal Navy, he was, I hear tell, for sodomizing a cabin boy with a bloody belayin' pin, right smack in the old Adriatic. Them as knows, knows. It's the bovine warble to his voice as does it. Look, look, there're something in that wind that tastes like death. It's in the air, I feel it comin'.

Looking grim.

That ship there, from Eastern Europe, by the look of her. She's knockin' about the queerest way. As if no one's aboard. Alive, that is.

A very elegant black DOG *appears.*

Gettin' late, Miss Lucy, I'd best be back to the nuthouse or the loonies'll have Master Jack climbin' the bloody walls. They rattle 'im, they do. If it weren't for me, they'd rattle 'im worse, I expect. What's more, the pay stinks.

Exit. DOG *smokes a cigar as* LUCY *reads the ship's log.* MINA *enters and, curious, joins her.*

LUCY   From the log of the freighter *Demeter*:
6 July. We finish taking on cargo. Boxes of earth, four in all. Transport consigned to Whitby, England.

11 July. At dawn entered the Bosporus. Backsheesh.

13 July. Passed Cape Matapan. Crew dissatisfied about something. Scared, but would not speak out.

14 July. Anxious about crew. Men all steady fellows. Mate could not tell what was wrong. They only told him there was *something* and crossed themselves.

16 July. One of the crew, Petrofsky, is missing. Men say there is *something* aboard.

17 July. Olgaren says to me he saw a tall thin man who was not like any of the crew, come up the companionway and go along the deck forward, and disappear. Searched the ship. Nothing.

24 July. Another man lost.

29 July. Another tragedy. Krupa gone.

30 July. Only self and mate left.

1 August. At midnight, I went to relieve the man at the wheel, and when I got to it found no one there.

4 August. Still fog, which sunlight cannot pierce. I am alone, and in the dimness of the night I saw it—him! And if we are wrecked mayhap this bottle may be found and those who find it understand . . .

Bottom of page ripped and bloody.

MINA How very strange! An immense dog has leapt from the wreck, there on the beach. My, what a remarkably large and attractive dog. Where do you suppose such a great brute beast came from, and who do you suppose will feed him?

VAMPIRETTES *dance and sing the song "Who do you suppose is going to feed him?" (repeat).* LUCY *exits.*

You seemed so tired, Lucy. I like to watch you when you sleep. Some of the "new women" writers will one day start an idea that men and women should be allowed to see each other asleep before proposing or accepting.

VAMPIRETTES *(Mocking her.)* Poor Lucy, I suppose she will be sleepwalking again. Then tomorrow she will be drained. A brave man's blood is the best thing when a woman is in trouble. All this puts me a brown study, and I think of poor Jonathan, sucked dry as a puckered flatworm. Poor crazy Scardanelli! I believe I shall require an opiate.

They spy SEWARD *and* VAN HELSING *approach the Black Dog Tavern.*

VAN HELSING This Dracula know me as "Porker" known by charcuterie. I going to extirpate malign of cancer wampyr. Drive stake through grisly undead heart. Garlic in mouth after chop off head. Hard work. Need saw. Chain. Hammer. Rope. Worktable. Wampyr have cunning brain, but child brain. As for instance, of monkey with hand in cookie jar. Ha. Dracula now in England. How do I know? Examine raving zoophagous patient Scardanelli, formerly normally respectable one Jona-

	than Harker. He engaged to find house for Count Deville, alias Dracula. He have, so to say, telegraph wire to primordial will of our wampyr.
SEWARD	You mean this wampyr is in England?
VAN HELSING	Here. There. Maybe even in Whitby, where we stand. Manifest of undead ship *Demeter*. Four boxes of grim, fine-mashed Carpathian mold. Of what use to England? Make sand castle? No. Is bed of wampyr. Nice, cozy earth smell. Kinda dig into and relax. Do inert wampyr business. At dawn wampyr must sleep. All these boxes are sent to old house. Somewhere unclear from soggy manifest. Surrounded by a big wall. Built of heavy stones. Solid, Gothic, solemn. Third mortgage. Must find, make poopy with holy water. Garlic. Undead no atheist.
SEWARD	Simmons! He works the docks on his days off. He might know where the boxes were delivered.
MINA	*(Joining them.)* Jack, if you don't mind. All this commotion. My stomach. Don't you think I could have just a little?
SEWARD	Be quiet, Mina. If we are to get to the bottom of this strange business which for your own protection you must know nothing about, we must have absolute discipline.
VAN HELSING	Give her the medication, John.

He gives her chloral, and she retires discreetly to take it.

VAN HELSING	Poor Lucy have all signs, too. Watch for unnecessary foreigner with biting habit. On throat vein. Find and destroy the undead pest. Before further harm. Squalor of harbor slum make good home for *nosferatu*. Where do we find your assistant?
SEWARD	He's probably in there. The notorious Black Dog Tavern.
MINA	*(Rejoining them.)* Does all this looking for boxes in unpleasant neighborhoods have something to do with Jonathan's malady?
SEWARD	You shall know it all before long, my dear.
VAN HELSING	Wampyr hate me because I know his virus and prepare learned article on same. Published in Louvain. *Annales*

	des Endocrinologie-Diabolique. Winner of Hubert
	Prize in '97. Good year.
Two	*(Emerging from the Black Dog.)* A moment of silence
Vampirettes	for poor Jonathan.

A street scene in front of the Black Dog. Seward *goes inside in search of* Simmons. *The others wait. A* Girl *with a beautiful hat. Oompah music. Punch and Judy version of "Dracula." Men carry a huge box and put it down.* Quincey *arrives, late as usual. He and* Van Helsing *smoke cigars to be inconspicuous.* Mina *nods off.* Dracula, *disguised as a bat, enters and follows after the* Girl. Quincey *sings "The Battle Hymn of the Republic" for the locals, who roar in approval.* Seward *returns, dragging* Simmons, *who is drunk, by the collar.*

Simmons	Well, guv'nor, I forgits, but it was empty.
Seward	How did you get into the house if it was empty?
Simmons	The old gent that engaged me opened up. Curse me, but he was the strongest chap I ever struck. Why, 'e took up 'is end o' the boxes like they was pounds of tea . . .
Seward	Just shut up and tell me the number of the house.
Simmons	What with all the beer I can hardly remember the county.

Seward *throws him down.*

Seward	A total waste of time.

Meanwhile a furtive copulation in the alleyway. Cross-fade to Lucy's *seat high over Whitby on the East Terrace. She and* Dracula *sit in the gloaming.*

| Lucy | Count Deville, you are quite the most experienced man I have ever met. Quincey is sweet. You don't know Quincey, but he is sweet. In the American way, with great, earnest quacks and gulps. Cows' eyes. Marmalade, really. Odd, I can't imagine him undressed. Though I cannot help but imagine Simmons that way. Jack's man, Simmons? Big, round, stiff Simmons. My, you are the smoothest gentleman. I hear the ladies of Paris are pretty and saucy. Do you think I am impertinent, my dear count? You may call me Ishtar if you like. Bobo calls me that. Pity my friends aren't more sophisticated. We could all go for an outing over the |

wold, or have a glorious dinner party. However, they lack savoir-faire. But today they're all down to Whitby Harbor on some queer business. A place filled with immoral back alleys. Gin Lane. The Black Dog Tavern. It is strange. The man always finds the girl alone.

Pause.

I feel a curious tingle when I am with you, Count Deville. Lizst does that to me also. What a fine, hairy man you are–even the palms of your hands. I am a silly girl, aren't I? Who could imagine a big, long man of your vast experience interested in a silly slip of thing like me?

DRACULA   Quite the contrary.

Kisses her.

LUCY   Do it again.

Kisses her.

I won't tell. Whatever happens.

Kisses her again.

Oh, that's a darker kind of sweetness. But I like it, I really do. Oh, but there isn't much time, so you must do it all now, because no one must discover us together. Mina would throw up. Oh, I won't tell anyone, but you must show me what to do and how . . .

Bites her.

Oh, my . . .

Bites her and sucks.

Oh, this is how it is.

Pause.

I'm bleeding a little. Is that all right?

Pause.

I think I am very fond of you.

Back to the Black Dog, only now we're inside. Loud. Crazy, Chaotic. VAMPIRETTES *are performing.* VAN HELSING *has some news and is trying to get to* SEWARD. MINA *has gone.* QUINCEY *has passed out.*

SIMMONS   Do you recall the old days at the Fortress at Mbululand? The native girls with their long, naked legs, and spent three-ten Greener cartridges tied up in their hair?

SEWARD   Oh, do shut up, for God's sake, Simmons.

Oompah music.

SIMMONS   Remember how we used to go at it high in the Andean
                  Sierra? Panpipes and the young Indian girls. Busy at
                  both ends of that fine, strapping one, eh, master Jack?
                  Bonka bonka bonk.
SEWARD   Simmons, you do recall the queerest sort of things,
                  after all.

More bad music and general vulgarity.

SIMMONS   Don't suppose you recall the stews of Tangiers? Oh,
                  pretend you don't. The swish of silk and the tinkle of
                  little silver bells about the ankles of little girls. Bonka
                  bonka bonka bonk.

Total tasteless pandemonium.

VAN HELSING   Lucy is ill; that is, she has no special disease, but she
                  looks awful, and is getting worse. I fear it is you know
                  what. Wampyr.

*Scene becomes LUCY's bedroom. VAMPIRETTES enter, make
vampiric gesture and trail out. SEWARD and VAN HELSING enter
and rush to her.*

SEWARD   My God! This is dreadful. There is no time to be lost.
                  She will die from sheer want of blood.
VAN HELSING   There must be transfusion of blood.
SEWARD   I am younger and stronger, Professor. It must be me.
VAN HELSING   Then get ready at once. I have my bag. I must prepare.

As they set up, QUINCEY enters.

QUINCEY   Lucy's in a bad fix, I hear from Simmons.
VAN HELSING   Sir, you are in time. You are the lover of our dear miss.
                  She is bad; very, very, very bad.

QUINCEY almost faints.

                  Nay, my child, do not go like that. You are to help me.
QUINCEY   What can I do? I'd give the last drop of my blood to
                  save her.

SEWARD becomes downcast.

VAN HELSING.   You are a man, and it is a man that we want.
LUCY   (*Sitting up.*) What's the matter with me anyhow?

VAN HELSING mixes a narcotic for her. MINA staggers in.

VAN HELSING   Now little miss, here is your medicine. Drink it off, like a good child. See, I lift you so that to swallow is easy.

Pours it down her throat.

VAN HELSING   You may take that one little kiss while I bring over the table. Friend John, help me.

They bring the table and avert their eyes so as not to see the kiss. MINA *stares shamelessly.*

He is so young and strong of blood so pure that we need not defibrinate it. Your miss (*To* QUINCEY.) wants blood, and blood she must have or die. John was to give his blood; but now you are here, and you are more good than us, young or old, who toil too much in the world of thought. Our nerves are not so calm and blood not so bright as yours.

QUINCEY   If only you knew how gladly I would die for her.

VAN HELSING   Good boy.

Stabs him with the needle and exits. SEWARD *takes chloral and staggers out into the hallway.* MINA *follows. A furtive copulation on the staircase. The transfusion continues and, elsewhere,* SCARDANELLI *sits in his cell, being mad.*

QUINCEY   Miss Lucy, I know I ain't good enough to regulate the fixin's of your little shoes. Won't you just hitch alongside of me and let us go down the long road together, driving in double harness?

LUCY   I don't know anything of hitching and such. And frankly, I find your interest in my shoes in somewhat bad taste. And as for the long road, I'm not yet broken to harness. But I'm eager to try . . .

He passes out from lack of blood.

Shall we meet tonight behind the Black Dog Tavern? That's where, so I hear, the poor girls go when the heat seizes. But you mustn't tell a soul. Promise?

Sees he's passed out.

Quincey, sometimes you are the very cipher of a man.

MINA *and* SEWARD *break off from their embrace.*

MINA   Jack, may I ask a special favor? I was wondering if I might see him again. Even if there's little hope. My

	stomach is feeling a bit more stable now. It's just that I must know more of his condition.
SEWARD	There has been little change.
MINA	Just once more . . .
SEWARD	He refers to himself as Scardanelli and says he possesses a master who is God and is near but difficult to grasp. Eats flies. Feeds them to spiders. Ate a bird once. A nice little sparrow that never hurt anyone. Another time he attacked me with a chair. I suffered a wound, here, upon the arm. It bled. Before that idiot Simmons could restrain him, he was on all fours lapping up the blood like a kitten. Quite batty. His linen is most rank. Very well. It's not as if he's been kept prisoner.

He enters JONATHAN's *cell.*

	A lady would like to speak with you.
JONATHAN	Why?
SEWARD	She is going through the house and wants to see everyone in it.
JONATHAN	Oh, very well, let her come in, by all means. But wait just a minute till I tidy the place up.

Eats all the flies and spiders.

Let the lady come in.

Sits down on the edge of the bed with eyes down and eyelids up. Ming enters.

MINA	Good evening, Mr. Scardanelli.
JONATHAN	You're not the girl the doctor wanted to marry, are you? You can't be, you know, for she is very ill.
MINA	Oh, no! I have a husband of my own. I am Mrs. Harker. Do you remember Jonathan Harker?
JONATHAN	Ah, it was your husband, poor Jonathan, who was sucked as dry as a parched cerement in the land beyond the forest.
MINA	We have had no word from my husband for some time now. But we would like to know where he is.
JONATHAN	Then what are you doing here?
MINA	I am staying on a visit with Miss Lucy Westenra.
JONATHAN	Don't stay. For the master is near and at hand.
MINA	We must find your master, for he has taken the soul of my dear husband, whose acquaintance you have surely

	made. You must surely recall the name Jonathan Harker?
JONATHAN	Ah, yes, his father was the inventor of a burnt rum punch much favored on Derby Day. All they serve me here is mamaliga.
MINA	Do you recall the name Jonathan Harker? You must try* very hard.
SEWARD	Mina, it's useless.
JONATHAN	Indeed, Mrs. Harker, don't stay. It is perilous to be here when the moons creeps over the grass and stands before me in all her nakedness. Look at you! Thin already, like the tea after the teapot has been watered.
SEWARD	Mrs. Harker, it's time for you to go.
MINA	Good-by, and I hope I may see you often, under auspices pleasanter to yourself.
JONATHAN	Good-by, my dear. I pray God I may never see your sweet face again. May he bless and keep you.

She goes out and weeps. SEWARD *follows and comforts her during the scene below between* LUCY *and* SIMMONS. *The former is still in bed, recovering from her transfusion.* QUINCEY *is gone.*

| SIMMONS | The master's an odd duck, ain't he? Bet he'd like to put his swizzle to you, and he's not the only one either. Workin' at this bloomin' place's makin' me loony myself, I reckon. Master Jack's a prig of the first water when 'e's not gassed out on the old chloral hydrate, and that's a fact. You want to play your Ishtar game in the garden tonight? Your lovely Wilhelmina is always makin' a nasty mess of the house and grounds with her continual regurgitation. And you know who's got to clean up all that filth. Reliable old Simmons here. Why, me mates at the Black Dog call me the rare sot for putting up with the lot of 'em: mooncalves, naturals, bloody gooney birds, I swear. Lookin' at you's got me pecker up, I do declare. I'm hot for a piece anytime, Miss Lucy. And that's the long and short of it. And that old cheese-monger from Hamsterdom leaves a regular splotch of piss every time he plants his fat arse. It's enough to make a bloke fly off his bloomin' nut. |

JONATHAN, *framed in the window of his cell, sings his song.*

| JONATHAN | There is hair growing into my head. |

There is hair growing into my head.
There is hair in the air;
It stands on a chair.
And then it grows into my head.

INTERMISSION.

Late twilight on the East Cliff overlooking Whitby. LUCY *and* QUINCEY *sit at her favorite seat. Below, a reprise of the puppet show.*

LUCY

Oh, I do feel so thin I barely cast a shadow. Do you know poor Mina throws up every day? Yes, she does. Every single day. It is quite revolting to be with her on these occasions. One must pretend not to notice. Her weak stomach must have something to do with the lamentable state of poor Jonathan. Quite changed, they say he is. Do you suppose he is still capable of love? In the physical, gymnastical sense. Doesn't look it, to be sure. Looks quite the shorn sheep. But I have heard from Simmons—you know Simmons? Jack's man?— that the mad are sexually indefatigable. Very goats at it. He described to me quite remarkable feats of copulation among the idiot population of his previous place of employment: Lady Gresham's Home for the Feeble Minded. It was no point to stop the poor dears. They would, if prevented during sensible hours, get to it, clandestinely, at night. Till the very floors creaked. The doctors tried strait-waist coats, but the poor dears would roar and howl so it was more than decency could bear. And, goodness knows, what else would you have them do? The girls were quite clumsy and incapable of acquiring the simplest stitch—I am referring to needlecraft. The men absolute unlicked bears, lost to all possibility of Christian improvement. Simmons kept meticulous records of the more wonderful feats, the most appalling and exuberant lubricities. Simmons calls me Ishtar on our little walks over the wold. I make poor old Dr. Van Helsing do that, too. He turns red as a beet, but he does it. Do you know he is quite incontinent? He must wear a sort of India-rubber night suit to avoid embarrassment. He calls it an attribute of a certain class of genius. Caesar. Alexander the Great. Willem the Silent. Bed-wetters all. That's what dear Van Helsing has told me. I call him Bobo. Then he pretends to do an examination of me—all because of my dreams, my apparent anemia, and the irritation about my throat.

Darkness. Pause. Wolf cries.

Lately, I have been restless at night, Quincey. Very restless.

Sings a phrase or two from her song.

I like when Simmons talks to me about the inmates at Lady Gresham's. It seems quite an exasperation being a young girl and knowing one is not supposed to know certain things, and precisely the sorts of things one wants to know. Bonka bonka bonka bonk.

More wolf cries. DRACULA *alone in the sky.*

DRACULA I am pure *otherness*. The ridiculous little sham of human conceit does not involve me. I am pure absence and am immune to the petty anxieties that trouble the shallow waters of humanity. I hear the music of other worlds and understand the deadly elegance of absolute nullity. He who opposes me becomes the fruit of my ceremonial banquet. I burn no bones before the altar of strange gods. I waste no blood in obscene and futile rites of propitiation. I am clean. I am honest. I do not suffer the inexact furies of the moving world. My dream is vast, empty, stationary, most cunningly articulated, infinitely mutable and transmutable. It was me and my kind, the high lords of Ckm Ckm, who have opened one inch the door of perpetuity, and slipped beyond, leaving behind on the doorstep of your civilization only the pathetic corpse of a dead rat. Nothing, absolutely nothing. For I am pure *otherness*.

Blackout. Lights up on another transfusion for the unfortunate LUCY, *who is near death.* SEWARD *and* QUINCEY *pace and fret.* VAN HELSING *breaks down. He raises his hands over his head in a sort of mute despair, then beats his palms together in a helpless way. Sits down on a chair and, putting his hands before his face, begins to cry, with loud, dry sobs.*

VAN HELSING	God! God! God! What have we done, what has this poor thing done, that we are so beset?
SEWARD	What does it all mean? I am beginning to wonder if my long habit of life among the insane is beginning to tell upon my own mind.
VAN HELSING	No. Today you must operate. I shall prepare. You are weakened already.

Takes off coat and rolls up sleeve.

QUINCEY	Jack Seward, I don't want to shove myself in anywhere where I've no right to be*; but I love that girl. What is it that's wrong with her? The Dutchman said, another transfusion of blood. That both you and he were exhausted. Is that not so?
SEWARD	Then please don't, you blithering idiot.

Pause.

	That is so. What of it?
QUINCEY	I take it that both you and Van Helsing had already done what I did yesterday. Is that not so?
SEWARD	That's what we're tying to tell you, Quincey.
QUINCEY	I guess Miss Mina was in on it, too. Four days ago she looked queer.
SEWARD	Oh, shut up, Quincey, for God's sake.
QUINCEY	And how long has this been going on?
SEWARD	About ten days. What of it?
VAN HELSING	My friend John, be more calm. Our American Quincey, he have the child brain, but not malign.

MINA *staggers in, looking strange.*

SEWARD	Oh, Quincey, you are an absolute . . . cowboy! If only you would pay attention, you might keep abreast. It is the work of a vampire.
VAN HELSING	The wampyr Dracula.
QUINCEY	What's a "wampyr"?
SEWARD	Vampire!

LUCY *lifts her little finger in the vampiric gesture.* MINA *responds involuntarily.* LUCY *dies. All regard her with horror.* VAN HELSING *crosses himself as we hear the* VAMPIRETTES' *chorus of "o, a, u."*

VAN HELSING	Just as at the scholomance high in the air over Lake Hermanstadt, the college of the undead. She is one of them now, God pity her.

Cross-fade to the sky high above. VAMPIRETTES *sing their song and dance.* DRACULA *flies up to join them. One turns to him.*

VAMPIRETTE 1   Kckcptcktpu, ungld, vigboaou, o, Drkloa.

DRACULA   Tkctt, Bttl Krrk, Mcuaugan.

VAMPIRETTE 2   Qqqst?

DRACULA   Nx krrrrrcafxuoaoau.

Nx grglc.

LUCY *joins them.* DRACULA *raises little finger. All raise little fingers. They greet her.*

VAMPIRETTE 3   Allillillillu, sstssh. Blld.

They all sing.

O, a, u.

Cross-fade back to LUCY'*s room with her casket. Candles. Dirge.* MINA, SEWARD, QUINCEY, *and* VAN HELSING *all hold wilted flowers.*

MINA   Just like poor Jonathan, sucked dry as a pressed hibiscus. A moment of silence for Jonathan.

Dirge continues as all exit. Pause. DRACULA *and* LUCY *dance the "Silverton Polka." Blackout. High on the East Cliff again. Gaslight.* MINA *and* SEWARD *sit in the twilight.*

SEWARD   Since our encounter, I have felt a strange new impulse, Mina. This monster, whatever he may be, has made me value my Christian soul the more. My days working with the twisted relics of lost reason have affected me, I fear. I must know if this thing truly exists. Van Helsing, I know, shall once more reap the recognition and rewards of our labors, if they do yield fruit. It is my lot; yet, perhaps, now, with the surety of your friendship, I can accept that lot. My father, you see, was a Hebrew, yes, a Hebrew of the Adelphi Theater type. All that that phrase projects into one's brain: the Asiatic gown and fez, the greasy coin, the garbled injunction to buy cheap and sell dear; these instincts I have sought to transcend, through good Christian fellowship. Quincey and his crew, etc. But I cannot, I also confess, entirely escape my nature, even though it is other than I wish. Other than I do, in the bright days of my faith, deserve.

MINA   Oh, Jack.

SEWARD   So I shall, when this nasty business be done, take up
                the faith and seek out representatives of the Church of
                Latter-day Saints, so that, God willing, I may journey
                to Africa once more and convert the dark man, and
                cleanse his wounds. And all within my brain will be
                "level with the horizon," as Van Helsing says. A feeling
                I have not known since the old days at Mbululand.

        Pause.

                I don't know, Mina. I really don't know.

MINA   It somehow eases me to write it all in words. To record
                it all, simply or not so simply, in figures of speech.

SEWARD   You're a pretty figure of a girl, Mina.

MINA   Was I very wanton?

        Pause.

                Oh, but Jack, you shouldn't have followed me. I came
                up here to be alone, for I am very sad. I miss Lucy, and
                I had hoped for so long that there was nothing perma-
                nently the matter with Jonathan. See the lights scat-
                tered all over the town, sometimes in rows where the
                streets are, and sometimes singly; they run right up the
                river and die away in the curve of the valley. Over there
                the view is cut off by the black roof of the old house
                next to the asylum. Isn't it the place they call Carfax? A
                band on the pier is playing a harsh waltz, and farther
                along the quai it sounds like a Salvation Army meeting
                in the back street. Neither of the bands hears the other,
                but up here we can see and hear them both. It is like
                that with Jonathan. There are two of him. But all the
                time I wonder where the true, good, Christian soul of
                him is, and if he is thinking of me. I can't help it. I wish
                he were here.

        SEWARD *shuffles about awkwardly.*

                So I sit here thinking, thinking I don't know what.

        Tolling bell. Wolf cries.

                I suppose I should try to get some sleep. Good night.

        She exits. Blackout.

DRACULA   *(Singing.)* Dust: my friend.
                Fine, black sand.
                Old red plush

of a coffin
lid's inside.
Ten thousand years.

Blood: my food.
Old hats and
coats ago.
Where am I?
Ten thousand years.

Lights up slowly on MINA's *bedroom. Wolf in window.* DRACULA *in doorway. He seizes her and drags her to the center of the room, opens his shirt, and cuts his own vein with a fingernail. Pause. He forces her to drink "like a kitten." She does so.*

DRACULA   Flesh of my flesh, blood of my blood. Drink.
Pause.

            Good. When my brain says "Come" to you, you shall
            cross land or sea to do my bidding.

Cross-fade to padded cell. JONATHAN *is in a pool of blood.* SIMMONS *discovers him. Rushes out and returns with* SEWARD.

SIMMONS   I think, sir, his back is broken. See, both his right arm
            and the whole left side of his face are paralyzed.
SEWARD   Go and fetch Quincey, and send for Van Helsing.
SIMMONS   I can't understand two things. He could mark his face
            like that by beating his own head on the floor. I saw a
            young woman do it once at Lady Gresham's before any-
            one could lay hands upon her. Bloody waste that was,
            as she was a rare piece. And I suppose he might have
            broke his neck by falling out of bed, if he got in an awk-
            ward kink. But for the life of me! If his back was
            broke, he couldn't beat in his head; and if his face was
            like that before his fall . . .
SEWARD   I think that will do for now, Simmons . . .

VAN HELSING *and* QUINCEY *enter.*

QUINCEY   My God, what happened to him?
VAN HELSING There is no time to lose. His words may be worth many
            lives. It may be that a soul is at stake.
SEWARD   We shall operate above the ear.

Applies a brace and bit to JONATHAN's *head.*

JONATHAN   I'll be quiet, Doctor. I have had a terrible dream. And it
            has left me so weak that I cannot move.

SEWARD	Go on.
VAN HELSING	Tell us your dream, Scardanelli.
JONATHAN	All day I waited to hear from him, but he didn't send me anything, not even a blowfly. He promised: "All these lives I will give to you and many more if you will fall down and worship me." But he came for her, for when she came to visit me this afternoon she wasn't the same.
VAN HELSING	You are referring to Miss Lucy?

VAMPIRETTES' *vowel chorus.*

JONATHAN	No, I am talking about Mrs. Harker. She reminded me of someone. A face from long ago. Before I discovered fright in the dark interstices of the Borgo Pass. No, I must be mistaken. I know nothing of solicitors and their pretty wives. I like people with plenty of blood in them.

Groans.

So when he came tonight from Carfax I was ready for him. I have heard that madmen have unnatural strength; and as I knew I was a madman—at times anyhow—I resolved to use my power. He felt it, too, for he had come out of the mist to struggle with me. He slipped through it, and, when I tried to cling to him, he raised me up and flung me down.

SEWARD	We know the worst now. He is here, in this house.

They let JONATHAN *drop to the floor, and then rush to her door.*

QUINCEY	Should we disturb her?
SEWARD	We must. If the door is locked, we must break it in.

They bang on the door.

Mina, are you doing something in there you don't want us to see?

She opens the door, her face covered with blood.

MINA	I was sleeping, Jack.
SEWARD	In God's name, what does this mean?

JONATHAN *(sings his swan song.)* "There is hair growing into my head," etc.

The MEN *join him for a chorus. He moans and dies.*

MINA	He's dead.

VAN HELSING	God's will be done.

LUCY *suddenly appears, lifts her little finger.* MINA *responds involuntarily.* QUINCEY *faints dead away.*

LUCY	Come with me, Jack. I want to kiss you and comfort you in my arms. Come and we can rest together.
MINA	*(As in a trance.)* He stepped out of the mist and said: "You may as well know it is not the first or the second, time." And then he began to do it, and I felt my strength fade away.
SEWARD	Is this really Lucy's body or only a demon in her shape?
VAN HELSING	It is her body, yet not it.
LUCY	Oh, Jack, my love. I'm so glad to see you. I have seen things you would never believe. I have flown over London and Whitby. I can see through your eyelids into your brain; I can see what you are thinking. You are so unhappy in this place. Come with me. I have always loved you best. We are going to a wonderful land in the West, where there are no boundaries to one's will, and every type of energy is free to take on its own shape. Here you can only dry up, and be an inmate of your own brain. You must come with me.
VAN HELSING	Not for your life.

He holds up a wafer. She retreats in horror.

SEWARD	What is that you are using?
VAN HELSING	The host. I brought it from Amsterdam. I have an indulgence. Come, we must follow quickly and catch them all before daybreak.
SEWARD	She is headed for the ruined chapel of Carfax. Across the wold. Quincey, for God's sake, wake up.
MINA	I took the opiate you gave me, Jack, and was dreaming of poor Jonathan, lost in the land beyond the forest.

All rush out. Blackout. Chorus of VAMPIRETTES' *"o, a, u." Lights up in the ruined chapel of Carfax. Dim.* LUCY, DRACULA, *and the* VAMPIRETTES *and their coffins.* VAN HELSING *enters. A* VAMPIRETTE *attacks him. He holds up the host. All fall back in disarray.* QUINCEY *and* SEWARD, *also with hosts, block the other exits. The* VAMPIRES *are trapped. Pause.*

DRACULA	You think to baffle me, you with your pale faces all in a circle, like calves' heads in a butcher shop. You think

JONATHAN you know who I am. But my name is . . . TREMEN-
DOUS. Ask your friend. Ah, where is poor Jonathan?
(In a ghostly cameo.) He is no more. For he straddled
two worlds, and for his arrogance was torn apart.

He vanishes.

DRACULA Scardanelli! Would he had drunk the dark wine of eternity and joined us who . . . simply ARE.

The MEN *advance on him.*

I must speak clear. England, with its sedgy pathways
and stone fences, pleases me not. The blood is poor
here, and I confess to a distaste for the bowler hat,
which is such a passion in these parts. Miss Lucy West-
enra . . .

He throws her to them.

You may have her, but you must not interfere with our
departure.

Gestures grandly. LUCY *blanches in horror.*

The warlike days are over. Blood is too precious a thing
in these days of dishonorable peace; and the stories of
the great races are as a tale that is told.

QUINCEY *lunges at* DRACULA. *Slices him with his bowie knife.*
Money pours out.

Foolish, Mr. Morris.

Slices vertically with one swift movement of his fingernail. Red sand
spills out. QUINCEY *collapses and slowly dies.*

Your land intrigues me, for there are fewer crucifixes
there, and little garlic, with its noisome flower. If you
must know, it is there me and my kin are journeying.
America! Aboard the steamer *Paducah.* The crew is fat
and flushed with blood. But you are a peasant. Die like
one. I go now.

He and VAMPIRETTES *warily begin to withdraw.*

LUCY You must not forsake me. I have given up everything,
my honor, my faith, my people, my blood, my very life.
All for you. They will snuff me out with no more com-
punction than boys kill cats. Drkloa, o, ccplp!
Qmmnll! Oh, remember how much I adore you, my

fire, my creator, my God, my sin. AM I TO SUFFER
THE ABSOLUTE REJECTION OF MY LORD AND
MASTER, FOR WHOSE SAKE MY SOUL SHALL
BURN FOREVER IN THE FURNACE OF HELL!?

The MEN *close in on her.* DRACULA *exits.*

> Mina! Mina! You mustn't let this happen. The blood is
> the joy, and I don't want my ridiculous Christian soul.
> Oh, Mina, I have flown, flown high above London and
> Whitby! Stop them! Mina! Mina! Oh, please stop
> them.

Dawn. She falls helpless to the ground. MINA *looks on in horror
as* VAN HELSING *takes up a mallet and stake from his sack.*

VAN HELSING	It will be a blessed hand that sets her free.
SEWARD	Tell me what I am to do.
VAN HELSING	Strike in God's name and send her to the stars.

Amid shrieks from both WOMEN, SEWARD *drives the stake
through her heart. She lies still. Pause.*

VAN HELSING	He said the steamer *Paducah,* did he not?

The MEN *rush out, roaring. Pause.*

MINA	Poor dead Lucy. Poor dead Jonathan. Sucked dry as a harvest pipping in the fastness of Dracula. A moment of silence for Jonathan.

LUCY *arises and joins* MINA.

> Kcm. Kcm. Xxxghn. Drkloa.

*They hold hands and sing a reprise of "The Land beyond the
Forest." End of play.*

Appendix 1. A text for the puppet show. DRACULA and a GIRL.

DRACULA	Listen, my dear, to the children of the night.
GIRL	Why may I not go this evening?
DRACULA	Because, my dear, my coachman and horse are away on business.
GIRL	But I would walk with pleasure. I want to get away at once.
DRACULA	And your baggage?

GIRL I do not care about it.

He lunges at her.

Oh, oh, my god. He has placed his reeking lip upon my throat and bitten me!

Attacks DRACULA *with a mallet.*

Whirligig   (1988)

CHARACTERS *(in order of appearance)*

    MAN (XUTHUS)
    GIRL (Michelle)
    BUS MAN
    SISTER (Jennifer)
    GIRL HUN
    GIRL HUN

The play takes place in the present, in a waiting room in a rural bus station and in outer space.

Whirligig was commissioned by the Shaliko Company with the help of a grant from the New York State Council on the Arts. It was premiered in New York City on April 5, 1989.

Note: The occasional appearance of an asterisk in the middle of a speech indicates that the next speech begins to overlap at that point. A double asterisk indicates that a later speech (not the one immediately following) begins to overlap at that point. The overlapping speeches are all clearly marked in the text.

Act One

Scene 1. A waiting room in a rural bus station. A block of lockers up left. An open door up right with a view of an open field and a starry night. The silver MAN *stands in the shadows with only his legs visible. A* GIRL *with green hair enters with two immense suitcases. She stops, lowers them to the floor, and pauses. She unwraps a stick of gum and slips it in her mouth. For a long time she is expressionless. It is as if she senses the presence of the* MAN, *but is unsure of what to do. A big grin appears on her face. She whistles a snatch of a song. She stops and we hear the night wind in the trees outside.*

GIRL

I dreamed I had a wicked sister . . .

Pause.

She was a girl Hun. She rode her pony, up there
in the sky. She rode across the vast empty spaces
the sky is filled with. Across millions of miles
of empty sky, sky so empty and clean you could
never hope to fathom it. A whole horde of girl
Huns rode with her, harrying all the meek ones
of the outer worlds. They wore only rags; bows and
arrows were their weapons. They obeyed no laws
and had no rules. For nourishment, they dug up
disgusting roots and ate them raw. They laid strips
of raw meat on their ponies' back, under the saddle
as they rode. Slap, slap, slap. This makes the
meat soft. My sister, she was the leader of the
girl Huns. In the horde all are equal. Except the
Shanyu, my sister, who was a little more equal. The
Shanyu interpreted the will of Tengri, god of the
girl Huns. Slap, slap, slap, as they rode. Their
eyes shine bright as balefire in the dark, in the empty
reaches of outer space. Their flag is a bent stick

	with nine foxtails nailed to it. Tengri is the only god, and my wicked sister is the Shanyu. Everyone in outer space is afraid of the girl Huns . . .
Pause.	
	Ride, ride! Steppes, plains, steppes, endless forest of the outer dark. Ride, pony! Ride the darkness. Ride on stones, ride in woods, ride in the wind, ride where there is no wind, no stones, no woods . . .
Pause.	
	Searching. No road. Where. No where. Ride nowhere.
Long pause. She whistles.	
	You can come out now.
Pause.	
	I wasn't talking to myself.
MAN	Pardon me, I happen to be in the shadows here.
GIRL	I noticed.
Pause.	
MAN	May I join you?
GIRL	Suit yourself.
MAN	Your hair is green.
GIRL	Yup.
MAN	Interesting. . .
GIRL	I dreamed I had a wicked sister.
MAN	What is "dreamed"?
GIRL	Skip it.
Pause.	
	I don't have a wicked sister. I have a good sister. Barf.
MAN	Of course. I heard only a part of the story . . .
GIRL	Smile, curtsy, straight A's. Special goody-two-shoes. Barf.
MAN	The woods outside are cold.
GIRL	Dreams bomb. I'm fed up.
MAN	Your hair is green.
Pause.	
	You are a very happy people.
GIRL	Happy? God. Money. Junk. Cars. Crud. School. All of it baloney.
MAN	You look happy.
GIRL	Fuck happy, fuck family, fuck America.

MAN	What is "fuck"?
GIRL	All-purpose noun, verb, adjective, adverb, pointer, name,
	fate, accusation, punishment, black box, verbal dump, dark
	delight, toxic word waste, a hole in the head.
MAN	Oh, I see.

Pause.

GIRL	Darkness. Spooks. Monsters. Ghosts. Nameless evil bugaboos.
MAN	You must teach me the secret of your happiness.
GIRL	(*Laughing.*) Just look at this dump of a country.
MAN	The surface of things is obscure.
GIRL	(*Laughing.*) Funny thing to say . . .
MAN	See, you are happy.
GIRL	I am not. I am running away from home.
MAN	What is "home"?
GIRL	Home is where you're from.
MAN	Oh, I see.

Pause.

	I am from a place faraway, but it is no longer existing.
GIRL	Dad? Sixties type. Lawyer. Acid head, hippie, "way-out,"
	"cool, man, cool." The Beatles, ugh. Law school, tunnel
	vision, career in venture capital. Suits, hats, coats.
	Condos. Fuck the poor. Senator Moynihan. The pope. IRAs.
	Hippie yuppie. Huppie yippie. Yawn . . .

Pause.

Mom, the hippie honey. Short skirts, long skirts, short
skirts again. Castro, Che Guevera, born-again, Jews for
Jesus, puke. Moral majority. Likud. Jogging. Condos for
Christ. The West Bank. Summer home somewhere.
CDs and money market. Double yawn . . .

Pause.

I ran away from home. Two thousand miles. Home
sucks.

Pause.

I'm going to the desert.

MAN	What desert?
GIRL	Any desert. Libya, Chaco, Morocco, Arabia. Mongolia, home of the Huns. Patagonia. Anywhere. Anywhere out of here. Here sucks.
MAN	My world is sand world of Plinth.
GIRL	Yeah, and I'm Madonna.
MAN	What is "Madonna"?

Pause.

GIRL	What's "Plinth"?
MAN	Sand world of Plinth. Far away. Very old place filled with stuff. Colorful tents, gasbags, flying sandwiches, as you say. Slight accident. Advanced nuclear fusion project. We call it "the big boo-boo." Gizmo out of control on thirty-seventh level. Kablooey. No more jamboree on Plinth. No more Plinth. Sadness. We are scattered among the planetoids. Thousands, thousands upon thousands. Most dead. No more rock-'n'-roll.
GIRL	No more rock-'n'-roll?
MAN	No more rock-'n'-roll. Hop from one planetoid to next, as, for instance, Mitake Mura, Dikan'ka, Elmer.
GIRL	What's Elmer?
MAN	Elmer is a small world in local argot, of where I am from. Name of Elmer is different on Elmer. I am Xuthus.
GIRL	Funny name, Xuphus.
MAN	Not Xuphus, Xuthus.
GIRL	I won't tell you my name.

Pause.

MAN	So be it.

Pause.

	The surface of things is obscure.
GIRL	(*Laughing.*) Xuphus the obscure.
MAN	What are those?
GIRL	My stuff. Suitcases. Possessions. Just a lot of junk.
MAN	You travel light.

GIRL	I travel light. Girl Huns, remember?
MAN	Where I come from we are very sad, even our sex is an occasion of great mourning.
GIRL	You really like America. I hate America.
MAN	Elmer is worst, and Hektor, and garbage world of Dr. Spock. Unspeakable. Hektor is shaped like a dumbbell.
GIRL	America is full of Fascists.
MAN	Elmer is full of broken glockenspiels.
GIRL	My suitcases are very heavy.
MAN	Like fate.
GIRL	Tell me something, Xuphus.
MAN	Sure, lady.
GIRL	Tell me why the world's so fucked up.
MAN	That word again. I do not able to parse that word.
GIRL	I have nothing to say about America.
MAN	Elmer is more worst, that is why I have come.

Pause.

GIRL.	Girl Huns, ponies, night, sigh!

Pause.

Murder, mayhem, slaughter of
innocence, rock-'n'-roll. Death.
Death, departure, pilgrimage,
Mecca, Moluccas, sea-green.
Robespierre, revolution, raunch,
ranch, Ronald Rubout. Death,
destruction, blast force, crater,
lime pit, death star, wipeout . . .

Pause.

Girl Huns, feathers, foxtails, spurs.
Joyride, hangout, hangar, blimp,
moon, monster, master, mistress.
Beyond the beyond and beyond that.

Pause.

Xuphus, tell me why.

Pause.

Xuphus, goofus, doofus, toothless,
Xuphus the obscure.

Pause.

Howl, scream, shriek, bellow, barf,
and die.

Pause.

Gambol, dart, spring, drop dead . . .

Pause.

Passion, wheelbarrow, hook and ladder,
burn up, burn out, blow up, and
croak . . .

Pause.

Drive, dislocate, discombobulate,
disappear, disc, discus, flying
saucer, fear, fly away, furniture,
fin, finish, reappear, nowhere,
somewhere, not here, nope, never,
naysayer, nix, Nixon, Ahab,
mud, monster, mule, mugger . . .

Pause.

Are you a mugger, Xuphus?

Pause.

Skip it . . .

Pause.

Where was I?

Pause.

Banks, box, motor, profit, sleazoid,
cheapskate, thrift, virtue, value,
timeless, elegance, Cadillac, warlock,
cannibal, time, slime, drop dead . . .

Pause.

Screwed.
Walk, run, drop dead.
Escape, hurdle, are killed, rot.
Kill X in the name of Y.
Blast the sand-nigger,
dance on the bones, Uncle Sam . . .
Uncle Somoza,
South Africa, Israel, Russia,
beanbag, blowup, drop dead.
Little, littler, littlest.
Bomb, blast, bright, nothing.
Black, white, blast, nothing.
Star wars, blast, brightness, nuts,

drop dead, are dead, nothing.
Condos, Broadway, box seats,
    blockhead, money bin, blast,
    bright, barf, drop dead, nothing.
Boy, girl, blast, feathers falling,
    are dead, nothing.
USA, Europe, Yemen, Tierra del Fuego,
    Antarctica, Albania, are dead,
    zero.
Zero the ozone layer.
Zero the Museum of Natural History.
Zero the pink tennis shoes.
Zero the green hair.
Zero the heroes, Ollie, Poindexter,
    rolling uphill, are dead, blast,
    brightness, nothing.
Zero the last things rolling uphill,
    zero the republic, zero the
    heat death, zero the whole
    hideous wipe-out machine,
    Xuphus.
Zero the blowup, zero the heat
    death, fried city of standing
    corpses, earnest readers of
    journalism, somnambulism.
All dead, rolling uphill, seeking
    the white light, religion, popes,
    real estate, all rolling uphill,
    brightness, are dead, no after-
    life, no up, no down, no angels,
    no pretty times, no sweet divinity,
    no, nothing but cinders, soot,
    rocks, nothing and more nothing
    and a lot more of it, nothing,
    never, not, no, zero. Zero forever.

Pause.

Except the girl Huns, hunting.

Pause.

Fury, swiftness, brightness, fun, freedom,
    fury and more fury.

Pause.

Contempt, warlock, bitterness. Hatred . . .
All of it rolling uphill . . .

Pause.

Antigravity, wonder, awe . . .

MAN   Weirdness.

GIRL   You could call it weird.

Long pause.

MAN   I am a weird.

Pause.

I am a weird. One of the few left. The
way of the weird is an open road, a
road that always turns away.
One world after another. Now
a green world of woods, people
like you, happy to run away, among
the forest of lights, the city, or
here, amidst the wild prairies, you,
with two suitcases, all you possess.
Maybe tomorrow a stone world as old
as the chroma of the sun's furnace,
and as empty as a dead man's dream.
Or perhaps a bright, crystal world,
an M-type metallic planetoid, bright
as burnished gold, inhabited by
shiny beings of glass, strange beings
who dream in little polygons of light,
and when they talk they make a little
noise like a teapot's whistle.
Maybe you can tell what the suitcases
are for and what they contain.

*Girl opens one. Silverware clatters out. MAN falls down in wonder.
We see his face, which is also silver, for the first time.*

What beautiful implements! What are they for?

GIRL   Swag, loot. It's called silverware.

GIRL sees that MAN is silver

Like you. Hey, you. You're silver.

MAN   I am a weird.

Pause.

The color, you mean. I am partly

	metallized. It helps absorb random
	energy when one is lost, out there,
	a frequent happening in the old days.
	It is a folly, applied from within.
	Folly, fooly. Foil. Electrolysis.
	Now it is of cosmetic utility only.
	We who do the work of weirding
	have a big pleasure in this silver.
	But your implements are wonderful.
GIRL	Family silver. I'm going to pawn it
	so I can go to the desert. I'll
	never come back. Never.
MAN	With such beautiful implements I would
	not come back, too. Never.
GIRL	I'm going to resist the impulse to ask.
	I'm not going to ask you the question.
MAN	I am glad. I am transparent by
	nature, even though I am a weird.
GIRL	I refuse to ask you.
MAN	I am almost happy, the bliss you
	emanate is contagious.
GIRL	DON'T YOU WANT TO KNOW WHO I AM?

Pause.

| MAN | No. |
| GIRL | Right . . . |

Long pause. The MAN FROM THE BUS COMPANY *enters and delivers his monologue.*

BUS MAN	Ladies and gentlemen, the Amalgamated
	Odd Fellows Bus Company of Grayways,
	Iowa, is sorry to report we have
	canceled the 1:00 A.M. for Grayways
	and points west. Ladies and gents,
	we are most sad to inform you the
	bus in question has done blowed up
	and is no more. Furthermore, folks,
	we are plumb wore out and
	would like to call it a day, but
	owing to the problem with the, ah,
	aforementioned bus, mysteriously,
	spontaneously combusted out by

the dump near Milwacky, we are
stuck, like you, in this dustbowl
shithole till Lord knows when.
Christ, it's enough to push a sane
man to drink, and a drinking man
plumb over the edge into the purlieus
of outright insobidy. Nameless,
hopeless, dark-finned, incurable
insobidy from whence no man has
returned, but in the shackles of the
mad, screaming bloody murder,
gibbering fit to kill, in Lower Malarkey,
or Glossolalia, language of the doomed.
And, further, there ain't no bus to
Crow, Port Tobacco, Loyalsock, Baraboo,
Washington, Salem, Cheecago, Webster,
Troy, Utica, Carthage, Beanbag, Thorpe,
Hog Eye, Noodle, Oblong, Santa Claus,
Rabbit Hash, Bumblebee, Wink, Zigzag,
Jackass Gulch, Gouge, Hang Town, Bug,
Humbug Flat, Defeated, Raccoon, Okay,
Custard, Brindle, Dead Man, Horsetail,
nor to Puppytown, by ways of Centipede,
Paint Pot, One-Eye, Puke, and Rattrap,
nor through Chucklehead, Shinbone,
Dead Mule, Ground Hog's Glory and Poverty
Hill, where nothing don't grow no more
owning to a radioactive constitution
of stroobontium seepage down there,
deep in the ground-water thing . . .
'Cause, like I say, the bus done blowed
up, burned like a son of a gun, and
ain't no more.

Pause.

However, you can take your ticket to Grayways
and apply for a refund but,
just between you and me, I
wouldn't bother, 'cause it's a
waste of time, aside from which
how you gonna get there in the
first place without you got no

wheels, and me, I tell you, the
first thing I do on payday is
cash my check quick because
it's like the Good Book says:
don't count your chickens
before saving up for a rainy day,
and seeing as how today is payday,
I'm henceforth outta here . . .
Goo'night, ladies, goo'night, gents.
If by chance another bus do come
by, tell 'em Fred is dead, and
watch out for that fatal, itchiferous,
insidious insobidy and praise the Lord.

Pause.

Now there just might be a bus show up
for Elmer. Elmer, or Waltraut, Sphinx,
Erika, Argentina, Thule, 1940 W-L, Hay,
Kutuzov, Murakami, Ahti, Ops, Gogol,
Muazzez, Hathor, James, Cuffey, Teucer,
Vanderlinden, Goethe, Alex, Khufu, Bus,
Hus, Kosmodemyanskaya, Galahad, Smithers,
Beer, Shao, Lick, 1931 PH, Ethiopia,
Thais, Galatea, Hedwerthia, Tyche, Isis,
Amphitrite, Metus, Vala, or Hohensteina.
Just imagine taking the bus to Bus . . .
You think on that, kind gentlefolk,
but I wouldn't count on it. Why? you ask.
Them places are not on no map neither,
them places are up in the night sky.
Least how it's rumored they are . . .
Strange, a bus to Bus! Goo'night,
sweet prince, goo'night, ladies.

Starts to go out, stops, and looks at them sternly.

You two look funny. Weird. Strange.
Foreign. Not from here. People like
you, people not from here, people
who don't belong here, that's for sure.
They take their life in their own
hand, and they have a fool for a doctor.

*Exits through the open door upstage, wanders few paces farther,
blows his brains out, and collapses under the starry sky.*

GIRL	Are you sure you don't want to know who I am?
Pause.	
	Shit. I asked you. I demeaned myself. Fuck.
MAN	Surfaces are obscure.
GIRL	You're not really human, are you!? Wowee! Great! Splendid. You're wonderful! What are you? Are you a machine? A robot? Are you going to kill me? Let me see you do something weird. Please. Just one little piece of weirdness. Turn me into whatever you are. You're a machine, I just know it!

The GIRL's SISTER *enters.*

SISTER	Here you are, Michelle. Well, what have you got to say for yourself?
GIRL	Go away, Jennifer.
SISTER	I have absolutely nothing to say to you, Michelle.
MAN	Blackout!

Scene two. The same. SISTER *lectures* GIRL.

SISTER	Michelle, Michelle. This is madness.
Pause.	
	I have absolutely nothing to say to you, Michelle. Do you hear me? Nothing. Have you ever considered, Michelle, the sheer amount of garbage, every day? How long it took Grandfather to become rich? Really. Do you imagine you are the only one? With problems. Michelle. Can you imagine what I might be going through?* Have you considered the past and future? Have you given thought to sheer human stupidity? The sky. The earth. The sea. Have you thought about the sea, and about what lies at the bottom

of the sea? Shipwrecks, Michelle. Ghostly,
bloated, dead, the drowned. Thousands
of them, with staring eyes, with starfish
in the eye sockets, and coral in their
waving hair, emerald hair. Green hair,
like yours, Michelle. But they have
at least earned their green hair by
going down with the ship. They at least
have fought the good fight, and the sea
will never, never yield up their secret
tragedy. You, on the other hand, are no more
than a fearful ingrate. A leech on the body
politic. You do not go to church, you
do not send aid to the contras, you
do not join the family in our
choral readings of the *New Republic*.
You are apathetic, you do not follow
current events except from this
insane perspective of radicalism,
this insane PLO terrorist line you
repeat to shock us, your father
and mother, the cat and dog, all
shocked but not surprised, Michelle.
For you are bad seed, Michelle, the
black sheep, pariah, outcast, the family
failure, the disgrace, the wicked child,
the ne'er-do-well, the satanic changeling . . .
I have always known this, but I tried to
protect you from your evil nature, which is
sick and vile and vicious; and yes,
I had my secret motives, too, for Mom and Dad
would be crushed to know what a monster they
had begotten and brought into this world and
reared and nurtured with all their love, all
unknowing. But I knew, even, yes, even
when you seemed normal. I knew full well
you were not. Your associations among the
dark underclass. Scandalous. The dead beats.
Drug addicts. Perverts. Social undesirables
and rejects. Losers, Michelle. Have you thought
about the stock market? Real estate? The need

to accumulate, heap up, hoard, and conserve?
Have you considered the feelings of your
betrothed, North Mainwaring, who I warned
against your aberrant, sick nature, though
he would have none of it, being under the
spell of your wiles, yes, I warned him it
would come to this, while he could have had me,
who understood his sensitive nature, and need
to be alone, in the wilderness, for long periods
of time, with ducks, and decoys, and guns.
Have you thought about Smith College,
about Bergdorf Goodman, have you
considered our holidays at Key West,
Lake Tahoe, the rough anfractious rocks
off the coast of Maine, have you considered
reputation, the bottom line, public morality,
risk of AIDS through normal (I dare not
imagine it!) heterosexual relations with a
horde of unsuitable partners, have you
considered the fragility of credit, belief,
trust, social glue? God help us, Michelle,
have you thought about money, hard-cash money?

Pause.

GIRL

You rotten-minded, little good-for-nothing slut.
(*Begins to overlap* SISTER *at* *.)
This is my good sister, Jennifer.
Jennifer, meet Xuphus. Xuphus, meet
Jennifer. Jennifer is a normal American
cunt. She can't stand the idea someone
might not want to be like her. She hates
anybody who is different, or looks different,
or aspires to strange gods. She thinks
the Arabs should unilaterally accept UN
Resolution 242. She thinks South Africa
is America's best friend in Africa. She
believes in God, Somoza, Swaggart, and Margaret
Thatcher. Look at her, Xuphus, she's a closet
religious maniac who wants to be reborn so
badly she'd blow the world up gladly. Pleasure
is lost on her, simple fun means nothing to her.
Human life horrifies her unless it's a famine

on TV that reminds her how much America is
not doing . . .

SISTER's tirade continues. GIRL puts up with it for a time, then:

Drop dead, Jennifer.

SISTER drops dead. Pause.

MAN	Your mother, she is dropped dead as you commanded.
GIRL	She's not my mother, she's my sister. Wow!
MAN	She talks to you like she is your mother. You often do this command to drop dead?
GIRL	I was struck by lightning when I was a kid. Maybe I'm special.
MAN	Kids struck by lightning often have strange powers.
GIRL	She can't be dead. She was hardly alive.
MAN	A sensitive nature perhaps.
GIRL	She's too shallow and materialistic to be dead.

Pokes her SISTER with her foot. Pause.

She sure looks dead.

MAN	I can feel the body cooling.
GIRL	Now what do I do? Shit. Why did she have to follow me?
MAN	I suggest we dispose of the body in one of the lockers.
GIRL	Good idea.

She drags her SISTER along the floor.

Would you mind giving me a hand?

MAN	With pleasure.

*They stuff the body into one of the lockers, but are unable to secure
the door. So SISTER's feet protrude.*

Your mother is massive for such a slight frame.

GIRL	All the right-wing periodicals she used to read. Turns the brain to lead.
MAN	Such a happy people. Perhaps now you will teach me the secret of your happiness.
GIRL	You're crazy. Go away and leave me alone. I'm a murderer. Yikes. Now what am I going to do?

| MAN | Persist. Then go out in silence. Like the rest of living things who must croak. Even the dung beetle persist. |
| GIRL | I don't want to go out quietly. I want to make a loud noise. |

Pause.

	Are you really from outer space?
MAN	From the sand world of Plinth, which was blown up in an accidental blast at the central fusion station, as I said. Then, like all my kind, I am in a perpetual pilgrimage from one world to another. Amongst, as you say, the asteroid belt. I travel much, frequent-flyer advantage. Bad joke. From Elmer to Roswitha, from Roswitha to Pia, from Pia to Wolfiana, from Wolfiana to Erda, from Erda to Helio, from Helio to 1935X, from 1935X to McCuskey, from McCuskey to Wild, from Wild to Whipple, from Whipple to Zu Chong-Zhi, from Zu Chong-Zhi to Zulu, from Zulu to CrAO, from CrAO to Sy, from Sy to Toro, from Toro to Kacheuvskaya, and from Kacheuvskaya back to you know where . . .
GIRL	I have no idea.
MAN	Back to Elmer. And so on. Very tedious, but necessary to avoid what we call the madness of small worlds. Even so, it is hard.
GIRL	Are you for real?
MAN	We want to learn why people are so happy on Terra.
GIRL	YOU CALL THIS HAPPY!?
MAN	On our world, Elmer, remnant of Plinth, we are very doleful, dour, sad.
GIRL	I have an idea. Xuphus, take me with you.
MAN	Even our sex is sad, as I have explained.
GIRL	Boy, does she ever look dead.

Jennifer, oh Jennifer.

Do you have a cigarette?

MAN   I am not smoking.

Pause.

It is forbidden on Elmer. As on
Fanny, Voloshina, Wirt, Bistro,
Scobee, Durer, and Vondel. It is,
however, permitted on Niepce,
Redddish, Karin, Kron, Goto, Tuulikki,
2009P-L, and Sawyer Hogg. But
it is not, however, permitted on
Elmer, which is where my basic
behavioral grid was installed.
Sorry.

MAN *gets up.*

GIRL	Where are you going?
MAN	I am going back.
GIRL	Take me with you.
MAN	It would make you, like us, sad.
GIRL	It would make me very happy.
MAN	Space in the vehicle is confined and not many.
GIRL	I don't mind.
MAN	I have to think on this.

Pause.

GIRL	Well?
MAN	I think you have become, like me, sad.
GIRL	I have not. I only want to escape.
	I am a murderer.
MAN	(*Standing tall.*) Indeed. Further, you want to join the girl Huns, who are a great menace out there. You are your wicked sister. Your good sister is the one you have murdered.
GIRL	All I did was say "drop dead."
MAN	In all religions of this world, to think a bad thought, or say a bad thing, is to make accomplishment a fact. Bad thought, bad mouth, bad act. Thing thought, thing

said, thing done. As for instance: Bad
(happy) thought, "drop dead," good sister
are killed, crash, thump, bounce, bounce,
bounce, dead. What a happiness for you!

Pause.

Religion makes you feel good feeling
about the world. As though it were not
truly there.

GIRL   Where?

MAN   Here.

GIRL   What?

MAN   The world.

GIRL   Shit. I'm fucked.

MAN   Step on neighbor's face. Good feeling.

GIRL   I hate this fucking world, I hate it.
What's done is done.

MAN   Not necessarily.

GIRL   What's that supposed to mean?

MAN   You can undo certain events, as,
for instance, happy murder of
good sister. You can change good,
happy events till they become sad,
too. As on Elmer, or even more
loathsome worlds of Gorgo, Yrsa.
Thusnelda.

Pause. MAN *sits down.*

Like the lamentable bad sex of Elmer.

GIRL   All I want to do is get off this dump.

MAN   I can undo the murder, but it will make you
sad.

Pause.

GIRL   I don't believe a word you've said.
You're a fake.

MAN   I am a weird. After word comes weird.
It is an old proverb.

GIRL *begins packing up the silver.*

GIRL   You are one of them, a Fascist cur.
I'm getting out of here. I am going
where no one's ever been before. I

am going where people don't creep
low all the time and cheat their
neighbor of the last dime. I am getting
out of this cheesy, rancid banana republic.
The biggest banana, and the cheesiest, the
lowest, the creepiest, the most conniving.
The whole damn political climate makes me gag.
And you're a fake, a fucking bad joke.

MAN   As you wish.

      MAN *snaps his fingers. As before, the* SISTER *enters.*

SISTER   Michelle, Michelle.
MAN   Blackout!

Act Two

Scene one. The same.

SISTER   Michelle, Michelle. This is madness.
   Pause.

I have absolutely nothing to say to
you, Michelle. Do you know how
foolish you are, how retrograde?
Have you considered the sky, Michelle,
all the pretty things that float and bob
in the wind? Have you considered
nomenclature? Have you thought of all
the ages, heaped one upon the other
like Ossa upon Pelion? Have you
considered the torturous ascent of the
species, of mankind, through all the
eons, from a one-celled bacterium,
through all the viscous, sticky
stages, through the finny and four-footed
curtain raiser, amidst the Permian bogs
and mists and fogs, then the Triassic,
Jurassic, the Cretaceous.

   She roars.

Then wee, little, rat-faced humanoids

stealing reptilian eggs, gleeful little
entrepreneurs . . .

She nearly swoons.

Surely you have not considered all
this, Michelle. Therefore you are damned
in the face of God, and thrown out of the
family hearth, as though a leper, a pariah,
yes, an outcast, one despised and hated, from
whom no good is expected. Become a bag lady,
Michelle. Become a street person and share your
needles with the underclass, the wretched of the earth.

Pause.

Become one of those whose name is not
spoken. Become one of those whose bones
are crushed beneath the armored heel of
divine virtue. Become an insect, or a
horde of insects, as in your wild, obscene
fantasy of being a girl Hun, with which you
terrorized your Uncle Jack, now fresh in the
grave, whose only wish on his deathbed was that
you be restored to sanity. But no, no, you
have become unclean, one of the enemies
of the true way, the Judeo-Christian
tradition, Michelle, have you given
thought to the Judeo-Christian tradition?

Weeps.

You will creep low, Michelle,
among the foul and slimy things
that dwell in darkness.
Your dreams will be fog
and noxious gases from
the unholy pismire of eternity.
Divine wrath and retribution
will haunt you, Michelle,
and snap at your heels
and harry you all your
days till, exhausted and
feeble, you roll into a
cold, wet ditch and die.

Screaming.

	All this, Michelle, all this . . .
GIRL	Drop dead, Jennifer.

SISTER *drops dead again. Pause.*

	My God, I don't believe it. I did it again.
MAN	Much as before, she is dead. You have killed her twice.
GIRL	I just can't stand Jennifer when she gets in a snit.
MAN	Now you are more happy than before.
GIRL	Did you do that? It was you. It was your fault. You brought her back.
MAN	The surface of things are obscure.
GIRL	Give me a hand.

MAN *and* GIRL *haul the* SISTER *away and stuff her body in another locker. Now there are four feet protruding.*

	There. It's done.
MAN	You did not believe I could undo the twisted skein of fate.
GIRL	I feel awful. All I wanted was to run away from home, and here I've gone and murdered my sister, twice.
MAN	Many people would envy you. I am made happy watching your natural human excess.
GIRL	I feel rotten. Now I'm really doomed.
MAN	Do not worry. All religion is, as you say, baloney.
GIRL	How the hell do you know?
MAN	I know. I know much. I am a weird. We know these things. All is hocus-pocus. The truth is inenerrable. Religion is baloney.
GIRL	What is "inenerrable"?
MAN	It means "unable to be narrated."

Pause.

	The feet are intriguing as they stick out from the metal boxes.
GIRL	Now you've got to take me with you.
MAN	You would have to comb your hair

	our way. You would have to learn
	to walk our way. You would have
	to learn to dress our way. It would
	not suit you. It would make you sad.
GIRL	I feel a total repulsion for everything human.
	All I want is to get away. We're all yahoos.
MAN	You have not convinced me by your
	reasoning. There is a virus of humanity
	that resonates amidst the jangle of your
	voicing. It is what I like. But perhaps
	I should stay here and become like one
	of you, a killer, a bigot, a secular humanist,
	or some combination of these, with my special
	powers I could become a member of the thought
	police, a TV evangelist even.
GIRL	You're starting to talk like a Fascist again.
MAN	The universe is inherently Fascistic.

Pause.

GIRL	I don't believe that. The universe
	isn't inherently anything. That is
	a cynical, reductive position. And
	one typical of a person unwilling to
	examine the political implications
	of his own discourse. Alas, you are
	all too human, and a reactionary
	on top of it all. I am disappointed
	in you, Xuphus.
MAN	You would not be happy on Elmer.
GIRL	I doubt it, if everyone there thinks like you.
MAN	We do not "think." We reflect light along
	various vectors of force.
GIRL	That's a cop-out. I'm getting out of here.
	You're a fake.

MAN *snaps his fingers.* SISTER *enters once more.*

	Oh, for Pete's sake. You don't mean
	we have to go through this again.
SISTER	Michelle, Michelle. I can't believe it.
GIRL	Make her go away, Xuphus.** Make her go away
	or I'll do it again.
MAN	A language virus has infected her. As a

	consequence we are no longer
	on the same modality. Sorry.
SISTER	*(Starts to overlap* GIRL *at* **.)
	Michelle, I have absolutely nothing

consequence we are no longer
on the same modality. Sorry.

SISTER   *(Starts to overlap* GIRL *at* **.)
Michelle, I have absolutely nothing
to say to you, you little pinko rat
fart. You treacherous little whorelet!
How dare you try to escape? America
needs airheads like you, America
needs cheese, America needs corn.
America needs hog-belly futures. When
you try to escape you commit presence
in the name of absence, you waffle,
you devolve, you infect the gene pool
with alien mumbo jumbo, you tarnish
the national flatware, you appoint
yourself an unindicted co-conspirator,
you become a garbage truck chasing a
Good Humor truck, ** you become the perfidious
Chinese general Pang Chao, who chopped off
the heads of the Hsiung-Nu, the first Huns,
and that, Michelle, that ain't beanbag!

Pause.

What do you have to say for yourself?
Nothing. Absolutely nothing. The earth,
have you considered the shape and the
weight of its elephantine folds, twisting
and writhing beneath your wicked feet?
Have you paid the slightest attention
to the doings of the damned who labor
forever, without recompense, in the
ovens of hell? Have you considered the
doings of the Devil, your consort, for
I can see with my own eyes that this
strange man you refuse to introduce,
is the Adversary himself and no other—

MAN   I am Xuthus, the Obscure.
SISTER   *(Overlapping him.)* —and that you have sold your soul
              to him
to pay off your vast gambling debts,
and the cost of your recent abortion, and that
through his agency you plan to enter law

school, even though your GREs were truly
mediocre. Yes, Michelle, and you sold
your soul to him, that's how you came
to be nominated for homecoming queen,
even when you professed to have no such
interest in such things, when I would
have died for the honor . . .

    Pause.

GIRL   *(Starts to overlap* SISTER *at* **.)*
Jennifer, you had better stop
shouting at me because I am
not your ordinary little sister,
Jennifer, no I am more than you ever
bargained for and if you think
my patience is not limited then
you are quite mistaken, Jennifer,
a heavy price indeed so you'd better
watch out. I mean, like, CAN YOU
IMAGINE WHAT IT WOULD BE LIKE?
TO BE EATEN ALIVE BY FIERCE, WILD
ANIMALS, YES, TO BE SEIZED AND HELD
DOWN BY SHARP TALONS, FANGS, AND TUSKS,
THEN HOISTED ABOVE THE GROUND,
    FLAILING
AND SCREAMING ALL THE WHILE, HELD IN
THAT ANIMALISTIC GRASP, THEN CARRIED
ON THE RUN, OVERLAND, THROUGH BUSHES,
BRIARS, POISON IVY, DEEP INTO THE FOREST,
WHERE THE LAIR OF THE CREATURE IS, THEN
DROPPED DOWN, MAIMED AND BROKEN,
    BLEEDING
AND SUFFERING FROM INDESCRIBABLE
    WOUNDS,
HORROR, AND AGONY. THEN, PIECE BY PIECE,
TO BE TORN APART, DISEMBOWELED, AND
DEVOURED ON THE SPOT. WELL, THAT IS
YOUR FATE IF YOU PERSIST, for I am
of the Tribe of the Beast, of all the
underclasses, of all the disinherited
of the world, and I want nothing from
you but to watch the look on your face

when you come to realize that George Bush
is the author, yes, the sole author
of the Iran-contra mess, and that
under the administration of his unmentionable
predecessor all the many political denials
of this contemptible banana republic
reached critical mass, and we all, yes all,
but you in particular, became political
has-beens, Jennifer.* Yes, has-beens! Truly!
All relics of a great dream gone sour.
JENNIFER, YOU'VE LOST IT TOTALLY, AND
YOU'D BETTER SHUT UP.

SISTER *(Subdued; starting to overlap* GIRL *at *.)*
No, Michelle, I think you are a
totally worthless person and that
you will surely come to a bad end.
And that's that. I have no more to
say. I'm done. I have spoken.
It is finished. I'm going. The
die is cast. Done. Nothing, Michelle,
I have nothing to say.

MAN Truly wonderful.

GIRL Jennifer, you asked for it. And now you're
going to get it. Jennifer, * drop dead . . .

SISTER *(Overlapping* GIRL *at *.)*
No, you drop dead, Michelle.

The GIRL *looks stunned, then drops dead. The* MAN *and the* SISTER
*look at each other for a moment in silence, then drag the body and
deposit it in yet another locker. There are six feet now in view.
Pause.*

MAN She was a very worthy antagonist, but
in time we have defeated her.

SISTER Fucking barbarian, she got just what
she deserved.

MAN The girl Huns may have more agents on this
world, I fear. I hear their invisible
ponies at night, pawing and whinnying
in the distance, hidden.

SISTER Well, this one is finished.

MAN It is good she was low on ammunition.

| | We would be busy all night with your clones. |
| Sister | You must prepare the ship, while I file a report. Our orders require we be airborne by three. Hop to it, Xuthus. Yes, Excellency. |

Pause.

| Man | But, isn't it right for us to take a little moment to savor our victory? |
| Sister | Yes, perhaps you're right. |

She relaxes.

	This ridiculous Terran getup, these idiotic baggages. These frightful shoes.
Man	I have champagne hidden in the woods out there. Would you like?
Sister	Why not? It's about the only thing on this hideous cheese bucket worth the effort. Bring on the champagne!

Man *goes out the upstage door.*

| Man | (*Off.*) I have left it in a cool spot, beneath a cold stone in a burbling brook. |

Pause.

	Back on Elmer I will rest.
Sister	I'm up for a promotion. Then it's off to the beaches of Valeska. Valeska's one of the least expensive of the bright worlds.
Man	(*Off.*) I have not heard of this Valeska. For my holiday I visit family on Hamburga, the dark side. It possesses an excellent system of underground grottoes, hot waters with health-making minerals. But then I am low-class, a mere weird.
Sister	The Huns have not ventured that far into the Trailing Trojans, I surmise.
Man	(*Off.*) No, they regard it as low priority, owing to the clouds of soot. But we are used to soot. It is strange, I am having trouble locating this

	magnum of Dom Perignon. Perhaps over here . . .
SISTER	I am weary of small worlds, Xuthus, so I shall move to Vesta once my promotion comes through. This is my seventh girl Hun. I'm an ace.
MAN	(*Off.*) Lucky for you.

He reenters.

My name is still on the proscribed list,
hence I am not permitted beyond the
Tilting Line from Marlu to Winchester,
nor beyond Jole, Brunsia, Manto,
Monachia, Hippo, Geraldina, Alekto,
Chaika, ITA, Skip, 1969 QP, Onnie,
Bronslawa, Stroobontia, China, Seki,
Harris, Amber, and Linda Susan. Nor
am I ever invited to elegant parties.
It is because my skin color is offensive
to the High Lords of Vainu Bappu. If
I was not made stupid by centuries
of servility and were not a slave to my
wicked cravings I would turn traitor
and join the girl Huns against you.

He goes out into the night again.

SISTER	Such thoughts are treasonous, Xuthus, watch what you say.
MAN	(*Off.*) I am your trusted servant, madam, you would not betray me.

Pause.

Where did I put that bottle of champagne?
I am become cretinized.

SISTER *snaps her fingers and the* GIRL *wakes up and wiggles out of the locker. She looks stunned but then recognizes her* SISTER, *both* GIRL HUNS. *They smile.*

SISTER	Sometime you must tell me the whole chronicle of the madness of small worlds, Xuthus.
MAN	(*Off.*) The old stories are pointless, madam.

All you needs to know is that the surface
of things are obscure. Aha, I think I
have rediscovered the champagne, it is
closer to where I have buried the vehicle,
amongst the prickle thorn and poison ivy.

The SISTERS *don their Hun hats, which were in the other suitcase.*
The other feet belong to more GIRL HUNS, *who join their comrades.*

SISTER   I would in particular like to hear the whole
                tale of the seven worlds.

We hear a cork pop.

MAN   (*Off.*) Ah, that is a sad, sad tale. Even
                for the sad people of the Caldiera
                that story must not be told, ever.

GIRL HUNS *deploy with bows and arrows.*

SISTER   Still, I should like to hear it from
                your lips.

MAN *enters, dressed as a waiter, with champagne and glasses.*

MAN   Whoops.
SISTER   Yes, Xuthus. We are taking your spacecraft.
MAN   You think you have fooled me, but
                you have not fooled me. You may
                have defeated me, but you have not
                fooled me. I have seen this approaching
                all along, all the way from Agnes to Jubilatrix,
                all the way from Jubilatrix to Ara, all the way
                from Ara to Frostia, all the way from Frostia
                to Pittsburghia, all the way from Pittsburghia
                to Sara, all the way from Sara to Stereoskopia,
                and all the way from Stereoskopia to Dudu.
                It was clear to me, even then, even on Dudu,
                that I would encounter you, then,
                at the appropriate time, you . . .

Points to the GIRL.

                her sister in crime would appear, and then
                together, you would betray me and then
                destroy me . . .
Pause.
                . . . but not yet, please, as I am getting

around to my point, which is a difficult
point, one requiring a certain room for
purposes of expatiation, not to mention a
certain mood of serenity in the teller, not
to mention a certain intellectual curiosity
on the part of the hearer, you two, girl
Huns, unused to a learned discourse on the
higher subjects, by one such as me, a weird.
For I may be a mere weird, but we weirds
have our sense of honor, and this honor
forbids much.

Pause. They point at him.

God curse those who do what is
forbidden. And chief among the things
which are forbidden are the combing of hair
not our way, the eating of food not to our
taste, the enactment of dramatic scenes not
to our liking, and the rubbing out of our
very being, when we have merely been
engaged in the working out of our destiny,
as described in the Big Book of Tlooth,
who you may not reckon as amounting to
a pot of piss compared with your god
Tengri, but I assure you it is not so,
because Tlooth was before Tengri, and
Tengri learned how to comb her hair, and
learned how to swagger so . . .

He demonstrates.

not by mimicking the wild creatures
of the steppes, the wildernesses, and the
Outer Dark, bears and tigers and rhinodraconopeds
even, but by imitating our god Tlooth, who
is called Tlooth for good reason. For Tlooth
is truth made manifest and angelic and eternal.
And the truth is eternal, that is why it is
called the truth. Truth, Tlooth, the same.
The curse of Tlooth is to be feared because
Tlooth sees far and possesses a big stick.
Think of it before you crush me under your
heel like an insect . . .

Pause. They point at him.

> Think of the big stick of Tlooth, and how
> it will fall upon you like fate, for he
> will avenge me.

Pause.

> For even if he will not avenge me,
> it is in questionable taste to abuse one
> of us, the weirding ones, because we
> injure no one and are meek, and we
> possess beautiful shoes, and hurt no one
> except when we give in to our wicked cravings,
> which are wild and warped, it is true,
> but if the truth be told, as Tlooth would
> have it, they are also wonderful, and if we
> have on occasion given in to them, you surely
> did not complain, never on Mildred, Tea, not
> on Yangel, Shimazu, Oongaq, 1951 RJ, Bonsdorffia,
> Shane, or Shaposhnikov. Nor on the wastes of
> Gondola. Nor among the painted screens of Fulvia,
> where golden hummingbirds witnessed all we did,
> wicked as it was. Wicked as it was, you never
> said no, though you despised me for it,
> and refused to discuss it because you were
> above such things, or so you said, when you
> were sated and had had your fill. And when we
> tried it your way it was not so good, because
> it was far better our way, because we are not
> so proud as you, and not so stuck-up and bent
> on conquest for its own sake, and as for your
> wicked sister with the greenish hair, all I
> can say is she did not fool me for a moment
> also, and her physical aspect is almost sufficient
> to cause me to make an unpleasant remark.
> Nor did you fool me for a moment neither.

GIRL HUNS   *(A choral curse.)* DROP DEAD!

MAN *drops dead.* GIRL HUNS *all point fingers out, and announce:*

> Blackout!

Scene two. Aboard the spacecraft. The GIRL HUNS. *We see only their eyes. They sing their song and accompany themselves on plucked bowstrings.*

GIRL HUNS   Under the sign of the nine foxtails,
             Trap the weird and make him dead.
             Turn our backs
             and forge ahead . . .

Two GIRL HUNS *repeat the above lines over and over while the others continue.*

Plinth . . . Mitake Mura, Dikan'ka, Elmer, Hektor, Dr. Spock,

Roswitha, Pia, Wolfiana, Erda, Helio, 1935X, McCuskey,

Wild, Whipple, Zu Chong-Zhi, Zulu, CrAO, Sy, Toro,

Kacheuvskaya, Fanny, Voloshina, Wirt, Bistro, Scobee, Durer,

Vondel, Niepce, Reddish, Karin, Kron, Goto, Tuulikki,

2009P-L, Sawyer Hogg, Thusnelda, Gorgo, Yrsa, Valeska,

Hamburga, Vesta, Marlu, Winchester, Jole, Brunsia, Manto,

Monachia, Hippo, Geraldina, Alekto, Chaika, ITA, Skip, 1969

QP, Onnie, Bronslawa, Stroobontia, China, Seki, Harris,

Amber, Linda Susan, Vainu Bappu, Caldiera, Waltraut, Sphinx,

Erika, Argentina, Thula, 1940W-L, Hay, Kutuzov, Murakami,

Ahti, Ops, Gogo, Muazzez, Hathor, James, Cuffey, Teucer,

Vanderlinden, Goethe, Alex, Khufu, Bus, Hus,

Kosmodemyanskaya, Galahad, Smithers, Beer, Shao, Lick,

1931PH, Ethiopia, Thais, Galatea, Hedwerthia, Tyche, Isis,

Amphitrite, Melus, Vala, Hohensteina, Agnes, Jubilatrix, Ara,

Frostia, Pittsburghia, Sara, Stereoskopia, Dudu, Mildred,

Tea, Yangel, Shimazu, Oongaq, 1951 RJ, Bondorffia, Shane,
Shaposhnikov, Gondola, Fulvia, and mythic Gray-ways . . .

The blackest of blackouts.

Crowbar   (1989)

_____

CHARACTERS *(in order of appearance)*

    FIRST GIRL
    SECOND GIRL
    MAN
    MR. RIOSO
    CHORUS OF GHOSTS
    FIRST WOMAN
    YOUNG MAN
    SECOND MAN, J. HENRY FRUITNIGHT
    THIRD WOMAN
    GHOST OF DAVID BELASCO
    GHOST OF OSCAR HAMMERSTEIN

Crowbar was commissioned by En Garde Arts as a piece of site-specific theater written for the old Victory Theater on Forty-second Street in New York. It was premiered on February 17, 1990.

Note: The occasional appearance of an asterisk in the middle of a speech indicates that the next speech begins to overlap at that point. A double asterisk indicates that a later speech (not the one immediately following) begins to overlap at that point. The overlapping speeches are all clearly marked in the text.

The interior of the Victory Theater on Forty-second Street. Audience on stage, within the gloom of the empty house. We spy the FIRST GIRL *in a puddle of light, then the* SECOND GIRL *nearby. The* FIRST GIRL *is playing cat's cradle. They speak in whispers.*

FIRST GIRL   . . . and they buried the gold they stole from the drunken
                     knights of olden times; they buried the loot out
                     back under the outhouse or apple tree; and craftily
                     hid their crimes; they heaped up and hoarded and spoilt
                     everything they touched. They reared up banks and
                     factories and fenced in the common lands, as though
                     this were their right. They plotted and schemed and
                     connived all down through the ages. Aside from all the
                     ruin they visited upon the poor, the unemployed,
                     the hungry, and their mothers, sisters, and wives,
                     they brought nothing into the world but cunning,
                     the mindless, heartless hoarding of wealth and
                     property and the fruits of other people's labor;
                     and grotesque bad taste, the latest fashion in ladies'
                     hats, religious idiocy, the armaments industries,
                     the slaughter in the Philippines, Africa, all over.

Pause.
                     That's the long and short of it.

SECOND GIRL   Father Gallagher will have a thing or two to say
                     about your reasoning, I imagine.

FIRST GIRL   The devil scratch his hump on the hook of Father
                     Gallagher's nose.

SECOND GIRL   You ought to consider the state of your immortal soul,
                     sister Jennie.

FIRST GIRL   And there are some books you ought to read, Mary.
                     Dark, deep books full of the truth. Marx, Proudhon.

Pause.

	They closed the theaters, too, you know. In England.
	After the death of Elizabeth the Great.
SECOND GIRL	But who will help me? Father's a drunkard. Poor
	Willie cannot dress and feed himself. And mother . . .
FIRST GIRL	I promise to send money from Germany. The Socialists
	care about common folk like us. Only you must
	promise
	not to read the jingoist newspapers any more. And you
	mustn't say a word to Father Gallagher, I mean Rabbi
	Baruch . . .

Pause.

	Funny mistake.
SECOND GIRL	Funny mistake indeed!

A whistle from the darkened wings.

FIRST GIRL	Just a moment, Archie.
SECOND GIRL	Why did you call me Esther? You're Esther.

A puzzled pause.

I'm Cecile. As for Mary, she's dead.

A ghostly cry from the CHORUS. *Blackout. Music and slide show. A middle-aged* MAN *enters, well-dressed in turn-of-the-century clothes.*

MAN	Where is she? Where is she, in heaven's
	name? and what are you staring at,
	miscreants, the lot of you! I know
	she's in here, I saw her dart in
	just as intermission began. She
	has purposely evaded me and her
	mother, and avoided my authority.
	In heaven's name, a theater is no
	place for a young girl, as everyone
	who is anybody knows. Where is she,
	by God, tell me! One of you must
	have seen her enter these premises
	only a few moments ago. For I was
	behind the upper balcony and forced
	one of the windows, the oval portico
	which faces the street, for I knew she
	would make for this place, for I have
	read her secret diary also, and perused

its contents; therefore I am apprised of her
plans. Motivation is the key to unraveling
the secrets of human nature.

MR. RIOSO *has appeared behind him. The dead* CHORUS *also appears in the house-right aisle.*

MR. RIOSO Welcome to the theater. Perhaps you
wonder why things are arranged
so queerly. The people there, dead.
The place empty and deserted, the
faint tingle of an unknown alarm, a
strange scent of bad deeds long ago
accomplished, an evil and sarcastic
tinge to the air, the peculiar sensation
of a barely perceptible fluttering of
wings and paradoxes. All these uncanny
effects are of the nature of the place.
All of this is for you, Mr. Pretzel.
All of this, all.

He gestures widely. The CHORUS *begins a slow soft-shoe, chanting.*

CHORUS Time is empty air.
Pause.

 To be or nobody.
Pause.

 All theaters are haunted.

MR. RIOSO All theaters are haunted, everybody
knows that.

MAN How the devil did you know my name?
Maybe I have made a mistake. Perhaps
in my nervous state I have entered
the wrong theater.

MR. RIOSO No, Mr. Pretzel, you have not entered the
wrong theater. This is opening night
for *Sag Harbor,* a drama by James A.
Hearn, the inaugural production in
this, the Theater Republic, Mr. Oscar
Hammerstein's new house. Both Misters
Hammerstein and Hearn have just addressed
the audience, in eloquent and conversational
terms, the former regarding his hope

for his new theater, that it be dedicated
to pure and noble things; the latter, in
order to express his hope that his new
play draw well in New York. The day is the
twenty-seventh of September, nineteen
hundred. The weather is fair and mild,
the winds shifting gently from the northerly
to the southerly.

Pause. Pretzel regards the CHORUS *as it chants.*

MAN   Sir. I know perfectly well who I am,
               and where I am, and what I am about.
               What I do not know is who you are,
               though to be frank I care not a pin;
               or where my daughter is, whom I fear
               for, in this wild, outlandish place;
               and for her honor, which is mine
               also, and for the state of her nerves,
               which are delicate, as she is easily
               rattled, high-strung, and subject to fits.*
               As was her mother, my wife.
MR. RIOSO   I am Mr. Rioso, and your daughter, Cecile,
               is there, high in the second balcony.

CHORUS *stops.* MAN *looks up. The* GIRL *appears. Smiles.*

MAN   Cecile. It's your father. Will you come home?
GIRL   No, Father.
MAN   And why not, pray tell?
GIRL   Because I'm dead, Dad.
MAN   What in the name of heaven does she mean?

VEILED WOMAN *appears in lower box left. With a candle.*

WOMAN   Don't you recall, Horace, how bitterly
               you teased her? Telling her she was
               a changeling, the devil's child, telling
               her she was adopted, and that we
               would return her to Germany, from
               whence she came, from the foundlings'
               hospital at Darmstadt, forever a foreigner,
               with no American citizenship, except
               in her heart?
MAN   Who the devil are you?

WOMAN	Your wife, Matilda, Horace. Whom you chained to the floor, yes, chained for five long years to the floor, at West Eighteenth Street, where we lived. Till my mind went awry, and I became, for all purposes, a raving maniac. A soul lost to reason. Don't you recall who I am, Horace?
MAN	Dimly. The memory is not distinct.

The GIRL *pipes up. She's closer now, leaning over the balcony.*

GIRL	You claimed you chained Mom to the floor because of her passionate addiction to opium and other intoxicants. But you know very well that you chained Mother to the floor because she objected to your treatment of sister Mary's suitor, Philip Sutton, a perfectly sensible, normal, and intelligent lad, gainfully employed as a cutter and polisher of diamonds at Louis Strasburger and Sons, of Maiden Lane. For when Philip begged for Mary's hand you pointed a large, double-barreled shotgun at him, and swore venomously, so he dropped to the floor in a dead faint, and never recovered. Poor boy, he died some weeks later in the facility at Elmira, where madness is on the rise. Do you tell me you do not remember these events? Do you, Father?
MAN	What on earth are you talking about? I have never heard of any Philip Sutton, and everybody knows that Jennie died two months ago, a dreadful suicide by an overdose of medicine. Enough medicine to kill two grown men.

A YOUNG MAN *enters.*

YOUNG MAN	And who do you think the baby was

	who was cut to bits with an axe and
	disposed of in the East River earlier
	that day, you bloody poltroon?
MAN	Who the devil are you?
YOUNG MAN	I am Frank Moore, as well you know.
MAN	Who the hell is Frank Moore, that I
	should know him?
YOUNG MAN	I am your son.
MAN	I have no son.
YOUNG MAN	You have one now, you cad.
MAN	I have none, I swear on it.
YOUNG MAN	I am your son-in-law. For sweet Jennie and
	I were married. Secretly, at Saint Wendacious
	of Murphy Street in the city of Hoboken. I
	have the papers as proof.
MAN	Sir. I am flabbergasted.
CHORUS	Sir. He has the papers as proof.**
Pause.	
	Time is empty air.
Pause.	
	To be or nobody.
Pause.	
	All theaters are haunted.
The YOUNG MAN *disappears.*	
MR. RIOSO	All theaters are haunted, Mr. Pretzel,
	everybody knows that.
MAN	I swear I know nothing of these things.
WOMAN	You know very well, Horace, but
	you are a coward and a liar, for
	after you had driven me stark,
	raving mad I would go and wander
	far and wide, yes, go and wander
	far and wide among the outer boroughs
	even; so that I was known as the
	"white woman of Bay Ridge," because
	of the spectral appearance of my dress,
	particularly in the moonlight; so
	I was a ghost before I had even died.
	I was the "white woman of Bay Ridge,"
	which you must remember having read

	about in the newspapers, Horace.
MAN	That's the first thing anybody has said
	that makes sense. Yes, I recall
	reading about the "white woman
	of Bay Ridge" in the newspapers,
	but how was I to know that was
	you? And all the time I thought
	she was in the kitchen baking apple pies.

A strange MAN *enters.*

SECOND MAN	Why is it when the police find a man
	dead or unconscious on the street
	they always diagnose the case as one
	of intoxicants? Is it possible for them
	to conceive that some people do exist
	who do not indulge in intoxicants? It is
	about time that our "wise" police learn
	that other causes besides overindulgence
	in intoxicants can produce unconsciousness
	and the habit of lying dead in the street.
	Mr. Peck's case, as reported both
	in the *Herald* and the *Tribune,* is a case
	in point, and only the most recent example
	of this asinine perversity.
MAN	Who the devil are you, and why do you
	come stomping in here, making such a row?
SECOND MAN	I am J. Henry Fruitnight, and I have
	written a letter on this matter to the
	editors of the *Times.* Say, I have caught
	a distinct odor of clam pie, clam pie and
	gingerbread. And no wonder! What is all
	that clam pie and gingerbread doing, all
	heaped up like that on the stage? Never
	seen the like of it.

He exits, muttering.

Stupefying . . . prodigious . . . asinine . . .

The FIRST GIRL *enters dressed as a Western Union boy.*

BOY (GIRL)	Telegram for Mr. Charles Peck.

MAN *snatches it and reads it. Meanwhile, the* BOY *looks around in wonderment.*

Mr. Oscar Hammerstein's new Theater
Republic, which opened last night, is
beyond question one of the most
attractive, comfortable and well-
conceived buildings of its kind in
the United States.

Looking about her.

The decoration of the interior, in
which greens and reds are combined
with much gilding, is exceedingly
rich, while the chairs are wide
and easy to sit in. The acoustics
are good, and the ornamental dome
is very handsome . . . The ventilation
appliances were at fault last night,
but this doubtless will be rectified.
It is unfortunate that the entrance hall
from the street is low. A tall man
surmounted by a tall top hat has
nothing for it but to ignominiously
duck when he comes to the doorway.

Pause.

So what's in the telegram, Pops?

MAN Michael O'Connell was found dead yesterday
in his room at 322 West Fifteenth Street,
where he had lived two weeks. On his
bureau was found an empty medicine bottle,
and an open letter, on which was written:
"Oh, my poor head! Will it ever get
better? I have had that awful pain
for the past seven or eight weeks, and
have lost nearly seventeen pounds
since July. A fortuneteller told me
I would live to see thirty years. I have."

A sad moment.

BOY (GIRL) Willie Mcleer, you know, was arrested for
stealing a dressed pig from the Penn Yards
near the foot of Sixth Street.

Raspberry. Goes out.

MAN	*(Deeply moved.)* Michael O'Connell, you see, was my natural child by Martha O'Connell, who worked in the theater, with Mr. Belasco.
CHORUS	With Mr. Belasco?
MAN	With Mr. Belasco, and that is the root cause of my antagonism to the theater.
MR. RIOSO	Motivation is the key to unraveling the mystery of the human soul.
CHORUS	Time is empty air.

    Pause.

	To be or nobody.

    Pause.

	All theaters are haunted.
MR. RIOSO	All theaters are haunted, everybody knows that.
MAN	Nothing. NOTHING. Nothing will come of nothing.

He sits glumly.

	That telegraph boy who was just here, that was no boy, that was my daughter, Mary. Why does she mock me so?
WOMAN	There is an old Albanian proverb: Behind every hero is a traitor.
MR. RIOSO	If you pass the Independent Subway Station at Twenty-third Street and Eighth Avenue you will not fail to have noticed a strange door marked "Night Forces Structure."

A tall MAN with a tall top hat enters from the lobby, bends low to avoid the low ceiling, and seats himself in the shadows of the mezzanine. Simultaneously, another WOMAN appears in the balcony, muttering to herself.

CHORUS	*(Repeating at intervals.)* One single demon knows more than all of you.

The SECOND GIRL enters from left wing.

SECOND GIRL	If you ask me, it's the devil who's behind all this rumpus. The devil gets into young people's heads, and makes 'em

do what they want, like smoke cigars,
play blackjack, and join the theater.
Doesn't matter how smart you think
you are, the devil's smarter, and he's
behind a whole lot of modern devilishment.
Like that devil Carl Schurz, and his
talk of that devil Aguinaldo, and
all those Filipinos, devils ever last
one of 'em; and those devil goldminers
out in Leadville, Colorado, yeah,
the ones that shouted down Governor
Roosevelt the other day. Demoniacal.
Devils in the streets, devils in the banks
and courts of law, devils in the mills
and factories churning out the work
of the devil: anarchy, strikes, sedition.
People from the old country with strange
hats, and beards, garlic, and animal shoes.
You can always tell the devils because they
all wear animal shoes, furry, with cloven
hooves, like animals; like all those people
on the stage there, all those devils, just
a-sitting there, thinking smutty thoughts;
doing the work of the devil; using the Lord's
name in vain, and never doing a thing
without listening to what the devil says,
because if you look hard you can see little
furry devils leaning over all their shoulders,
whispering smutty thoughts into their ears, up
there, concocting dark delights and crazy
works of evil, all of 'em,* with their
furry little ears, and their animal feets.

The CHORUS *whispers behind the audience, into their ears. A*
ghoulish light appears in the grate below the stage.

MAN	Oh, be quiet, will you, Bertha, for Christ's sake. Matilda or Martha, whoever you are!
MR. RIOSO	This strange door, this strange door bearing the cryptic legend "Night Forces Structure," marks the entrance to the ghost world. From there, they scratch their way, through unknown tunnels and passages, here,

to the basement of this place, exhausted. Why? The
souls of the dead are hungry for stories of the
dead, and fires, disasters, catastrophes of every
kind.

Pause.

Motivation is the key to unraveling the mystery of the
human mystery.

WOMAN   *(Blows out candle.)* As I was saying, behind every
                 traitor
is a hero. There are plenty, believe me,
even in places like theaters, where
forgetfulness is a law, and gratitude
an implication of folly. The only thing,
after all, that separates us from
Periclean Athens, Elizabethan England,
Dantean Florence, is so much empty
air; air that we take into our lungs
when we talk about freedom, as though
we meant it, and were not talking about
money; because most people, face it,
are stupid, and couldn't tell a play
from a pineapple. Also, there is the case
of those few hapless idealists who believe
in fucking, hopeless, idealistic fucking;
but they are even more unfortunate because
the flesh doesn't wear well once we are dead.
People who think too much about fucking
after they are dead have problems; people
with problems don't interest me anymore.
I would like to know a few simple things,
things that had a bearing on my life, my
life before I came to America from Poland,
a country that does not exist most of the
time, and that, when it does, is regarded
as something of a joke, even by the sophisticated.

Pause.

I'm just a disillusioned ghost who wants
to understand what the meaning of all
this is. Because I don't know, and after
ninety years of being a theater spook one
gets to be tired of perplexities, and changes

of management; and the theater syndicate,
and Mr. Belasco (who time has not treated
well), and Minsky's Burlesque, and Harry
Houdini lowering elephants into artificial
lakes under the stage (there's still an
artificial lake under the stage, I'm not
kidding, there is!), and *The Girl of the
Golden West,* and *Abie's Irish Rose,* and
forty years of porno flicks and chop-and-
slice karate films. Mr. What's-his-name,
to whom I was . . . with whom, shall we say,
I incurred matrimony, has two daughters,
you see: one is always threatening to kill
herself if we return to Germany; while
the other continually threatens to run away,
back to there, with her brother, so she can
implement her Socialist dreams (she is under
the interesting delusion that Germany offers
a more fertile soil for social progress than
the United States, and this in nineteen hundred!); and
whatever for I can't imagine, since we are
Polish, and not German, and just between us
I wouldn't go back if you paid me, and I'm
thoroughly dead and know what I'm talking
about. Although, the part of Poland we are
from is called Germany now, so she has a point.

Pause. Quietly.

Also, there is the question of time; also,
there is the question of what time is, and
how it manages to do what it does, and how
it erases all things, especially those
that are important and mean so much to us
we could never articulate them if we tried;
also, how it leaves us only with reminders of
what we would rather forget, at best; or what
we did that we are ashamed of, and managed
to hide, just barely, even if for only a
little while, while those we hated and
despised, and who hated and despised us,
were laughing behind our backs; even when

	we were children and first got involved in theater: the abandoned Punch-and-Judy show in the attic, remember? Also, why everything that time touches is so ephemeral, and involved with death; also, why talking about it, like this, or like someone who knows what they're talking about, makes us look so stupid. Like now, with me, a dead person, talking. Can you imagine?
MAN	Whatever are you driving at?
WOMAN	Haven't you guessed by now?
MAN	I believe you have connived with my children against me.
MAN IN TOP HAT	(*Standing.*) You fool! Your name is not Horace Pretzel. Your name is Charles A. Peck, and you were sandbagged to death last night at the corner of Seventeenth Street and Ninth Avenue, having been seen, in the company of certain rowdy women, at certain saloons, saloons frequented by lowlife types and the habitually bibulous. I am Archie Kinsolving, alias Philip Sutton, your murderer.

He strides out, as FIRST GIRL *and* SECOND GIRL *enter and approach.*

MAN	Then what, in heaven's name, am I doing in a theater?
GIRLS	Because you hate and despise theaters.
	Pause.
MAN	(*Wonderingly.*) Why, then. I suppose I must really be dead.

He lies down. They cover him. Pause.

MR. RIOSO	Ladies and gentlemen, as the intermission has turned out to be a little longer than we had expected, we shall help the time to pass with a choral recitation of yesterday's fires.

CHORUS *recites a litany of yesterday's fires. Musical interlude: a fake funeral.*

CHORUS	1:15 A.M.: 432 Eighth Avenue; John Lewis; damage $5. 1:45 A.M.: 99 Sheriff Street; August Jopowitz; damage, $150.

3:55 A.M.: 28 Fifth Avenue; Amos R. Eno; damage
$10,000.
8:30 A.M.: 44 Franklin Street; George Leyers;
damage slight.
10:05 A.M.: 301 West Thirty-sixth Street; Wright and
Ryan; damage $30.
12:50 P.M.: 202 Stanton Street; Minnie Elderman;
damage, $50.
6:10 P.M.: 126 Second Street; Louis Lustgarten;
damage $5.
7:30 P.M.: 205 West Eighty-fourth Street; William
Lyons; damage $50.

The funeral ends. Long pause. Both GIRLS *wander about in the dark theater.*

FIRST GIRL	The baby they found all chopped up was my sister's, not mine. I work in a shirt factory. Is that the real color of your hair?
SECOND GIRL	No, it's pretty mousy. The actual color, I mean.
FIRST GIRL	(*Pointing to the* WOMAN.) That lady? The one standing in the box,

she's the mistress of David Belasco,
and she lives in a secret apartment
located somewhere above the dome up there.

Points with a flashlight.

SECOND GIRL	Do you believe in God?
FIRST GIRL	No, not much. My family's Irish Catholic, so I got force-fed religion. Kind've ruined it for me. But I like the spectacle. The sense of theater.

Pause.

But I only go to church on Christmas Eve.

SECOND GIRL	My real sister became a nun to meet men. I mean, I do have a real sister in real life. Or I did when I was alive. Always said to myself I'd like to live in a theater when I grew up. Lo and behold, it all came to pass: when I grew up and died I ended up here, and now I live in a theater.
FIRST GIRL	So it did.

                You sure that's not a wig, I mean, it's
very convincing for fake hair, but it
looks a little too real. The highlights
and stuff.

SECOND GIRL   I'm not the wig type.

FIRST GIRL   I wasn't saying you were the wig type.

Their identities begin to wander.

SECOND GIRL   I was just saying it looked fake, you
know? It's hardly the same thing. You
don't have to get in a snit about it.

FIRST GIRL   What about the baby you murdered?

SECOND GIRL   No, it only looked like a dead baby.
Actually it was a dressed pig I stole
from Willie Mcleer, who stole it himself,
from a meat locker somewhere down on Horatio
Street. Cutest little dressed pig, with a
little derby, and little spats, and a little
bowtie. Adorable.

Pause.

FIRST GIRL   I don't believe anything I read in the newspapers.
I am a confirmed skeptic.

SECOND GIRL   I've been studying aboriginal cultures, from the
outback, western Australia. I read an article
that said their shamans sing one song all their lives,
and when they die they become the song they've sung
all their lives, and fly off, all around the hard,
flinty places of the desert, as pure song, and people
hear them and think they're echoes.

Pause.

                Then they go mad, the people who hear them, I mean.

FIRST GIRL   Yet, there is abundant evidence from their songs
and cherished traditions that Australian
aborigines are by no means destitute of some qualities
in which civilized men glory, such as the power
of inventing tragic and sarcastic fictions, the
thirst for religious mystery, contempt for pain,
and reverence for departed friends and ancestors.

Pause.

SECOND GIRL   I'd rather be what we are than an echo.

FIRST GIRL	Then, what are we?
SECOND GIRL	Beats me.
FIRST GIRL	Doesn't it feel cold in here?
SECOND GIRL	Yeah, so what? It's winter.
FIRST GIRL	I forget, is winter when it's cold, or is that summer?
SECOND GIRL	Winter is when it gets cold.
FIRST GIRL	Are you sure?
SECOND GIRL	You can take it from me.
FIRST GIRL	Who do you suppose that old rhinoceros is?
SECOND GIRL	Some bigwig. Look at those shoes.
FIRST GIRL	Did you have any hobbies, when you were growing up? As a kid, I mean.
SECOND GIRL	I grew up in a Socialist family. We weren't supposed to have hobbies.
FIRST GIRL	What's a Socialist again?
SECOND GIRL	Share the wealth. Common ownership of the means of production. Equality.
FIRST GIRL	Is Governor Roosevelt a Socialist?
SECOND GIRL	I don't think so. He's an American.

Pause.

FIRST GIRL	What's wealth again?
SECOND GIRL	Wealth is *stuff.*
FIRST GIRL	Oh, that's right. Stuff.
SECOND GIRL	All the stuff that is, that's wealth. All the stuff that's heavier than mere mortality. All the stuff that sinks to the bottom.
FIRST GIRL	Right, right. Now I remember. Weight. Solid weight. Massive. Ponderous. Heavy.

Pause.

	All the stuff, or just some of it?
SECOND GIRL	Most of it, except for the cheesy stuff. The stuff that's not worth anything, the stuff nobody wants, the stuff nobody has any use for. Like old theaters and stuff.
FIRST GIRL	Now I got it.
SECOND GIRL	It's awful creepy in here.
FIRST GIRL	You're talking that way again. Stop it.
SECOND GIRL	Okay.

Pause.

	What exactly is a theater again?
FIRST GIRL	Kinda big place. Red walls.
	Like the inside of the human heart.
	Only bigger, and not as empty.
SECOND GIRL	Okay. But not as empty. I got it.

Pause.

	Don't be angry, but who are you exactly?
FIRST GIRL	Suicide. Wanted to be in the theater. Folks said
	no. Said I'd meet the wrong kind of people. Became
	a bad girl. A pro. Didn't last long at that. Took
	some medicine. Enough medicine to kill five grown
	men,
	they said. Bother the taste of it! Found my body on a
	hook in the East River.
SECOND GIRL	Sad. I got in the family way. Boyfriend's a yegg.
	Was, that is. That's a safe-cracker. After I was
	dead he slit his throat, but didn't die. Later they
	hanged him, twice. For the murder of Charles A. Peck.
	The first time he didn't die. Archie Kinsolving was
	his name. Loved the theater. Worked here backstage,
	his day job, that is.
FIRST GIRL	What's your name?
SECOND GIRL	Forget. Something like . . . Flora . . . Floris.
FIRST GIRL	Rita's mine. Rita Mingus.

Pause. The CHORUS *has assembled and begins a slow, slow soft-shoe.*

CHORUS	Welcome to the theater . . .

The GIRLS *dart out the door in terror. So does the corpse of Mr. Peck.*

	Perhaps you wonder why things
	are arranged as they are. The
	people, dead. Everything, cold
	and dead. The theater, a wreck.
	All of this is for you,* because
	of you, against you, all of this
	is time's work. Time is empty air.
Pause.	
	To be or nobody.
Pause.	

All theaters are haunted, everybody
knows that.

They sit.

MR. RIOSO   But the truth is, the dead will find no
peace here because this theater, their
abode, their tenement and abode, is to be
reopened, as of this night, and their souls
are to be evicted, driven out into the blackened
wind of America, an America they will not recognize,
an America that has changed beyond description.

THIRD WOMAN   I don't know about that, but I do
know this is the longest intermission
I have ever heard of. I returned from
the powder room and, as you see, have
taken my seat. I would not miss the
opening night of Mr. Hearn's new play for
all the world. I am a great admirer of
Mr. Hearn, and of Mr. Hammerstein also.
Also I intend to go backstage and ask
Mr. Lionel Barrymore for his autograph,
as he is a fine young actor. But I do not
understand how it can take so long for them
to prepare for the second act. The first
act was perfectly acceptable, but I have
many questions about the piece, and what
it means and how it is supposed to be . . .
understood. I would like to know which
of the two young men the charming young
girl is truly in love with; although
I do hope it is the older, since they
are to be married; also, I hope there
can be a general reconciliation among
them; also, I am intrigued by the
idea of a courtship between an elderly,
meddlesome, prodigiously warm-hearted
and slow-speaking scallop fisherman and
the spinster who fears to get married
because she has read the book of Genesis
and found all the "begats" alarming;
also, I would like a little reduction

of the garrulity, and an avoidance of
music-hall humor, much as the speech
about the man who went swimming and
returned in a barrel, as sophisticated
theater-goers, I'm sure we would all . . .
we would appreciate this; also some
moderation of the too intimate talk
about married life, as this too might
be an affront to the sensitive . . . also . . .

Pause.	
Mr. Rioso	Are there any other hopes you have for the second act?
Third Woman	Well, no. . . . Although, now that you ask, I would also hope that there be no mention of the First and Second World Wars, the Great Depression of the thirties, the annihilation of the European Jews, also, the atomic bombing of Japan, the various Third World client wars of the forties, fifties, sixties, seventies, eighties, and so forth, as all of these unpleasant events might not be germane, strictly speaking, to the hopes and fears of the simple fisher-folk of Sag Harbor, and their humble lives; also, that temptation would clearly be there, or here, so to speak, since it has been nearly ninety years since the conclusion of the first act . . . and therefore we are rapidly nearing the millennium that the Pentecostals have been desiring, also those who prefer the nullity of the future over the insanity of the past; also those who cannot help but prate over the end of this, that or the other, the end of ideology, of history, of nature (when we know perfectly well these things aren't going anywhere!); and also, the prayers of those with a liking for round numbers. But *two thousand* does have a bit of a hollow ring to it, doesn't it?

MR. RIOSO	(*Patience wearing thin.*)
	Anything else, you'd like, from the second act?
THIRD WOMAN	Yes, I should also like them to bring on a
	real clam pie and real gingerbread, when they
	do. Because it is quite obvious these things
	are called for, given the kinds of common fisher-
	folk represented, and the kind of pictorial realism
	of the play—a tendency encouraged also by Mr.
	Belasco, I am told. Therefore these things ought
	to be real, and not false, when they appear,
	this clam pie and gingerbread,* I mean. We in the
	audience ought to be able to test the veracity of
	this gingerbread and clam pie, by our noses.
MR. RIOSO *and*	(*In a clam pie apotheosis.*)
the CHORUS	Yes, Mrs. Clara C. Lester, the clam pie shall be
	brought in smoking hot from the kitchen. The pie
	shall have been baked in a huge dish, and Cap'n
	Dan'l shall dish it out to everybody, who shall
	thereupon eat. They shall all eat excepting
	Freeman Whitemarsh, who has not been crossed in
	love, and therefore shall not eat. The pie shall
	be the real thing, and so shall be the gingerbread
	that follows. You shall be able to smell the cooked
	clams, and if you are hungry, and like to smell cooking
	in the theater, you shall be delighted.

A blissful moment, interrupted by the reentrance of the MAN.

MAN	Pardon me, there is another matter
	that concerns me, because I was
	enjoying the intermission when it
	occurred to me that I am not Charles
	A. Peck but Frank Worth, who was
	arrested for speeding in Central
	Park by one Aloysius Bugler, a sergeant
	of the New York City Police. As I was
	apprehended by Sergeant Bugler, I lost
	my temper and exclaimed: "I am Frank
	Worth, of East Twenty-first Street,
	I am worth over one million dollars,
	and I will not stand for this outrage."
	Sergeant Bugler persisted in his deluded

sense of duty, and before I was able to
remonstrate further I burst a vessel,
here, in my head and succumbed on the
spot. Informed of my demise, my terrier,
Spot, lost her wits and attacked, in a
cage, a golden eagle belonging to our
neighbor, the naturalist Jankow, from
Lubeck. Jankow's pug, Kaiser, finished
the work Spot had begun, and Jankow lost
his specimen. Had I been alive I would
have offered to pay for the loss, and my
apologies. I died a bachelor and, being
a confirmed atheist, left my entire fortune
to Saint Wendilly-by-the-Water, with the
proviso that my gift be used exclusively
to refute the pernicious superstition
concerning the immortality of the human
soul. It did not occur to me that my wishes
in this regard might not be observed.

FIRST GIRL *and* SECOND GIRL *appear in the upper box.*

FIRST GIRL	Did it occur to you, Frank Worth,
	that I, Emma Cottrell, took poison
	and died from it, and no one
	knew more about the matter
	than that I had died, and my name
	and nothing more, and no one cared?
SECOND GIRL	Did it matter to you that my
	eye was cut in two by a piece
	of glass in a loud and terrifying
	factory, and that I died of an overdose
	of carbolic acid some time later, me,
	Esther* Loesche, a girl of no importance?
FIRST GIRL	Did it matter to you, Frank Worth,
	that after the failure of my elopement
	I died of an overdose of medicine,*
	enough medicine to kill a dozen, fully
	grown men, they say?
SECOND GIRL	Did it matter to you that after
	the meteor explosion in Rahway
	I began to speak in tongues, and

my mother, father, aunt, and uncle
began insanity proceedings against
me, me Rebecca Stary, who was sent
to the facility at Elmira, where
madness is on the rise, and I died
of an overdose of a lethal substance,
a substance I found in a bottle with
no label; or that my brother, Will,
aged twelve, was sent to prison for
the death by gunshot of Fred Wood,
who drowned in a barrel of rainwater,
or Carl Fraydee, aged fifty, whom he
mistook for a woodchuck and shot dead?

FIRST GIRL *and* Or the death of William Rice the day
SECOND GIRL after he had given Albert T. Patrick,
his lawyer, checks amounting to three hundred
and fifty thousand dollars; or

FIRST GIRL, the death of Fanny Russell, wife of
SECOND Ray Russell of the banking firm of
GIRL, *and* Brown Brothers and Company, in a squalid
CHORUS room in a cheap lodging house, after
seven years abject slavery to opium;
or the death of Henry J. Barbour,
found dead in a Brooklyn hotel, whence
Helen Southgate, not his wife, also
suffering from a bullet wound, has fled;
or the death of a young baby chopped to
bits with an axe.

With full voice.

OR: THE DEATH OF DAVID ALLISON, CASHIER
OF THE TRADERS INSURANCE COMPANY OF
BROAD STREET, HARASSED TILL HE COM-
    MITTED
SUICIDE, SO HIS WIDOW ALLEGES, BY A
SCOUNDREL WHOSE NAME SHE PROMISES TO
GIVE THE GRAND JURY NEXT MONDAY . . .

Pause.

MR. RIOSO Namely, Mr. Frank Worth, who I believe
is among us.

FIRST GIRL I may not know who I am, and I may be dead, but

	I will always be a Socialist, a proud, defunct
	bluestocking, and** one day there will come the
	republic worthy of our dreams . . . worthy
	of our labors and sacrifices . . .
SECOND GIRL	You see what comes of your blasphemy, Mary?
	We're trapped in the devil's coal chute,
	and I am afraid all those people are ghosts.
	What in heaven's name will become of us now?
MAN	What poppycock! I won't stand for this.

The ghost of DAVID BELASCO *enters. He and the* MAN *tip hats as the latter exits muttering out to Forty-Second Street.*

	Outrageous . . . idiotic . . . rubbish . . . a scandal . . .
CHORUS	One single demon knows more than all of you.

The first MAN *enters again, maddened. Pause*

MAN	Out there, that's not America. That's not
	America! Where are we, by God, and
	what have we become? Are we all mad?
	That's not the America I know. THAT'S
	NOT AMERICA!
MR. RIOSO	(*Quietly.*) Oh, yes it is, Mr. Worth, America
	is an empty theater and the streets
	outside, and that theater is haunted.
	The national anthem may be heard.

We hear it, from the CHORUS, *scattered singly, all over the theater.*

	moaning and rustling about in the
	rusty drainpipes, under broken seats,
	and under creaking staircases . . . hither
	and thither . . . It shall tell us what we are
	to do, to avoid being too much ourselves.

The MAN *produces a crowbar from under his coat and throws it down at* MR. RIOSO's *feet. Pause.* MR. RIOSO *hastily exits.*

WOMAN	The younger dead like to ensnare and
	deceive the older ones, who are ignorant
	of more recent things and therefore are
	also more gullible. Why? Who knows?
	Who cares?

Pause. The MAN *puts on his hat and salutes the* WOMAN.

MAN	Fickle, thy name is woman.

The Man *exits. The* WOMAN *laughs and exits.*

CHORUS MASTER	But in reality our Mr. Rioso was one George Washington of West Twenty-eighth Street, number unknown. Washington was employed in the renovation of the Theater Republic, shortly to be reopened as the Belasco Theater; he was accidentally killed by a crowbar that fell from the roof garden in the process of construction above: the roof garden was designed as a Dutch farm. A windmill was built on top of the theater's stage house. Beside it was a miller's cottage, with a stork's nest on one chimney and an attached stable with two cows. Beside the stage house on the auditorium roof was a duck pond, over which was built a rustic bridge. The wall fronting the street was built up above the roof line and decorated to look like a ruined castle. Beside that was an imitation grist mill with a working water mill. Washington was laying tile on the floor far below while workmen were installing a wooden beam above, near the ruined castle. One of these men was using a crowbar. His foot slipped, and to save himself from falling he dropped the crowbar and caught hold of a fake weathervane. The crowbar fell to the floor. It struck Washington on the head, fracturing the skull. The body was removed to the morgue. The workman who dropped the crowbar was William Gorman of number seventy East Twelfth Street.

BELASCO *appears high in the balcony.*

BELASCO	Wrong, wrong, wrong, wrong, all of it

totally wrong! It was the oppressive grip
of the theater syndicate that forced my hand.
By their monopolistic machinations they had
threatened to shut me out of New York theater
altogether. This caused me grave
uneasiness. On the evening of January 7,
1902, I was in my little room in Carnegie
Hall, seeking to devise some means of
obtaining control of a New York theater.
There was a knock at the door . . .

A portentous pause. A MAN *enters.*

My visitor proved to be none other than
the theatrical manager Oscar Hammerstein.

HAMMERSTEIN   Mr. Belasco, the theatrical syndicate is
trying to crush me out of business.
Valuable attractions must have been
prevented from patronizing my houses
this season. I must have attractions.
You must have a New York theater
or find yourself helpless. I have one
in Forty-second Street, the Republic,
which I am willing to turn over to you.
I have come here on an impulse, on the
chance that you may be willing to take over
control of the Theater Republic.

BELASCO   Mr. Hammerstein, I shall be very glad
to take over control of your theater.

CHORUS   Five-year lease with an option for renewal.
Thirty thousand dollars a year and ten
percent of all gross receipts.

BELASCO *and*   Agreed.
  HAMMERSTEIN

They shake hands. Hammerstein exits.

BELASCO   I shall have to alter it. The stage is wrong.
The house is wrong, the colors set my teeth
on edge.

Pause.

Tore out the whole interior, leaving
nothing but the roof, and four walls.

A worried MAN *enters.*

CHORUS   A stranger presented himself to
          Belasco, demanding that he be
          permitted to inspect the property,
          and explaining that he held the
          mortgage on it.

BELASCO   I have nothing to do with the mortgage,
          that is Mr. Hammerstein's business.

MAN   God above me! I've got a mortgage
          on four walls and a hole in the ground!

He exits, tearing his hair.

BELASCO   The theater is, first of all, a place for acting,
          a place for the acting of plays; though to a
          majority of managers of our time, it seems,
          primarily to be a place for almost anything
          rather than *acting*—first of all, a place
          for the exploitation of their conceit and
          the making of money by any means.

Pause.

          Cost me a hundred fifty thousand to
          rebuild the place. Finest theatrical
          appointments. The stage floor was,
          in fact, an elevator, a movable
          platform fifteen by thirty, by means
          of which scenery and properties
          could be transferred rapidly to and
          from the cellar. The ropes for "flying"
          were counter-weighted, and working
          with a crank one man could raise
          pieces, which, in former times
          would have required six. Border
          and footlights were compartmentalized
          to prevent "spill," and all lamps
          in the theater were connected, "on
          resistance," so that all the lights
          in the house could be raised or lowered
          as required, gently, by degrees.
              The drop curtains were of
          Rose du Barry velvet. On the back
          of every chair, upholstered in silver-

green tapestry, was embroidered a
Napoleonic bee, which promptly
became "bee for Belasco" and served
as coat of arms on programs, and
the like. Torches, garlands, wreaths,
and festoonery framed the rich
tapestries on the side and rear walls
of the auditorium.

I have many plans for this
theater, ladies and gentlemen. In all
ways I desire to make this new
dramatic home of ours a dwelling
of refinement, good taste, good
entertainment, and good art. No
stone shall be left unturned, no
effort unmade to accomplish
that end. You cannot know what
it means to me to speak to you,
after thirty years of labor
in the dramatic calling, from the
stage of my own theater. Ladies
and gentlemen, I thank you, I
thank you . . . I can say no more.

Pause.

Oh, the impertinence of imperishable
dust, oh, the infamy of consuming
time!

He sits on the lip of the stage.

When I was a kid, I loved to get away
by myself. My dream was to have
a studio. I remember how I spent
my first three bits: I bought a packing
box and a piece of red cloth for lining,
and I put this in the cellar, where it
wouldn't get too wet, and I climbed
inside of it and dreamed for a long time
of the wonderful colors I should one day
be able to buy and hang about my walls.
From that I kept increasing and adding,

selling and buying more and more,
rarer and rarer things, until now . . .

He gestures.

CHORUS　　　One demon knows more than any of you.

Repeats, etc. Pause.

Motivation is the key to unraveling the secret
of human destiny.

Pause.

All theaters are haunted.

Pause.

To be or nobody.

Pause.

Time is empty air.

A long pause. Two beautiful WOMEN *dressed in white gowns pass
slowly through.*

BELASCO　　　America has too many lunch counters.

WOMAN IN　　(*Pausing.*) Too many lunch counters?
　WHITE

BELASCO　　　Exactly. A man who might otherwise
be a thinking man rushes into lunch,
grabs a sandwich, a glass of milk,
a piece of pie, and presto—he has killed
a *Hamlet.*

OTHER WOMAN　Must I, then, go back to Germany?
　IN WHITE
　　　　　　Pause.

BELASCO　　　(*Regarding the* WOMEN.)
They can speak little English. They take
care of my studio for me, and on a
Sunday you will always see them,
kneeling before the image of Christ, flanked
on either side by the beautiful thieves.

WOMEN *exit, and* BELASCO *follows.*

And again we shall climb from the
caterpillar into the butterfly, and from
that into something higher, and up
and on, until the fall set in.

Blackout. End of play.

7 Blowjobs   (1991)

CHARACTERS *(in order of appearance)*

> DOT, a receptionist in the office of the Senator on the Hill
> DELIVERY PERSON from Express Mail
> EILEEN, the Senator's administrative assistant
> BRUCE, the Senator's legislative assistant
> BOB, the Senator
> BOB JUNIOR, his son
> BOBBOB JUNIOR, an idea of Surveillance

The action takes place in the Old Senate Office Building during the late afternoon and evening.

I would like to thank the following for their generous support: the New York Foundation for the Arts, the John Simon Guggenheim Foundation, and the National Endowment for the Arts. I would also like to thank the Bellagio Study and Conference Center of the Rockefeller Foundation, and the staff at the Villa Serbelloni, where this play was written.

7 Blowjobs was premiered October 13, 1991, at Sledgehammer Theatre in San Diego, California. This play is dedicated—like *Sincerity Forever* before it—to those supreme clowns of our sad time, Jesse Helms and Donald Wildmon; and also to Representative Dana Rohrabacher and the Reverend Pat Robertson, because they have shown such an abiding interest in my work. These gents (God help them!) comprise the Four Harebrained Horsemen of our Contemporary Cornball Apocalypse.

Note: The occasional appearance of an asterisk in the middle of a speech indicates that the next speech begins to overlap at that point. A double asterisk indicates that a later speech (not the one immediately following) begins to overlap at that point. The overlapping speeches are all clearly marked in the text.

Act One

Scene one. The SENATOR'*s office on Capitol Hill.* DOT, *a not-so-busy receptionist, is seated primly behind. She smiles. She stops smiling. A furry blackout.*

Scene two. The SENATOR'*s office on Capitol Hill.* DOT, *the busy receptionist, is answering a busy phone.*

DOT   Hello. Senator X's office. Hello,
                        nothing of value inside, please.
                        Please don't steal our stuff . . .

Pause.

                        Yes. No. Maybe.

She hangs up. Pause. Phone rings.

                        Hello. Senator X's office. Hello,
                        nothing of value inside, please.
                        Please don't steal our stuff . . .

Pause.

                        Yes. No. Maybe.

She hangs up. Pause. Phone rings.

                        Hello. Senator X's office. Hello,
                        nothing of value inside, please.
                        Please don't steal our stuff . . .

Pause.

                        Yes. No. Maybe.

She hangs up. Pause. Phone rings. There is a knock at the door.

                        Phone. Door. At the same time, wow.

She tries to decide which to answer. She goes to the door. DELIVERY PERSON *enters. Phone rings. She smiles.*

                        Hello. Senator X's office.

The phone rings. She answers it.

	Hello, please.
DELIVERY PERSON	Package for the Senator.
DOT	(*To phone.*) Hello, please.
DELIVERY PERSON	Sign here.

She signs.

| DOT | (*To phone.*) Yes, hello, please. |
| DELIVERY PERSON | Thanks, lady. |

He puts down the package.

| DOT | (*To phone*). Yes, hello, please. |

He exits. Pause. She hangs up the phone. She looks over the package.

Maybe, maybe not . . .

She shakes the package. She listens to the package. Pause.

Maybe I should. No.

Phone rings.

Hello. Senator X's office. Hello,
nothing of value inside, please.
Please don't steal our stuff . . .

Pause.

Yes. No. Maybe.

Pause.

I said: Yes, No, Maybe . . .

Pause.

Yes, no, maybe, he is obsquatulated.

Pause.

YES. NO. MAYBE.

Hangs up. Pause.

Maybe I should. No . . .

Pause.

Yes.

She opens it. The package contains photos. She looks at them.

Eek!

She faints. Hits the deck. Blackout.

Scene three. The same, only a little later. Dot *is back at the phone.*
Bruce, *the Senator's legislative assistant, and* Eileen, *his adminis-*
trative assistant, are examining the contents of the package.

Eileen	What do you make of it, Bruce?
Bruce	The real thing.
Eileen	Serious . . . stuff . . .
Bruce	In basic English, I would say.
	The real thing. Serious stuff.
Dot	What do you mean? Cripes!
	It's hypoallergenic. I'm
	ill on account of it. Cripes!
Eileen	Bag it, Dot.
Dot	Cripes, you guys.
Eileen	Okay, Dot. Just bag it.

Phone rings.

Dot	Hello. Senator X's office. Hello,
	nothing of value inside, please.
	Please don't steal our stuff.

Pause.

	Yes. No. Maybe.
Eileen	The photographs decked Dot, Bruce.
	She fell down on account of them.
Bruce	Eileen, at best she's not up to
	much. Eileen, why does she do this
	thing? Why does she do this thing
	of "Hello. Senator X's office.
	Nothing of value inside, please"?
	Senator X is not Senator Bob's
	name, and this other stuff, crazy!
Dot	Bruce, I do this "Hello. Senator
	X's office. Nothing of value inside,
	please" thing at the request of
	Surveillance, who is afraid for
	Senator Bob's life after he said
	the speech Eileen wrote for him
	about the Arabs being an insect.

To the phone.

No, not you. Yes, no, maybe.

Hangs up.

	Bruce, you crossed my wires.
EILEEN	She's got feelings, Bruce.
BRUCE	Eileen, at best she's not up to much. Especially, if these photos* decked her.
EILEEN	Okay, bag it, Bruce. I've got feelings, you've got feelings, everybody's got feelings that deck them. It's normal to be decked by one of them when they are . . . like this . . .* Okay, Bruce? So just bag it.
DOT	The pictures aren't normal, but it didn't deck me, Eileen. I fell over on account of lunch hour having come and gone and no lunch. Cripes, Bruce!
BRUCE	Sorry. Sorry. I was . . . trying . . . okay?

Pause.

| DOT | But they sure aren't normal. Cripes! |
| EILEEN | Bag it, Dot, okay? |

Pause.

	Maybe they are a FACT of some . . . maybe they are an evidence . . .
DOT	Maybe it's a dilemma.
BRUCE	Could be. They are personal.
EILEEN	Quite. I would say so.

They look long and hard.

BRUCE	Are those people doing that?
EILEEN	They are not cows and pigs, Bruce.
BRUCE	I was being euphuistic, Eileen.
EILEEN	You're a scholar, Bruce.

DOT *joins them. They look long and hard.*

DOT	Maybe it's a dilemma. These two ones here. He's got to make a choice. Somehow. He has to.
EILEEN	Why do you say that?
DOT	Look at that, there.

BRUCE	True . . . Urgent . . .
EILEEN	And this arm here . . . Whose?
DOT	Is that a face, Eileen? Whose . . .

A long pause.

EILEEN	Wow. Look at that one.
BRUCE	Which?
DOT	That one there.
EILEEN	Wow. Is that one real?
BRUCE	Very funny, Eileen. Ha-ha.
EILEEN	I was not making light of it. I was just of a mind. Two actually, if this is what a person means when they are contorted, so to speak. As, uh, in the case of having sex, you know . . . Bag it, Bruce.
BRUCE	(*Pointing.*) You would call that, that?

Phone rings.

EILEEN	No, I would not call that, that. Did I call that an instance of that? No.
DOT	Hello. Senator X's office. Hello, nothing of value inside, please. Please don't steal our stuff.

Pause.

	Yes. No. Maybe.

Palming the phone.

	Is he in today, ever? Senator Bob?
EILEEN	Bag it, Dot.
DOT	You're getting heavy-lidded from looking at that.
EILEEN	We are not looking at that. We are just . . . ah . . .*

They look long and hard.

	That's unusual, that.
DOT	No, not you. Hello? Hung up.

She hangs up.

BRUCE	That?
EILEEN	No. That.
BRUCE	I don't think so.
EILEEN	I know what you mean to say. You mean to say you've had experience with that, with one such as that. Bag it, Bruce.
BRUCE	I was not saying that. I was saying something else.
EILEEN	You were making a claim. Ha!
BRUCE	I was not* making a claim.
EILEEN	He was making a claim, Dot.
DOT	He is always making claims, Eileen.

All look hard.

DOT	Cripes.
EILEEN	Why are they on a chair like that. With no clothes on?
BRUCE	Eileen, please. Can you not please use your imagination? This is a possible evidence. You are agitated. Please, Eileen, do not become agitated because you know how you get and how the boss feels about getting that way, when you do.
EILEEN	Bag it, Bruce.

They look. DOT *goes back to her desk. Pause.*

BRUCE	Anyway, that is not an arm. No, I would not say it is an arm.

Pause.

EILEEN	What are you saying, Bruce?

DOT *laughs.*

Bag it, Dot.

Pause. EILEEN *looks hard.*

	That is not that, Bruce.
	That is something else, because
	the light is not so bright
	in the photo. It's a somewhat
	dark place where they are,
	clearly, so a big mistake is
	possible. I think it's a . . .
	No. Maybe a . . . piece of clothing.
DOT	Bob will want to know what it
	is, and why you are taking so
	long at . . . it . . . This is . . .
	maybe important stuff.
BRUCE	He is not *Bob,* Dot. He is,
	you will recall, a Senator.*
	Hence the name is Senator Bob.
EILEEN	Oh, shut up, Bruce. You are
	an exasperating person, really!
BRUCE	Eileen, don't look at more.
	You're starting to get . . .
	you know . . . wiggly . . .
EILEEN	Bag it, Bruce. I am not.
BRUCE	Women get wiggly when they look
	at the real thing. We men do
	not, having been hardened by
	the war experience and hardship.
	Growing up in law school and
	the rest. Money, responsibilities.
	It's awful. I don't know how we
	put up with the pressure, but we
	do. At least some of us do, if
	we are not stabbed in the back
	by our women, and those on the
	Left and in the opposition party,
	those who want us not to succeed.
	It's true, all of it, I swear,
	Eileen. You are a sweet kid,
	but you don't know how bad
	a place the world is, having
	been a girl at some, I bet,
	Ivy League place, where they
	are permissive about stuff,

He points.

	about people who do that
	and that and THAT! CAN
	YOU BELIEVE THAT!? THAT
	A MAN WOULD DO THAT!? A
	FULL-GROWN MAN DOING THAT . . .
	Your background is too
	nice for understanding of
	how gross and disgusting
	people can be. I think you are
	a liberal underneath your
	clothes and underwear, all
	women are. Even Dot, who is
	more low than we, but has the
	privilege of working on this*
	staff. Even when it is awful
	work, it is exciting. But I
	know, I went to Bob Jones
	University and I know how
	people get twisted by false
	gods, and how a life of crime
	awaits all those who . . . get
	weak and . . . experiment with
	drugs . . . atheism . . . And
	the real thing . . . that, I mean
	. . . and THAT . . . I mean, will
	you get a load of . . . THAT!
	. . . Eileen, for Pete's sake.
DOT	(*Aside.*) I think I will change. I think
	I will not let this bother me.
	I think I will use this as an
	instance to my true, life purpose.
EILEEN	That is not *that*, Bruce, so
	just bag it. That is the . . .
	radiator, and not an active
	participant . . . So just bag it,
	Bruce, because where do you get
	off saying those things? Drugs
	are not on my résumé. Atheism
	is not on my résumé. Have you

looked at my résumé, Bruce?
You are a silly goose, Bruce.
So just bag it.

They look long and hard.

DOT	Look at that, there.
EILEEN	True . . . urgent . . .
	Wow. Look at that one.
BRUCE	Which?
DOT	That one there.
EILEEN	Wow. Is that one real?
BRUCE	Very funny, Eileen. Ha-ha.
BRUCE	(*Pointing.*) You would call that, that?

Phone rings.

EILEEN	No, I would not call that,
	that. Did I call that an
	instance of that? No.
DOT	Hello. Senator X's office. Hello,
	nothing of value inside, please.
	Please don't steal our stuff.

Pause.

Yes. No. Maybe.

Palming the phone.

	Is he in today? Senator Bob?
EILEEN	Bag it, Dot.
	That's unusual, that.
DOT	Bag you, Eileen.
	No, not you. Hello? Hung up.

She hangs up.

BRUCE	That? Are you asking
	is that an instance
	of that?
EILEEN	No. That.
BRUCE	I don't think so.
	I was not saying that.
	I was saying something
	else.
EILEEN	You were making a claim. Ha!
BRUCE	I was not making a claim.

EILEEN	He was making a claim, Dot.
DOT	He is always making claims, Eileen.

All look hard.

	Cripes.
EILEEN	Why are they on a chair
	like that. With no clothes on?

They look long and hard.

DOT	I was shocked by those photos.
	I do not see either of you,
	cripes, being shocked as I.
	I think you like those things
	they are doing, like that, the
	animals. I think you both
	want to look at that stuff
	too much not to be . . . cripes!
	Suspicious. And when the
	Senator gets back I plan
	to ask him for a raise, I
	did not come to the Hill to
	be exposed to a moral vice
	as with this experience, cripes!
	All seven photos remind me
	of what you're not supposed
	to think, each one worse
	than the other, and you both
	pretend to be Christians, cripes!
	I am truly shocked by this . . .

Points.

	Not to mention *that* . . . sick.
	I've never thought of bending
	over . . . like that . . . And wow,
	you sure are lapping it up, ha.
EILEEN	Bag it, Dot. This is work.
	Documentation of evidence.
BRUCE	I feel unstable, wow.

He sits.

EILEEN	What's wrong, Bruce, did
	the putty-tat from Puscaloosa
	poop his panties? You putz . . .

The real stuff got to you,
I can see, all seven, each
one worse than the other.
Wow, what a man! What
a tough-minded Young
Republican! No American
Enterprise Institute for you,
wussums. No, the real stuff
gives you the wiggles, too.
Brucie better take his crackers
and milk and curl up for his
little nap on his little blankie.
Wow! What a man! What
a tough-minded Young
Republican. No American
Heritage Foundation for you,
wussums. No. The real thing's
got you a little dizzy, huh?
Brucie better take his crackers
and milk and curl up on his
little blankie for his little nap.

Pause.

BRUCE   I felt unstable for a moment,
is all. Wow.

DOT   You sure are lapping it up,
both of you, cripes.

EILEEN   Bag it, Dot.

Pause. She and BRUCE *look.*

Do you think that is what
it actually looks like? Or,
how else do you explain
what it really is, if that's
not right? I mean, well,
if what we are seeing is
photos—of stuff—say . . .

DOT   The real thing, I would say.

EILEEN   But maybe doctored . . . maybe . . .

BRUCE   They sure look healthy to me,
Eileen. Ha-ha.

EILEEN   Very funny, Bruce. You are

a wit. Dot, Bruce is a wit.
Bag it, Bruce.

Pause.

BRUCE   The photos may be doctored
to emphasize that and that,
for instance, though . . . *why*
is beyond me . . . why they
would need to emphasize
that anymore than . . . that . . .
is unclear to me. Perhaps in
the light of day we can see
a clear evidence of tampering,
perhaps at the lab. Do we have
access to a lab of some sort,
Dot, do we?

Phone rings.

DOT   Hello. Senator X's office. Hello,
nothing of value inside, please.
Please don't steal our stuff.

Pause. *

Yes. No. Maybe.

Hangs up.

EILEEN   Dot is circumscribed, Bruce,
so don't bother her. But yes,
we do have a lab, but it is
not Congress's. The lab, I mean.
Congress does not have a lab
for this, but Surveillance does,
and that is the Surveillance
that watches out for stuff
just like this, bad stuff,
meant to injure the mind
and screw up public morals.
We need to be wary, because
stuff meant to injure the
soul exists aplenty, and people,
too. People who do this . . .
And this . . . And this . . .
and this one . . . wow . . .
I did not see that one.

BRUCE	That one, that was on the bottom, being the worst.
EILEEN	That one is clearly the worst. I did not think bodies did that. Bodies do not have things like that, on them. Look, Dot, look. Look at that thing there, there.
DOT	Wow.
BRUCE	That one is clearly the most . . . worst . . . But that thing is not a part of that body, no, Eileen, it's much worse. Because, see that body over there, that one? With the hair on, see it? There?
EILEEN	There? No . . . that could not possibly belong to that, it couldn't fit, on her, oh, my.
BRUCE	That part is not a part that is *on* anything, it is a part that is normally inside, it's not meant to be seen. See?
EILEEN	If it's not meant to be seen, that part, then I have never seen one, nope. I would know if I had, and so . . . Dot, take a look at this thing, here.
DOT	Where? That one? Which?
EILEEN	No, this part here. It's not what we think it is, maybe . . . Sweet Jesus, I hope for their sake it is not what it looks like, because that would make me ill. I knew some parts are capable of bending and being bent, stretched and wiggled in ways that suggest . . . all kinds of stuff . . . stuff that decent people try not to think about,

but the human anatomy, Dot,
how can it be so . . . unstable,
as to do that to itself, and say,
hey, I'm normal. I'm okay,
and just having a fine time, but
sweet Jesus, I hope for their
sake it is not what it looks
like because, they never told
us about this or that, at the
Dartmouth Review, when we
tore down the ugly shanties
of those colored people who . . .
you mean to say, Bruce, do
you mean to say, that part
there is normal, that is normal
only when it is inside that
other part way over there!?
Oh, no, I can't believe that . . .
That is not how nature is
supposed to be. They never said
that that could be bent or flexed
like that, at the *Dartmouth Review*
when we tore down the shanties
of the colored people, of the Indians,
and of the other liberals. Because
that part is not normal, that
part should not be distended
to such an extent that it flares
out like that. It might pop.
It might pop and burst and
the stuff inside, why! it would
trickle down the sides here, and
God, that part is not where
God intended, when he placed
it, modestly, nestled like a little
pink wildflower. Inside,
nestled like a little, pink
wildflower on the woodsy . . . thing,
there. In the soft, woodsy part.

DOT   It's not what you think, it's
not that, it's something else,

EILEEN

so calm down, Eileen. It's
only a picture. A picture can't
torture and rape you* . . . a picture . . .
A picture can too torture and
rape your mind, Dot, I mean
can't you imagine that, being
bent and wiggled and so
forth, and stretched and so
forth . . . like that . . . I mean,
look at that look on her face, the
pain, the intense anguish of the
poor thing. A picture can do
these things, I know it, and
so do you, which is why you
are here, and not down the hall
working for Senator So-and-so,
who represents a state where
the kind of behavior is all
too common, Dot. A picture
can too torture and hopelessly
maim the insides of you,
and can destroy the outside
of the inside part of you
like that poor girl there, that
Bruce is looking at, and not
helping me to argue the point
because that photo, like the
one before, and the one before
and the one before, and the
one before, and especially the
one before that, and the one
we saw first that now seems
tame—almost innocent, one
might say, by comparison—
have turned his brain to mush.
Look at Bruce, Dot, look at
his eyes, how empty and ill
they are, like an animal who
has seen too much of human
life ever to be an animal again.
They never, never told us about

the look in those eyes, at the
Dartmouth Review when we
were tearing down the shanties
of the colored people, and the
other people, Indians and the
rest. I feel tortured and maimed
by the impact of these pictures
upon the inside of my brain.
So just bag it, Bruce, and
you too, Dot, bag you, I
mean, bag it. Really, bag it!

DOT
Eileen, Eileen. Calm down,
Eileen, it's only a picture.
A picture cannot torture and
maim your heart. A picture
is a picture, Eileen. It
can't do that,

Points.

or that . . .
If you want to be destroyed
by a picture, a picture
will destroy you, like
Bruce here, but Bruce is
sick anyway, Eileen. We
both have seen how sick
Bruce is, at office parties,
Eileen. It's a fact. Cripes,
so don't get so worked
up. I have seen all this
before, back in Oil City,
Pennsylvania, we had this

Points.

and this and even that,
even though it was not so
swollen as that, and I
never saw such clear
photos of the whole thing,
and so many participants, all
in one room, at it, Eileen.
I knew such things happened
because it was a fact they

were not talked about, and
you can be sure that when an
activity is not being talked
about, it is going on. It is
definitely going on when it
is not being talked about,
because, Eileen, you go figure:
if you were an activity . . . like
that . . . or that . . . or even that
astonishing part there. That
one. And someone decent, say,
from the church, or an elderly
person in a position of power,
or a person in your family you
are supposed to look up to
for advice in troubled times . . .
Times like these, Eileen, times
like the ones the Senator has
talked about in the speeches
you have written for him,
and in the restrictive legislation
Bruce there—will you get a
load of whacko Bruce there!
Wow! What a sickie! What
a sex fiend's look in those
eyes, Eileen. Bruce, are
you drooling? Bruce is
drooling, Eileen, look at
the drool on his sleeve, oh,
God, I hope it's drool, oh,
please, God, let it be drool . . .
and Eileen, the point is . . . I . . .
was trying to say before Bruce
here, Bruce began to drool . . .
that if you were an activity

Points.

    . . . like that . . . or that . . . or even that . . .
that astonishing part there . . .
that one you said should be
more normal . . . if you were
such an activity, and a

person came up to you, even
a good person like the Senator
or the Reverend, a good decent
person who talks on the TV
about God and stuff and
how you should behave and
observe God's rules and listen
to the speeches you write for
the Senator and support the
restrictive legislation that
is drafted in this office, by
Bruce—sick, sad Bruce;
at least when he is not
drooling over dirty pictures—
would you not, being that
healthy, unspeakable act
simply reply: GO TO HELL!
MIND YOUR OWN BEESWAX
BECAUSE I AM HAVING A
GOOD TIME, THANK YOU!

Pause.

MIND YOUR OWN BEESWAX
BECAUSE I AM HAVING A
GOOD TIME, THANK YOU!
GO TO HELL! GOOD-BY!

The SENATOR *enters unseen.*

BRUCE   Dot, shut up. Eileen, shut up.
I am not a pervert, I am a
man who does his job. I
am examining these photos
because of them being sent
to the Senator, by a delivery
person, and therefore they
are evidence of a smear . . .
Yes, Eileen, I am capable
of seeing through these photos . . .
even this one . . . which I confess
is strong stuff. This one
is more than the real thing. This one
is abnormal, even by the sick

standards of the sex-obsessed,
subnormal person who took it,
and all the rest because, this
photo cannot harm you, it
cannot make you sick
if you are not sick already,
but if you are sick already
it can make you . . . more
sick than before. That is true, and
I resent that crack, Dot,
about me and my drool, Dot.
That was unfair. I was
doing my job of work here,
while you and Eileen stood
and yelled at each other
and then yelled at me. I
do not call yelling at
my colleagues "work," no,
but maybe I'm old-fashioned
and not "with it" as you
"hip" people say, as you "hip"
people say at your clubs
and discos, and at your
Dartmouth College, when I
did not come from no damn
high-class eastern liberal
establishment family but
was always working on my paper
route, Eileen, while you played.
Eileen, while you partied and
played I was lower-middle-class,
Eileen, and that hurts, Eileen,
that hurts because of not
being allowed to the country
club dances, where girls like
you wear white gloves and
are debutantes and do stuff
like "coming out" and stuff.
I know what that stuff
is, all that debutante stuff,
and how you all go on to

Dartmouth College with
all the other rich kids and
pretend to be conservative!
Yes, pretend, Eileen, pretend!
Because I went to Bob Jones
University, which is where you
go if you are the real thing,
Eileen, conservative, Eileen.
I know what that stuff
is, all that debutante stuff:
you wear white gloves and
are debutantes and do stuff
like "coming out" and stuff.
But Dot and me, we know,
because we have to work for
our daily bread, not like you,
Eileen, because Dot and me
know you're faking it
when you write those speeches
for the Senator, yes, Eileen,
your heart's not in it, Eileen.
Face it, you're an imitation.

EILEEN   Bag it, Bruce, just go bag it.
BRUCE   Because I bet you know
what that is . . . and that . . .
And that you've done that
with this and that, I just bet!
Because I know you rich
kids have access to good
drugs and stuff, and do
all the things that are in
these seven photos, yes,
I am not an idiot, Eileen.
Because all rich kids know
what that is . . . and that . . .
And that that thing there,
which is supposed to be
over there, on that one, is
the source of indescribable
joy if it has been over there
like that, in a sick and

twisted way, even if that
rich kid joy is loathsome
and morally reprehensible
and un-American and so
forth and so on, and I
bet these people here, these
sick and depraved people
in these photos, are friends of
yours, from Dartmouth
College, where you claim
you worked on the Dartmouth
Review, where you claim
you did patriotic activites
like pulling down the shanties
of the colored people, and the
Indians, and the liberals,
while all the time, Eileen,
you were up to no good,
doing stuff like this . . .
and that . . . and that . . .
and even this one here, wow.
This one sure got to me, wow.

All see the SENATOR *and fall silent. Pause.*

SENATOR   What in the name of Sam Hill
                   has happened around here? You
                   all look like you got poison
                   ivy on the back of your eyeballs.

         Pause.

BRUCE   These came in the mail* today, Senator.
DOT   They certainly did not come in the
                   mail. They were expressed here . . .
                   Cripes, Bruce!
SENATOR   What were expressed here today?
EILEEN   These. Take a look. You'd
                   better sit down before you
                   take a look.
BRUCE   That would be wise, Senator.
DOT   I did not sit down before I
                   took a look at them, only I
                   fell down. Then I got adjusted

and now I feel fine, but
these two, you would not
BELIEVE how these two have
been carrying on. I mean,
it's only a picture, and both
of 'em're having a fit, yup,
a regular conniption,* like
you never saw a thing such
as what people have between
their legs before, cripes!

EILEEN   Bag it, Dot.

He sits wearily.

SENATOR   Okay, okay. Show me.

BRUCE *eyes* EILEEN. EILEEN *eyes* DOT. DOT *eyes* BRUCE. BRUCE
shows them to the SENATOR. *Pause.*

EILEEN   I would advise deep breathing
if you feel faint, Senator.

Pause.

SENATOR   What kind of film would you say
it is? This here? Fast or slow?
I'm a bit of an amateur photographer myself.

BRUCE   *(Pointing.)* What is that, there, would you say?

SENATOR   What is what?

BRUCE   That. There.

SENATOR   That?

BRUCE   Yes. That.

SENATOR   Well, I dunno. Let me look.

Pause.

BRUCE   That is a blowjob.

SENATOR   That is not a blowjob. That is the pope.

He's got it upside down. BRUCE *helps him get it right. Pause.*

BRUCE   That is a blowjob, Senator.
We've got about seven of 'em
here. In this office. Someone
sent us seven photos of this
blowjob-type behavior,
and we're deeply concerned.

SENATOR   I still say that's the pope.

DOT   It does look like the pope—with no clothes.

SENATOR	I need my reading glasses, where in hell are my reading glasses? I always leave my reading glasses by the ant farm. Whose idea was it, by God, who the hell moved the ant farm? I can't do no reading without the ant farm, I mean the reading glasses I make a point of leaving next to, or on top of, the goddamn ant farm.
EILEEN	There they are, sir, in the ant farm. With ants all over them.

All look. Pause.

DOT	Boy, do they ever swarm when they swarm. Cripes. Do you suppose they are making a meal of your reading glasses?
SENATOR	(*To Eileen.*) Go clean these off. Who sent these photos, Bruce?
BRUCE	I . . . we don't know . . . sir.

An autocratic pause.

SENATOR	You did not bother to ascertain, Bruce, who sent them? You did not do this, Bruce? I cannot believe it . . .

He sighs deeply.

	Dot, who sent them?
DOT	Well, now, let's see . . . It's gotta be here . . . in the wastepaper . . .
SENATOR	What a bunch! What a royal bunch!
DOT	It think it was Senator So-and-so. The guy from down the hall . . .
EILEEN	See, Senator? Look. See? That thing there. And that one, too . . .
SENATOR	Oh me, oh my. That is a blowjob . . . * Wow!
EILEEN	No, Senator, that's not the blowjob. That is a borzoi dog

that is chained to the banister.
You can see, it's a split-level
den of iniquity, this den of
iniquity is . . . But the, ah,
the blowjob is over here, by
the ah, potted plant. Now, this
blowjob is a mild case compared
with this one there. This one
decked Dot, isn't this the one
that decked you, Dot?

BRUCE *rolls his eyes as* DOT *pipes up.*

	Bag it, Bruce.
DOT	Eileen, what a thing to say. I
	have seen worse than that back
	in Oil City, Pennsylvania. What
	got to me was that there . . . that
	fuzzy area,* no, it's not on this
	one, it's on the other one, that . . .
EILEEN	Believe me, Senator, this one
	decked Dot. She was out cold.
	And Bruce here . . . sick . . . Brucie . . .
	why, he got all, you know, wiggly,
	and this after saying how we
	women get wiggly when we see
	stuff like that . . . and that . . . and
	that. Well, just look at Bruce
	and tell me who the wiggly one
	is. Bruce there is drooling
	again, see, and that kind of
	abject drooling is as close to
	the state of being incurably
	wiggly as you can get, yes.
	And then there is this one . . .
	and this one, and that
	one . . . and that . . . and
	then this really scary one . . .
SENATOR	Oh me, oh my.
EILEEN	But for my money, this one
	is the worst: See it, there?
	Because we had a discussion,

	Dot and me, and Bruce, too,
	this was before he got wiggly
	when his drooling was under
	control, or at least he was
	better capable of controlling it.
SENATOR	Oh, my God, will you get a
	load of that. Is that, that?
EILEEN	Yes, Senator, that is that . . .
	And what's worse, Dot and
	I surmise that this thing here
	is the thing that is normally
	inside here, but—pardon
	my French—it got stretched
	way out to here by their . . . ah,
	exertions. Now, I certainly
	wouldn't know, but I do
	know that that there is not
	supposed to go all the way
	there. It is against the law
	of nature for a human thing
	to be distended like that, all
	flared out and in full view,
	and that look on her face . . .
BRUCE	That is not a look on her
	face, that is a look on
	his face. Face facts, Eileen.
EILEEN	Bag it, Bruce.
DOT	Cripes, Eileen, it's only a picture.
SENATOR	Dot, that is a picture of an
	unnatural act. That is an act
	we knew about when I was
	growing up, back in Mad Wolf,
	but we did not have a name
	for. Bruce, are you all right?
	Bruce is not all right, Eileen,
	get him a glass of water.
EILEEN	(*Aside.*) Dot is the secretary, I am the
	administrative assistant, why
	must I get Bruce the glass of
	water, it really bothers me . . .
	really, really, really, really . . .

SENATOR	Dot and Eileen would not be
	familiar with a kind of act
	of that sort, and I did not
	know the name of that act myself,
	although I knew it occurred
	to people who were not right
	in the heads, but the name of
	it, I did not want to know
	because the name of it was
	forbidden. It was unAmerican,
	and leads to saggy eyelids,
	and if you say to an act
	like that . . . calm down, boy,
	you are not acting right,
	why it will sneer at youand say: GO TO HELL!
	MIND YOUR OWN BEESWAX
	BECAUSE I AM HAVING A
	FINE OLD TIME,* THANK YOU!
DOT	That's just what I said, sir.
	That's exactly* what I said.
EILEEN	She said no such thing. Dot
	is such an errant exaggerator.
	Don't take a word serious, sir.
DOT	Is too, is too, is too, is too . . .
EILEEN	BAG IT, DOT.
Pause.	
SENATOR	Cool down, Eileen.
Pause.	
	And get him out of here.
Bruce comes to.	
	All I know is a monster case
	of blowjob like that means one
	of two things: smear or surveillance . . .
	We've got to find out which. Dot . . .
DOT	Yes, sir?
SENATOR	Call the Reverend and find me the
	file we have on Senator So-and-so . . .
	our surveillance on his surveillance . . .
DOT	Yes, sir.
SENATOR	Eileen, help Bruce clean out his desk.

EILEEN	Yes, sir.
BRUCE	I'm fired?
SENATOR	Yes, Bruce, fired.
BRUCE	But why? WHY?
DOT	But Senator So-and-so died day before yesterday, sir. You sent flowers to the widow, sir.
SENATOR	Flowers to the widow. Indeed I did.
BRUCE	But sir, why?
EILEEN	Bag it, Bruce.
SENATOR	Get that prevert out of here, Eileen.* A blowjob like that's got to be the tip of the iceberg. Either smear or surveillance. Good Lord,

Looking.

	would you get a load of that?
EILEEN	(*Aside.*) Dot is the secretary, I am the administrative assistant, why must I help Bruce clean out his desk, it really bothers me . . . * really, really, really, really . . .
BRUCE	But why, sir?
SENATOR	Because you are not right in the head, Bruce.

Act Two

The same. EILEEN. *The* SENATOR *and* REVEREND TOM. *The photos are on the table. It is night.*

EILEEN	This is it, Reverend Tom, this is it. Dot says this is it, this is the fatal blowjob, the blowjob in question.
TOM	It looks like a Pekingese to me.
SENATOR	You're looking at the wrong part, Tom. That's the part with the incriminating thing on its whatsis, the thing out there, wiggly, that part there.

All look hard and long.

TOM	No, that cannot be that, that really

cannot be that. Way over there.
Christ in a Christmas tree! I
mean, that defies describing, it
being all the way over there, how
in the name of saltpeter could it get
all stretched out like that . . . wow,
I mean, I seen some things, and
you would be amazed what you see
in the God business, because it
sure as hell is a business and it
therefore ought to be run as one, but
the soul—even the precious purity
of the Christian soul, even in
its infrequent state of being
saved, this human soul . . .
is attached to a human body . . .
by a thing, by a thing like
that . . . and there's the rub,
and that rub is where the
trouble starts . . . because
if you rub a thing like that,
a thing like this thing here,

Points.

up jumps the devil and the
devil is a creature of rubbing,
touching, stretching, and all the
damned contortions the human
body is heir to. It don't matter
what you do about it, you
are in a fallen state and . . .
to look upon a scene like . . .
that one . . . there . . . and that, wow . . .

He has to sit down.

EILEEN   That one is the one that did in
Bruce. That one, and the way
that thing there is. You see the
face between the other parts,
the leer there, on that face . . .
That did in Bruce, Bruce

started to drool at that . . .
That did not have that
effect on me,** though I am
no prissy type person, but
now this other one, I bet
you didn't see this one, did
you? This one here, this one
did something not right
to me in my head—part . . .
so I refused to look at it,
except for a little peek
every now and then just
to see if it's still there and
if it still has that powerful
effect on me so that my
knees knock and my head
swims and I dare not think
what else is going on, else-
ways and nowhere, where
it shouldn't ought to do.

TOM   Eileen, you are a picture of
what a soul ought to do
to be saved: Not to look at
the devil's work is the mark the
good Lord leaves on the water,
Eileen. The mark the good Lord
leaves on the water of life,
Eileen. You will be saved . . .
I believe you will, because . . .
you can resist the cloven
hoof on the forehead of your . . .
wom . . . wom . . . womanliness . . .

SENATOR   As for that Bruce fuck . . .
the dumb fuck was no damn
fucking good at all . . .

Pause.

As for that Bruce fuck . . .
the dumb fuck was no damn
fucking good. Nobody who ever
didn't go to no goddamn fucking
Bob Jones University was ever

worth an ounce of weasel shit
in the good Lord's silver spoon.
Tom, he had a pronounced
sado-momo-statistical drive,
and the leanings of this drive
could be observed in the men's
room, where he would look
at your pecker, if you were
not careful. That's right: look
right at your pecker. Everybody
who ever went to Bob Jones
University is a fairy, and
you ask how I know, I
know: he played tennis.
People who play tennis: fags.
Your typical Bob Jones–type
University-type student: fag.
And that's the fucking truth.

Pause.

I like my flacks Ivy League.
Ivy League flacks may be
faggy, but they know how to
network. Bob Jones University
flacks are fags and don't know
network from netsuke *and* they
are sado-momo-statistical on
top of that, and on top of
that they don't talk good, like
Eileen. Eileen, talk.
Talk some of that good
Ivy League talk for Tom.
Go on, don't be shy.

She smiles.

Go on . . .

EILEEN   I'd be delighted to . . .
SENATOR   See, Tom, see. That's what
I call high-toned talk. That
kinda talk I like because
that kinda talk is the coin

of the realm when it comes
to networking, ain't it so?

EILEEN *looks embarrassed.*

                She's the modest type, but it's true. So . . .

Pause.

                Dot said these photos came from
                down the hall. Senator Dick . . .
                Dick So-and-so. From the upstate
                of his state. The glacial part.
                Two days ago he died. Fell
                on the floor. Bam. Dead.
                It was a monster apoplexy, I hear.
                That is what it was I heard:
                apoplexy—was it not, Eileen?

EILEEN   That's what it was that you
                heard, Senator.* At least,
                that's what Dot said . . .

SENATOR   So the question is, was it
                a case of these photographs
                being an instance of him, ah,
                directing an act of smear
                at us, ah, me, my person, or
                is it an act of his surveillance
                on the lookout for a something
                he thought I ought to know
                before he up and kicked off,
                like that, bam, on the floor, dead.

Pause.

                So it's smear or surveillance,
                the way I see it. But which . . .

EILEEN   That's obviously the way we
                all look at it, here, sir.

SENATOR   Tom, it's an attack on public
                morality. And that means you.

TOM   If it's an instance of something
                we ought to go public with, we
                ought to go public with it
                then. But this Senator Dick,
                wasn't he one of us, Bob?
                I used to get a check from him.

	I used to pray with him, at
	the Holiday Inn at Beltsville.
	Good Christian gentleman, Bob.
	And his wife, Maybelle, a fine
	Christian lady, a little hard
	of hearing and not a looker . . .
SENATOR	Not a looker is mild, Tom. She's
	got a face like a Poland-China hog.
TOM	But Bob, Senator Dick was a fine* man.
SENATOR	A fag, Tom.
TOM	No, not Dick.
SENATOR	Senator Dick So-and-so: faggot.

Pause.

	It's true, Reverend Tom.
TOM	Indeed, the works of the
	devil exceed the number
	of digits in the mind of
	an IBM superfast computer.
	Praised be the name of the
	Lord Jesus Christ, amen.
SENATOR	Leastways, that's what I suspect.
	He was another pecker-watcher.
	He was a confirmed pecker-watcher.
EILEEN	But our surveillance tells us
	his surveillance was busy not
	with watching us, but was
	busy with watching Bob Junior.

Pause.

TOM	Bob Junior. Who's Bob Junior?
SENATOR	Tom, you know Bob Junior.
EILEEN	You must know Bob Junior.
SENATOR	My son, Bob.
TOM	Can't recall I do.

Pause. She looks at the photos.

SENATOR	Eileen, stop thinking that thought.
EILEEN	I was not thinking that thought.
TOM	What was that? You folks'd
	leave a poor man of God to

	guess what color the inside
	of a polecat's asshole is,* ah . . .
EILEEN	Beg your pardon, Reverend?
SENATOR	Eileen, call Bob Junior.
EILEEN	Now, sir? It's ten o'clock.
SENATOR	Call and tell him to get
	his butt here pronto.
EILEEN	Okay.

She dials.

TOM	Now, now, Bob. This don't
	smack of no damn smear. Why,
	Dick was one of us, our party,
	our God, our men's club.
	Just because he served in the
	other service, and not the
	one we are both veterans of,
	and lived upstate somewhere,
	there, of his corruptive state
	where people act funny and
	are likely to be Jews, colored,
	or émigrés from the Pakistani
	restaurants of New York City,
	and had a slight limp and
	a somewhat unnoticeable
	speech impediment owing
	to a piece of shrapnel in his
	head from the last good war
	this country had don't mean moosedick.

SENATOR	Like hell it don't mean moosedick.
	He cheats at poker and is a dyed-
	in-the-wool pecker-looker-at-er.
	Take it from me: Senator Dick: fag.

EILEEN	But the Reverend had a point, Senator.
	Why would Senator Dick want to
	smear you? It's not a reasonable
	supposition. You were close friends.

| SENATOR | That's where Bob Junior comes in, I'm afraid. |

BOB JUNIOR *enters.*

| EILEEN | Hi, Bob Junior. |

BOB JUNIOR	Hi. I'm Bob.
EILEEN	I'm Eileen. Remember? From the hog roast?
BOB JUNIOR	Oh, yeah. Hi.

Pause.

	Hi, Dad.
SENATOR	Bob Junior, this is Tom. Tom, Bob Junior.
TOM	Hello, Bob Junior.
SENATOR	Don't just stand there like a moron jack-off! Tom here is deacon of the Television Church of the Tachistical Wonder of Jesus Christ, Autodidact. Ain't it that, Tom? A real TV church.
TOM	Something like that, yes.

Pause.

EILEEN	Sit down, Bob Junior.

She hands the photos to the SENATOR. *Pause. He hands them to* BOB JUNIOR.

SENATOR	Bob Junior. Is that you?
BOB JUNIOR	That? No. That is a borzoi.
SENATOR	Not that, fool. That.
BOB JUNIOR	That thing, there?
EILEEN	No, Bob Junior, the Senator means that. There.
BOB JUNIOR	No, that's not me.
SENATOR	That looks like me. I mean you.
BOB JUNIOR	That doesn't look like me.
SENATOR	Bob Junior, come clean. If that's you just say so. It's okay. But if that's you, I'll kill you, boy. So come clean, for your mother's sake.

Pause. BOBBOB JUNIOR *enters. All look a bit puzzled as* BOBBOB JUNIOR *is identical to* BOB JUNIOR.

	BobBob Junior, this is Tom. Tom, BobBob Junior.
BOB JUNIOR	But Dad, that's not me.
TOM	Hello, BobBob Junior.
	Bob Junior, are you sure?
SENATOR	Don't just stand there like a moron jack-off! Tom here is deacon of the Television Church of the Tachistical Wonder

	of Jesus Christ, Autodidact. Ain't
	it that, Tom? A real TV Church.
EILEEN	Bob Junior, it's a very vital concern of ours
	having to do with a national security matter.
TOM	Something like that, yes.
	Pause.
BOB JUNIOR	Eileen, it's not me.
EILEEN	Sit down, BobBob Junior.

Hands him photos.

	I believe you, Bob Junior.
SENATOR	BobBob Junior. Is that you?
	Pause.
	I don't believe you, Bob Junior.
BOBBOB JUNIOR	That? No. That is a borzoi.
BOB JUNIOR	I know you don't believe
	me, Dad. You never believe
	me, Dad.
SENATOR	*(To BOBBOB JUNIOR.)* Not that, fool. That.
TOM	The boy's got a point, Bob.
	This here, the thing in question
	attached to the offending part
	over here . . . the part you, Eileen . . .
BOBBOB JUNIOR	That thing, there?
EILEEN	That's the part that decked Dot.
	Pause.
	No, BobBob Junior, the Senator means
	that. There.
TOM	That part only looks that way because
	it is not what it looks like . . .
BOBBOB JUNIOR	No, that's not me.
SENATOR	What are you driving at, Tom?

Pause. To BOBBOB JUNIOR.

	That looks like me. I mean you.
TOM	That thing there is not a blowjob,
	it's a borzoi.
BOBBOB JUNIOR	That doesn't look like me.
SENATOR	Let me see.

All look hard.

Hot damn, you may be right. But

that does too look like Bob Junior,
don't it?

Pause. To BOBBOB JUNIOR.

BobBob Junior, come clean. If that's you,
just say so. It's okay. But if that's
you, I'll kill you, boy. So come clean,
for your mother's sake.

BOB JUNIOR Can I go now, Dad?

BOBBOB JUNIOR But Dad, that's not me.

TOM It looks a little like Bob Junior, but
it also looks a little like the pope.

Pause. To BOBBOB JUNIOR.

BobBob Junior. Are you sure?

BOB JUNIOR It looks like Dad, too.

EILEEN BobBob Junior, it's a very vital concern
of ours having to do with
a national security matter.

SENATOR Shut up, Bob Junior. Here's fifty bucks.
Go buy a pair of shoes. Go and buy a pair
of normal, American wing-tip shoes and go
and throw those faggot shoes away, Bob Junior.

BOBBOB JUNIOR Eileen, it's not me.

BOB JUNIOR Thanks, Dad.

EILEEN I believe you, BobBob Junior.
Good-by, Bob Junior.

SENATOR I don't believe you, BobBob Junior.

BOB JUNIOR Good-by, Eileen.

BOBBOB JUNIOR I know you don't believe
me, Dad. You never believe
me, Dad.

TOM Good-by, Bob Junior.

Pause. To the SENATOR.

The boy's got a point, Bob.
This there, the thing in question
attached to the offending part
over here . . . the part you, Eileen . . .

BOB JUNIOR Good-by, Reverend Tom.

EILEEN That's the part that decked Dot.

SENATOR Good-by, Bob Junior.

Том	That part only looks that way because it is not . . . what it looks like.
Bob Junior	Good-by, Dad.
Senator	What are you driving at, Tom?
Том	That thing there is not a blowjob, it's a borzoi.
Senator	Let me see.

Looks hard.

Hot damn, you may be right. But that does too look like the pope.

BobBob Junior	Can I go now, Dad?
Tom	It looks a little like BobBob Junior, but it also looks a little like the pope.
BobBob Junior	It looks like Dad, too.
Senator	Shut up, BobBob Junior. Here's fifty bucks. Go buy a pair of shoes. Go and buy a pair of normal, American wing-tip shoes and go and throw those faggot shoes away, BobBob Junior.
BobBob Junior	Thanks, Dad.
Bob Junior	Wait a minute, who is this guy? I am Senator Bob's son, not this fraud.
Том	Don't get all hot under the collar, son.
Senator	It'd take too long to explain, Bob, BobBob.
Eileen	An idea of surveillance, Bob, BobBob.

Pause.

Good-by, BobBob Junior.

An odd pause. BobBob Junior *smiles and prepares to go.*

Eileen	Good-by, BobBob Junior.
BobBob Junior	Good-by, Eileen.
Том	Good-by, BobBob Junior.
BobBob Junior	Good-by, Reverend Tom.
Senator	Good-by, BobBob Junior.
BobBob Junior	Good-by, Dad.

Pause.

Senator	Good-by, BobBob. Good-by, Bob.
Bob Junior	Good-by, Bob. Ah . . . Dad.

An awkward moment.

BOBBOB JUNIOR (*To Bob Junior.*) Good-by, Bob.
BOB JUNIOR   Good-by, BobBob.

>   BOB *and* BOBBOB JUNIOR *exit.*

SENATOR   It *does* look kinda like the pope.
TOM   It couldn't be the pope. He's
                  still a Christian gentleman—
                  even if he is full-blown Antichrist.
EILEEN   Well, I think we can lay to rest
                  the idea of the thing being a smear.
                  If it is not Bob Junior, it is not a smear.
SENATOR   Looks like the pope. With no clothes.

>   *Pause.*

                  That means it's surveillance, but
                  is it his surveillance or ours? Dead
                  Senator Dick's surveillance, I mean.
EILEEN   Maybe this is a matter of a sort
                  that his surveillance wanted to
                  let our surveillance know about.
SENATOR   What's that supposed to mean?
                  Eileen, please, talk Ivy League.
                  That kind of talk is not what
                  I expect of you. That kind of
                  talk is Bob Jones University
                  kind of talk and that kind of
                  talk sucks hind-titty and not
                  only does it suck hind-titty,
                  it gets itself fired, like that
                  fag Bruce. You recall Bruce?
EILEEN   I recall the case of Bruce, sir.
                  You recall that it was I, sir,
                  who first told Bruce to bag it, sir.
TOM   Calm down, everybody, let's
                  not get excited. Indeed,
                  not only should we all not
                  get excited but perhaps we
                  should all get down on
                  all fours and pray to the
                  Lord for illumination from
                  this case of sado-botomy.

They all get down.

> Christ Jesus, hear us in
> our prayers and illumine
> the sick pathways of desire
> for bad things and cure us
> of what we should not
> think about if we want to
> avoid being chained to the
> wall of the State Home for
> the Criminally Insane and
> Lord Jesus, we have not
> gotten excited but have,
> as you can plainly see,
> gotten down on all fours,
> and are praying that you
> will come into the foul
> pismire that is the human
> heart and cleanse it of
> the odium of knowing far
> too much about the rub,
> that soft, seductive rub,
> the rub the devil delights
> in, and exploits for his
> fun and games, while we poor,
> lost sinners turn upon the
> spit and roast in the red-hot
> flames of . . . of what . . .
> of what has no good name . . .
> but might possibly come to
> mind, or may be invoked
> with reference to these vile
> photos of unnatural acts,
> photos of unnatural acts,
> capable of rendering a
> full-grown man *happy.*

Pause.

> Photos of unnatural acts
> capable of rendering a
> full-grown man happy
> should not only not get

us all excited but perhaps . . .
we should stay down on
all fours and pray to the
Good Lord of Stone and Rubble,
the Lord God of Goose Fat,
the Savior of our Common
Dementia, and our need
to be nailed to the Death Tree
like him, in the Son's agony
against the opaque Father, oh,
we should stay down on
all fours and pray to the
Lord for horripilation at the
mere thought of such an
act, even though in these
photos the things are not
in actual contact with the
other things, and therefore
the seven blowjobs are seven
unconsummated blowjobs,
but they suggest the worst,
worse than the actual act
would have done did and
had you come up to that
act and said in the voice
of faith: "Blowjob, you
stand in the need of
prayer, so get up off of
your knees, and pull
yourself up by your
underpants like a man
should, and be saved."
That blowjob, being a
child of Satan still in
his or her heart, would
leer, and say: "Tom,
GO TO HELL! MIND YOUR
OWN BEESWAX BECAUSE
I AM HAVING A GOOD TIME,
THANK YOU!" Thus the fate
of that blowjob would be

sealed, in the full horror
and knowledge of sin, and
photos of unnatural acts,
photos of unnatural acts
capable of rendering a
full-grown man *happy!*

He weeps.

Photos of homo-sado-mystical,
maso-sado-momo-dodo, beasto-
lesbo-sado-christmas-tree, eroto-
catamitical-beasty-phallic-momo-
centric, quasi-sodomitical-eroto-
maniacal-beasty-philo-pro-phallo-
centric, eroto-philo-beasty-centric-
momo-sado-ontological-proto-organistic-
hyper-pan-psycho-super-maniacal-dodo-
gomorrahmy . . . *Christmas-tree . . .

DOT *enters with beer and pizza.*

SENATOR   As for that Bruce fuck,
                the dumb* fuck was no damn
                fucking good at all . . .
REVEREND TOM   Hallelujah! Praise the Lord!

Pause.

EILEEN   Dot. Dot is back.
DOT   Good Lord, whatever has come
                over the denizens of the hog
                farm? All of you down on
                all fours talking about
                blowjobs and being happy!
                You all are lucky I'm not
                with the oppositional party!
                This would look like: smear.

All get up.

EILEEN   Bag it, Dot.

Pause.

DOT   Beer and pizza.
TOM   We were consulting the will
                of a higher authority, Dot.

DOT	I was chewing the fat with the receptionist over at dead Senator Dick's. Her name's Dot, too. I'm Dot White, she's Dot Black. So, we're sisters under the tablecloth of receptionist activities . . .
EILEEN	Come to the point, Dot.
DOT	It seems dead Senator Dick was under a surveillance for his part in a car-park deal in which his hands were not clean. Our surveillance, says the other receptionist, Dot, says the hands were definitely in the till, so to speak, at the time of the apocalyptoplectic attack which ended him. Dead Senator Dick was no dummy, he needed an object of public outrage for deflection of his own car-park scam problem. These photos are art, Dot says, the other Dot that is, art funded by a public agency and performed by artists in his own state. Dot does not say how he came upon these photos, but only that they were a contributory cause to his fatal apocalyptoplectic demise, God rest his soul.
SENATOR	Flowers to his widow, Eileen. Remind me please. Go on, Dot,* Go on.
EILEEN	(*Aside.*) Dot is the secretary, I am the administrative assistant, why must I "flowers to his widow"?

	Him being dead from a picture!
	It really, really, bothers me . . . *
	really, really, really, really . . .
DOT	Dead Senator Dick did not approve
	of this art even before it did him
	in, much as it did in Bruce—
	only worse.* Bag it, Eileen.
	Dead Senator Dick did not approve
	of this kind of art on the grounds
	of not being able to understand the
	moral implications touching upon
	its wiggly parts, the sheer
	touchiness of this and that and
	especially the ones that
	goosed Bruce and beaned Eileen.
EILEEN	One of them decked you, too, Dot.
DOT	It did not deck me, Eileen, I
	fell over on account of lunch
	hour having come and gone and
	no lunch—in the breadbasket . . .

Pause.

So: the public funding of immoral
art seemed a fine idea of
getting people not to think
of this car-park scam, on
account of how there are
more people in the car-park
scam than in the published
poet and funded immoral
art scam and they all vote.
So you see: it makes sense.
Even the car-park scam victims
hate immoral art more than
car-park scams, or so they
think when they are told how
to think by their moral betters.
That's where you come in,
Reverend Tom. You make the
people think religious thoughts
tending to the re-election of the

	saved and eternal damnation
	for the published poets, and the
	nonelect immoral acts . . .
	acts such as these . . .
TOM	You mean these
	photos of unnatural acts,
	photos of unnatural acts
	capable of rendering a
	full-grown man *happy?*
DOT	That is *precisely*
	what I mean, Reverend Tom.
	Acts such as these, funded
	by the American people, are
	immoral. These acts are
	immoral even though in these
	photos themselves the things
	are not in contact with
	the other things, ever,
	because they are clever,
	the acts I mean, and so have
	honored the letter of the
	law even though what they
	suggest is the worst. It
	is worse than the actual
	act would have done did
	had you come up to that
	act and said: "Blowjob . . ."
SENATOR	You can skip that part,* Dot.
TOM	We have more than covered
	that topic, Dot. In full.
DOT	So the fact that in these photos
	a thing does not touch any
	other thing does not matter
	because it's the thought that
	counts, as the other Dot says.
	And since the author of the
	act in question is few and
	a faggot, it means the logic
	is a circle squared, a perfect
	and undestructible argument.
	Ipso facto. Carpe diem . . .

Pause.

> Only he keeled over dead, did
> Senator Dick, and left you, Senator
> Bob, the legacy of his re-election bid.
> He did this having curried your
> favor, knowing your principled
> dislike of anyone a bit unusual
> in the American scheme of things.
> You, *too,* have a re-election bid to
> face, and your dislike of anyone
> who is a bit unusual, the poor, the
> queer, the colored, the women, and
> others who had their shanties torn
> down by Eileen while at Dartmouth
> is legend among many of them, the
> unusual, I mean, and they are many.
> These people do not like you,
> Senator Bob, they want your hide.
> Ipso facto. I would say
> take up the burden of dead
> Senator Dick's legacy and run
> with it. Reverend Tom can
> wrap it in the American flag
> of God versus crypto-sado-momo.
> And solve *his own* problem of
> hands in the till—a matter the
> other Dot apprised me of, the
> dear. Simply put: it'd be as
> easy as shooting whatever
> it is you shoot, in the bucket.

Long pause. Applause.

TOM   Christ in a tree, she's right.
             Bob. She's right. Gee, Bob.
EILEEN   (*Aside.*) Dot is the secretary, I am the
             administrative assistant, it
             really, really bothers me . . .
             really, really, really, really . . .

They all look at her. She falls silent. She smiles. Pause.

SENATOR   I think we got us a agenda here.

DOT	The pizza will turn to plaster. Eat, Bob eat. Eat, Tom.
SENATOR	Let's have us a drink. Eileen, get us the bourbon. The bourbon bottle ought to be buried in the ant farm, somewhere. Pour Dot a drink, Eileen. We got us a bona fide agenda here, hot damn. Pour Dot a drink, Eileen.

EILEEN *does as she's told.*

	Dot, you're gonna be my new legislative assistant. I need a mind like yours to draft all my restrictive legislation.* Dot, you got balls. Doesn't Dot have balls, Tom?
EILEEN	(*Aside.*) Dot is the secretary, I am the administrative assistant, why must Dot get to be legislative assistant? It really,* really bothers me . . . really, really, really, really . . .
TOM	Not only does Dot have balls, she has faith, Bob. Dot possesses the power of faith that surpasseth understanding, a faith that surpasseth all that wiggles and likes to be touched, rubbed, as well as photos of unnatural acts, photos of unnatural acts capable of rendering a full-grown man *happy!*
EILEEN	But Dot is not a lawyer, Senator.
SENATOR	Eileen, it's like the Good Book says: Ignorance of the law is nine-tenths of the law. Here's to Dot and the war against International Faggotry.

All drink. A slow blackout begins.

> Betcha didn't know: George Bush?
> Fag. Ronald Reagan: a faggot.
> General Schwartzkopf: a fairy.
> Senator Orrin Hatch: a damned
> homosexual. Alphonse D'Amato:
> a flagrant queen. Gerald Ford:
> fag. Richard Nixon: faggot.
> General Dwight David
> Eisenhower: fag. Woodrow
> Wilson: queer as a three-
> dollar bill. Abraham Lincoln:
> a faggot. George Washington:
> a confirmed sodomite . . .
> Napoleon Bonaparte: fag.
> Frederick the Great: fag.
> William the Silent: fag.
> Norman Conquest: fag.
> Julius Caesar: faggot.
> Alexander the Great: you guess . . .
> Cain and Abel? faggots.

Total darkness.

Terminal Hip   (1990)

Terminal Hip was premiered January 4, 1990, at PS 122 in New York City.

True ignorance approaches the infinite more nearly than any amount of knowledge can do.
                              —Henry Adams

1

Strange the Y all bent up and dented.
Blew the who to tragic eightball.
Eightball trumpet earwax and so forth.
Pure chew, loud thump and release pin.
Grabity gotta nail him too sure.
You don't not have no super shoes when as how
    you don't need not to never.
Ask for the labernath it's all over sure.
They got music there so bad.
They got music there as do the
    shame-ball double-up and fall-over
    three times running while it drills
    corrosive Z's on that there river bottom.
Technology comes here too am.
Cause if'n it less were it on stilts am too
    to buy air for the burning.
It makes hot tires and grabass thorns.
Sure you got to know winter hush slopes
    clear down the wedge till it topples
    on somebody else's property line.
Call that a question of cards.
Had to had sort of.
Allatime the nightless rider had to had sure.
All time sorta sank down on top of him.
    deserted loot, stuff, that and bad vegetables.
Ship the clandestine.
Open the what, wash the whole hog.
They got food as defies all measure.
The whole shebang rings a bell.
It flies up the chumney and comes out
    smelling like roses.
Meat course. Strange salad. Stranger wine.

Given in trust to whatsisname's acquaintance.
For the sky fills up with empties.
For the sky dreams of other empties than those.
For it has eyes for you and me and the crowe even.
For it are hongry.
And, face it, we are a darn pretty bunch.

Anyone can understand this, right?
Anybody with half a brain can trot the trot.
Any damn fool can winterize the octagon.
Any bojar walloon can strip the pentagon
      of its fluffy stuff and egg the wax.
Any airhead can play air guitar on X
      the beefy sand dollar hoohah.
Any cake X buys Y the faire.
Any cake wilde among the heart's ply.
Any self waxes on if are.
Slight the monster pavement suck.
To be an ointment the tear where was.
Any airhead serves the cause at at.
It charms the hot.
It zonks the charm hot.
Wire the air guitar on backdoor jive.
Flipper out, crazy tune in dynamite
      series of flip-up blackouts.
Hammer the thumb's ease.
Hammer the fried egg curse of devil dogs.
Snare the sweet sessions of elegant darkness.
Shall be not was hot for will have ought.
Find the mystic hand and hammer it onto
      the floor fried egg of the future airhead.
Wassail weasel shall was.
Corner on the corpse market heap door sucked.
Rambling movie of incoherent doors.
Trout season, Crazy Day, Hindenberg/Hydrogen/
      Ohio Matchstick Cooperation Fest.
Amber accessible cloud sharks on airhead
      tilt mode.
Fabulous Russian Grandmaster shall be done
      to by accessible American TV flip-up blackouts.

Salutations to the fruit farm from the nut farm.

Glimpse the cause and cry why an X.
Boat my terrors and blink as the boat
  boots it, glides, doped up, and is fried
  for all to see, in the C's underside, livid.
Quote the just Martian who oxidizes our
  earthly understanding stooped.
Peep down the daynight tube horror horror.
On TV airs the hogfarm snapshots.
On TV pears glide in hokey glue
  and pop up all tipped over.
Who greets glue heaps up aerospace.
Who packs ice doth TV warble on other
  sorta aerospace the low kind horror.
Comet creampuff wiggles her wet hair
  at the sun doodle.
Nox as inaccessible bojar night breathes O.
Nox my bad half goes updown blast
  that at hat's cat horror.
Who on whart is did been.
Who on fear drive locates with tremble the
  acute future hominoid also X also trouble.
Broach the blast and boots it
  the golden smash-up, silent at the center.
Who on earth, silent at the
  center.
Who on X by a hair's breadth, silent at the
  center.
Who on TV, baffled in shake-n-bake bag,
  silent as the center
Who on purple screen, interviewed by a set
  of teeth, offer meanings, cause, empty
  hand jive to public X monster horror.
Seek wisdom to redress, atremble, silent as a center.

Men like signs. Signs make sense of things.
Anyone can understand signs, right?
Anyone can up down when the
  sign says up down.
Anyone has a right to barge.
Glue has a right to wing the rat drive.
Nope has a right to claim feets.

Dot has a right to redot and grow a
    beard of the approved cut.
Hammertoe has a right to
    scratch ink.
Boils on low flame, ignites on fission,
    grabs the cat face on out-phase toxin.
Telephone has a right to listen.
Blue sky has a wall-to-wall creep wagon
    doing the warm donut on sharp Y, and
    has the rights to do so.
The rights crowd the barnyard hey.
Whisper the thing like was did.
How it crept in the hot sun.
Tamper with its carrion and weed the drive.
Poison the minds of willing elders.
End up on fruit and decay as perpetual
    adolescent foghorn barks.
For X is the mind of O.
And shoe was perpetual, a blitz of spikes.
They dazzled upright to wrong the
    weird placebos.
Political hegemony's a ledge of bedrock
    beneath the wide Silurian wedge of slate.
All the landlords are X gone to whye.
All their tintinnabulant alarms go off in
    furry unison as the lazy rains, the faraway
    hurricanos, belt their houses.

Ceaseless wanderer, fixed on the frame of cold
    wind and fire, orchestral, of iron mountains, go,
    go and ask your questions to the X, ply upon ply.
Never will the swatch tell true, as the
    button of interior rhyme, false, of coal.
Still: plod on, question, squirt, debamboozle,
    sand, darken, dwarf and die.
It are it all over again: sad longshanks and
    dour the blue face above the Corn Exchange . . .
Why Russia? Why Brooklyn? Why lard?
You're baseless, intransitive, a star-stomper.
Get into the has been bed and fold up the
    diadem of heavens, blue upon portly blue.

Azure of demon hope shall to shreds are.
Azure of blue as smoothest hickory.
Pup time on spotted wrinkle forks.
God of azure parks in special in between,
 all Holy Wormsfood am.
On X, on Y, the wreath of the searchlight falls,
 announcing new gas stations.
Find wings to your wetness, crisp, hoarfrost,
 a fatal jingle caught in midstep announcing
 cheese for the queasy millions.
For to axe the question mark you must renounce
 the azure blue baldachins of roaring hope's
 awful wagon shall be unto as it was did.
For to X the ? You must step into
 unknown and other shoes.
Unto what as it was did, did not go thus
 in them blue shoes?
For great big crime has a need of blue baskets O.

Wind of windup castles, skyscrapers, ski-
 jumps, strange oils and all dumped into
 J quite the am jar flamingo.
Paraphrasable snow job and easy does it.
Paranoid parafin inching up ne'er-do-well
 moon-stalks in garden did and easy does it.
Eruptive hounds and quite the easy does it.
Born-again woodwork eating Egyptian
 cheese and up and off and easy does it.
Untranslate the square fable into round hole
 and goose the never-say-die up-and-at-'ems.
Untranslate the honcho meat train and grow cats.
Blood the untranslatable clockwise cocksure.
Dense macaroni of strange winds!
Future boils and bedpans!
Slow energies ravening into pox of untranslatable
 Scutarene kickbacks, all glued to a wheel.
W sizable waste of it all was.
Tyranny of full, democracy of half.
Ride the X plate, and punt the dragon scheme.
For the tired oaf turns his back.

For the tired back of turn, turns back, smiles,
  and offs the oaf with sizable watering can.
The war we know shall be did in the name
  of the war we know not of, and easy does it.
The clear understanding of decent white men
  revolts under X and Y the prospect of infinite
  and ambitious chew.
Cantilever will machines, blind hexagonal
  pyrite stick horns, fly grates and hook dips,
  all leering to be understood.
An opaque and future wad of unchewable
  vegetation on semi-indestructible mission
  to pry loose huge plates of fire, and easy does it.

Libation to the not wing, low hum on Z coil.
So you ask are of all the pandas, which
  of you doth abound?
Some say are will, and shovel mouth.
Which pandas has pants?
Which pandas pushes the not wing?
Which pandas have plural endings?
Which panjandrums put out eyes, seek fire,
  hogtie hockey sticks on information overload?
Pure the panda nation.
Up to and including libation to the not wing
  and pick-up-sticks.
Shall be accordion.
Shall be ground ball X.
Fire up and melt down the infernal
  Z coil, up to and including pick-up-sticks.
Jumbo pandas, their minds in motion,
  screen the cosmic ground ball, as one,
  crye up libation to the not wing, put
  out the eyes of who, accordion likemost,
  pay their dues, gather no moss on the
  soles of their strange feet, heave and
  jar, sack the quarterback, lay waste to
  Wild Time, flip out, arrange themselves,
  in paranoid polygons, rev up, cut out,
  nail the sandman up to and including
  pick-up-sticks.

Godamighty them bugaboos shall strange
    shadow off the large wing-tips infer.
Purest Java, impure dialectic of panda stuff,
    showboat panda on ground ball overdrive.
All the understanding shot to a glass eye's
    rarefaction, a real eye's ghost.

Psych out the man who flies, bark up the wrong
    tree and bite the hand that feeds.
The will walls up the shall, coaxes gold from
    bitter pills, drives nails into hands of
    saintly stand-ins, golfs it, and goes mad.
The living reed retails living room, bending will
    and Idahos of fried potato.
The answer shall to all questions come, as
    X, and psych out the drop-kick.
The press release shall be Calliostro's sawn
    half of woman, replete with Sphinx lore.
Psych out the Sphinx lore, and learn radio.
Quite the parable Byzantine!
Quite the quadraphonic exegete!
Quite the lampshade turncoat!
Bark up the wrong tree, and discover Vendible
    Eden, psych out the snake, cut cheese and
    croak.
Will walls that bite the hand that feeds,
    discover evil in the heart's-sprung wind
    machine, blow it by the drag bunt try,
    wax bitter with sullen rage, grow up,
    cool out, find the Cheez Whiz, breathe
    in the heart's Himalaya and prorate damnation.
All the new shall be as advent of drip-dry.
All on a clothesline, a chorus of panda pants.
All in the high fruitcake that is the summer sky.
Bite the hand that feeds, and crucify the
    wholesale gossamer.
Bite the hand that feeds with a gross of wind-up
    mechanical teeth.
Bark up the wrong tree, and psych out the living
    paraphrase, X in the name of X'.

However, as a person who has taught the art
    of rhetoric at the university level for six years,
    I must object,
Pam, I wasn't cruel X.
The staff of the NY Institute would like to help
    you free of charge, let's face it, X is Y.
Box lunch announces when it's right to be blond.
Quite style fair occurs on duck press at weak safety.
Curious slime abjurs the ode to clutch trouble
    and like how them choppers!
Let's face it, lice lurk in seventh heaven.
Let's face it, grunting hair is a bad
    way of supreme being.
Let's face it, white out darks the hip drive.
And all X are asizzle.
And and are all X without no Y.
Bashed piles of hip shoes drive wedged
    ointment into heaven's annex.
Incredible dirt packs a rod and back aches.
Free for all, and the last one to the bank on
    cheese got chimp doilies.
Foaming men till the eastward pluck of yawn.
I crowe at the shadow's gloaming:
"Is that you, Monsieur M?"
It replies not but huge hates refries the hip
    cold and busts up snakes.
Juices sanctifies the surviving snake eyes.
Chthonic murmurs infect the bathing
    beauties, quarantine the other people,
    hide the sagacious extinct, and suck up
    pure platonium, it's a quark hoot yup.
For X stands mute at the end of dominoes' rattle.

Green and re-green, all on slo-mo power drive.
Grim ovoid, speckled with mud flecks, rise and fly!
Bogus, wrong-way, multi-angled, lewd, caved-in.
Your shoes are worth fifteen dollars a day, and buddy
    we'll pay you hard cash money for them shoes
    you got because we believe in giving hard
    cash money to people such as yourself who
    as gots shoes on they feets sure you bet.

X the miracle slide until as two clicks.
X the votive glide wave shall.
X the maneater womanhater Arab oil
    conspiracy rakes up so much scree.
Turbaned bojars contract for our USA-
    style asphalt and blow wampum.
Case study of Arab chew upchucks on
    laudible chain link and hangs over.
Portentous Arab glue rats on outtakes
    of terminal childsex scene.
Lustful Arab dildoes busy American
    teeth with inscrutable bear hugs.
Had to chop off Arab hats to breathe
    monster American beefcake and sings.
Your shoes ties knots in Arab gibberish.
Your shoes ply the nautical dilemma.
Your shoes send godly messages to Arab
    stink and scorch them X to will done be.
Your shoes celestial amplify the predrone
    amidst a clangor of dog fires.
Arabs see green in slo-mo power dreams.
Arabs greet Christ and deny the unsavory
    chew of childsex scourge.
Arabs in heaps wail to their grease.
O slime comes over them, and they to dust are gone
    done.

Reasonable speed says one is not chew
    nor Cain nor airport too.
We death to gilt bright brighteye the unique.
Glum we death to him are, too, a glass.
Guess we not as are did, which parallax is
    of the false practice, being two.
The cycle of one's a crying shame, a hindoo
    marvel, a political pox with no yet till.
Light pearls down the guilt chute in blue
    air's bay, bangs around, is huffed and
    dies awhite, somewhere, you thinking of it.
Off it a while ago, the urgent only occasion.
Up in the proud air, the only are.

S clear to V, mouths full of nothings, the
    wings done.
V clear to T and all mismatched, lacquered
    by unique excellence to show but O.
Tilted until the only terminally is controlled,
    useless to be an answer, a seagull, a no.
No one gear turns the chill, an elbow's ruins
    kills a dead fly, spills the eye's spray.
Curse of flight by absence quite.
Night dumped in its things, hats, guns.
Don't they groan so, the empty, in boxes.
Balls of leathers, stacks of rifles, rum.
Casks of lord knows what, unforgettable flowers,
    candies, tablecloths.
Sacks of grain, foul rags, distant places on old
    maps, strange books, colors, noises.
Roads bewitched by blue winds scudding there.
An engraving too small to fathom, a weak signal,
    a caretaker, a tenant, a ghost.
Only now, with the red dusk, there is a real one, too.

"I" wants to build a system, to perfect an art.
"I" wants to make sense of maniacal hubbub,
    that blat and sting, wandering X dome of
    crushed glass and cement ears onto stone.
Foreground corn flames up and acid tests
    no Arab plot to steam our children
    in weird craving and wild rice the stew.
Arabs steam extraordinary Jews and
    glide to X their maker using our American
    nose, as it will have did, on positron.
Mark the background eat its shameless
    portion, all cheese, all thousands of
    immigrant Santas, keening and braying
    the foul music of their mountainous swamp.
What glues grinds the heart out and the sun's
    pop.
"I" pops and charges disaster.
"I" pops and bears the foregone conclusion
    to a guilty grave.

"I" barfs, bellows, curses the light and
  croaks.
"I" overturns the good child's hamper,
  corrupts the fair-haired, consumes the
  stolen cheese with antic glee and Y.
The foreground am did while the background
  popped.
Thy murk, as it shows, gulfs the quelled
  saints of clarity, and boschs them with
  the foul music of Albanian Sword Troupes.
A slo-mo who freights the fear weight with gold
  chomps and tails the donkey with clouds of
  vacuous tranquillity, celery, and pick-up-sticks.
Pause.

2

Gotta move sideways, all balled up like so.
Bang on the metal part, easy on the safety glass.
Goose the hayride, set fire to the frame house
  where the dominoes are stored.
Bank on losing radicals their jobs,
  the whole kit and kaboodle.
Bad days move upon you, switch shoes,
  up and do no good, nor did, nor shall.
You get up slow, moving sideways like a
  hailstorm on a billboard.
Moving sideways to escape detection, confess
  to the wrong instinct, are clocked good
  by someone also all balled up, sounds like
  goose the hayride in cretin overdrive,
  see stars doing crazy eights, and wake up
  looking out your earhole, the whole kit and
    kaboodle.
Where the dominoes are stored melts down
  musical chairs and grammar box did.
Numerous wrong numbers lose radicals
  their job and shore up the will have ought.
Massive cloddy shoes crowd the gap and refry

tomorrow in today's name because roadblocks
assign numbers to who's on first, what's on
second, I don't know's on third, the whole
kit and kaboodle, till the balled
up orange blast clocks you good, all aero-
spaced, to smithereens wafting, seven miles
above the vast encrudded seascape O.
Strange new girl, with starred cheek, checks it out.

Dodging pandas, the Fridge pops a long one, blacks
out, blows cover, mesmerizes alien popover,
hotdogs after half a sack, names the name,
denies the Christ, heaves a Hail Mary, gambles
for His garment at the foot of the cross,
bails out, and buys time with slo-mo
mystic rendition of Old Man Time with
tweezers twixt his pointy ear flaps, doing
the warty ham on rye, and no beanbag.
Surface of fog's an airframe cottonball did.
To time the cottontails' hop they got this
doorframe of bad news, round as love is, till.
Momotum at halftime favors the harebrained
who transpose the door to lure mock ducks
into that ghastly cigar bag, but no cigar.
X is radiant, Y the critical hypotenuse,
both tent the deform, rot the upscale quotidien,
charm the novice with tales of slo-mo algebras,
allergies of beatific Alhambras, yokes of
miter's nappies and clawed remnants of blues.
The mendicant riddle comes late to the party at
foggy Del Mar, blows the password, ties one
on, is bumble-bee'd at cluster X, grinds out
a tinny quatrain, finds lost conical hat of
catfool, snaps cosmic base wire, dunces the wig
set, uncoils mock tail at whye the whilom,
keeks a halo, and hallows a good girl's disppearance.

The crystallization counts for nothing,
fogged up, covered up, set afloat a
demon ship upon a painted ocean.
Disappears in actuality, the fat man
comes on strong, the little boy beyond,

doing the comic, cosmic, bail-out, overly
goobered.
Co-opt the actor, garden-variety presidents,
axe-murder the apple tree, barnstorm
the money people, and yawn the yawn.
Pay off X in the name of Y, advance
career through artful changes, adopt
the right style at the key moment, name
names, shed friends and family in a moment's
magic, be born again, Mister Celebrious
Bankrupt the notorious autodidact.
Can't eat the crystal bough.
Can't eat the empty heart.
Can't eat the beautiful death and the
barf of Del Mar journalism ruins
the moment even before the ink runs
out and the night swallows up all
understanding, cats, hats, thumb-
tacks and returns the demon ship,
rebuilt, reborn, recycled, renewed,
relived, rebopped, reappeared and redead.
For the center of the world is full of dead pandas.

Xerox your face, cold war America, and blacklist pandas, the homeless, the sea at Del Mar,
and Philip Blotely, the whole kit and kaboodle.
Xerox the sea at Del Mar, lose radicals
their jobs and pandas their pants.
Xerox Xs and shall be unto, us'ns and
your'ns, the leastmost hindpart up to
and including pick-up-sticks, but no cigar.
Retrench the watchful dummy till the
rubber seal hots up 6,000° F. and no cigar.
Look out for what's up and coming, tilt
fabled gossip columnist till iron fist
on tile floor out of velvet glove clanks.
Hanker for exquisite experience, grease
the pig, powder the nose, uncork new
pitch, conceal the grease ball, accept
accolades in unknown tongues, name
names and drop the big one sure.

Religion names names and accuses Philip
  of what will be if he mighta could.
How he on X feigned Y, hounded the Savior
  all his days, inspired his Xification, got
  Him no gumballs, derided Him in His final
  agony, gambled for His garments at the foot
  of the cross, the whole kit and kaboodle.
Philip Botely shows symptoms X.
Philip Boxley has not been vaccinated against
  hypofluvia.
Philip Batley has hypofluvia and no cigar, you bet, sure.

The sea at Del Mar rolls over and drop kicks
  Paleozoic moonmen so.
Clouds of heavy water seek nameless squeegie fruit
  and burp over the bedrock, bankrupt.
Burp over the bedrock and bump the
  seaweed this way and that and did so.
All quite so moon-baked, gray, indigo,
  and wrestled across the road after humankind.
The noise coughs and stupendous darks.
Such as who, they play whales and X
  and names under the mystic undertow.
Clobbered will to some far other, not
  here, but yonder, battered am for sure.
Scaly moonmen infest the dreaming
  brownbag beach and get no chew.
They attract condo sightlines, who see them
  not, confuse infrared also, heap tubes
  of mystic toothpaste, abstract the minds
  of drowned autodidacts and authorize
  innuendo in the name of all in love there.
The sea at Del Mar harks back, barfs up
  the sunken blacklists of yore, speaks not,
  prickles the uncanny, taildives, booms flat
  making a poetic mishmash of all states.
The sea at Del Mar veils its wrath, undrapes
  antediluvian rebop, tumbles, tosses, acts out
  ungodly gong, hunches over and punts the ball.

Here at Del Mar myriad momotum activates
  the sandman's retreat.

Ghost of snows haunt our febrile
 female imagos.
Until what sheetrock shall have done with,
 blues the high balloon, boxes the lust
 excessive in steppes of incremental overbite O.
For that there blue dye was done with
 up to ears and topmost.
Presidents soothe the lagging cheese.
Presidents excessive croon to the moon in June
 and jubilate with successive Somozas.
Presidents' hands are saddened by photos
 of biped ballot boxes of Philippine bonzos.
Presidents' furry hands are clean.
X bangs the ivories in the name of what chews
 the inmost heart, that American stone.
Momotum woofs down ungodly ballot boxes
 in the name of Y.
Momotum's the necessary crock, it moonrakes
 shuttle's embers, staffs the handjobs, pats
 our brown brothers, paints the town red, greases
 the uncubed and dusky part of the world, loses
 radicals their jobs, maintains the upbeat, though
 a little off.
It offs the longterm for the shortfall, X in the
 same old name of Y, whye O whye.

Strange dark trees in strange dark meadow
 leap up and mystify scratch the demon itch.
Nine of spades, what waterway tours the
 black heart crispy like and crepes cake?
Too doors the halcyon linchpin.
As quite the shame flies, up dusts the blue
 dome, innuendo innoculates the dead sheep
 and then some rebarbitive momotum X.
"I" flies to Mexico to seek grotesque food
 and X the heart wing's creak O.
Bogus hats on stilts arrives, praying
 for end to cosmic allergies.
Bogus Stilton cheese revives, offers dead dog
 as permanent placebo, dwarfs the moondrunk,
 waxes the Studebaker, arms the wrong insurrection,

posts no bills, panfries rebop, mumbos jumbo,
   clinches the pennant, coordinates lumbago,
   denies the Christ, crawls before the empty
   throne, weeps and dies.
Delmar Beach walks upright and swallow a
   cow.
Delmar Beach masticates canned heat.
Delmar Beach blacklists the whole shebang.
The sea quaffs perpetual empties.
The sea barfs and blows up.
The sea decants mystic fragrance.
The sea is who, who's on first, I don't know's
   on third.

For terminal hip issues, deaf and dumb,
   on the western sea, far.
Sinister reweave hyphenates adobe.
Sinistra my sister.
Sister, sister, what's on second?
   Who knows? Who's on first?
To blacklist brothers and sisters and feathers
   until what steam, from what vent, loops the loop.
Aeropile, gradient and vector, cruise
   control, demonic allergies, and no
   damn pills and no commonsense.
Aeolipile.
Wrench.
Gloom button.
Heap.
The zero circle verves.
Luster of broken premise.
Gauze.
   . . . not wing . . .
   . . . X upon X′ . . .
   . . . wastes of times' . . .
   . . . inks . . .
   . . . ! . . .
   . . . ? . . .
Tintagel. Wolf Rayet. Squire's Castle.
A roar out of the past of the.
A royal pain in the butt.

And the shadow of the flying wing hides
   the question of names and immortalizes
   stealth, the secrets of our political betrayals,
   our toying and dalliance, our love of fog.
For the panda is a bear and not a raccoon.
For you must only examine the teeth and
   tissue and optic nerve of the panda to
   ascertain that it is a bear and not
   a raccoon or a snowman, or a senator
   or a lawyer or a real estate speculator.
For the mystery of sexual pleasure is a
   mental as well as a physical thing,
   and the panda enjoys munching on
   bamboo, a taboo for his carnivore cousin
   the bear, and his distant relation the raccoon,
   who eats out of garbage cans but is known
   in the Netherlands as the "wash bear."
For the shadow of the flying wing creaks
   overhead after the flying wing itself has
   disintegrated in a cloud of paper clips
   doing crazy eights, the whole kit and kaboodle.
Could be mighta have did if, insofar as it
   mighta could, each word with a daisy on it,
   dings, so light, so aromatic, like dew on a
   buttercup.
Who the moon bops hops on first.
What's on second, a barnacle goose of chronic look-
   see.
I don't know's on third, the flying wing
   of the written word.

Which was X shall be Y, so make my day buddy
   and blow cover.
Warped trees absorb alien chewing gum to French
   gumball machine. Apes inquire after X. A
   sort of conical hat and the man underneath
   the hat lurch. The letter Y. The letter E. The letter
   S is inscribed upon the gumball machine.
Bodacious splotch renders ugly the pink sky.
We who dream disgust ourselves. The fury
   crumbles. A nifty pornographic

alleyway fills up with dead ends and X
to X′ the whole shebang bazookas with video
redeye and parturient reggae.
We wander off, unable to be mythic
in the Del Mar mists.
"I" has a gun, so make my day
and move you rconical hat.
"I" has another gun, so make my day
and strike up the band.
"I" shall take my genius elsewhere, so make my day
and burst, crouch in the hole, denature
the toxic waste, pardon the jailed has-been,
forgive the grammatical shibboleth, deplore
chronic bottleneck, give head to passing horse-
man, communicate with mole people using
monster woofer, explore the down-side momotum,
rage over the maddening minutiae of the truly bogus.

X all the way to X′ and clean as a whistle.
Go and find a fishing pole, one far off, far off
in the night, far off as far can be.
Go and find a place to fish, by some sea
or other, a live not a dead sea.
The C is in, all the way clear across the
hole in the head, the dark forest, the
eternal promise of love, clean as a whistle.
Go then and fish and happily, with weed.
Go then and fish whatever, for the political
itch spills not, and what sick thing
that barks, it too must croak, born of bone.
Go and think up mutability, clean as a whistle,
even if the topic abhore thee.
What it is to go fishing, that too wreaks its
proud wrath on small children, stomps
on ripe fruits, wears the fake moustachio,
obliterates the New England secondary, un-
twists the salt shaker's cap, and crawls
forth from under the stall's door, it being
locked from within, of the men's room.
Go and ask then, what sick thing barks it out . . .
Pourqoui les moustaches, monsieur?

Why the, the one foot shorter, in the heel, than
     its mate?
Why the bat in the teacup's crack?
Why the boring mountain of laundry?
Why the cornball psychology?

Chance hunt for black flag, with smell of pine,
     Nuevo black flag, *con olor a piño*.
The Fridge parries Boston steamed dinner
     and pops the gap, manifold.
Crossbuck reverse slant play, overly goobered
     failed in the first half, but chance hunt
     for black flag gained the Chinese checkers.
Chance Hunt offers X tickets to the show's
Inkblot test as Fridge flies and blows cover.
Wait a minute. You got a pitcher on the team?
Wouldn't this be a fine team without no pitcher?
I dunno. Tell me the pitcher's name.
Tomorrow.
You don't want to tell me today?
I'm telling you, man.
Then go ahead.
Tomorrow.
What time?
What time what?
What time tomorrow are you gonna tell me who's
     pitching?
Now, listen, bud, listen, who is not pitching.
Who is on first. What's on second. I don't know's on
     third.
You got a catcher?
Yes.
The catcher's name?
Today. And tomorrow's pitching.
I think I got it.
You think you got it.
I'm a good catcher, too, you know.
I know that.
I would like to play for St. Louis.
Well, I might arrange that.
I would like to catch. Now tomorrow's pitching
     on the team and I'm catching.

Yes.

Tomorrow throws the ball and the guy up bunts
    the ball.

Yes.

So when he bunts the ball, me bein' a good
    catcher, I want to get the guy out at first base.

So I pick up the ball and throw it to who?

Now that is the first thing you've said right!

I DON'T EVEN KNOW WHAT I'M TALKING
    ABOUT!

Ladies and gents, the sea's a wet, perjured barricade
    and

who cares how the world got to be this way? And hey,

who's the wiser? What sheerness

acts as if X brinks? A flutter of fool's boat

tails the soul how of wood to. Small plane person

buzzes the sea why. O huge coil of wet wind

hurries it up, parks the head, drifts, puzzles it

this way and that. Bang out was. Perdition doth. The
    quest for

candy leads the cloaked one, superstitious

of flying wing, to absolute seacoast it.

Which were which. To drill a hole to salt

abyss. Cavern of dreams, bats, portents, crime, fake

flamingoes. All glimmers with X and O.

You find conical hat and off
    to new brinks.

Pandas pounce upon and eat
    enviable hats.

Pandas have done up the agate's eye.

Pandas has did the cosmic soft-shoe swell.

Pandas were what done shelved enigmas.
    and came up beyond the soul of wood.

Pandas part and leave they large tracks.

"I" cares not who the world got, who it is that
    is mesmerized, afflicts with bonehead clearness,
    spite's sheerness, the whole shebang and pick-up-
    sticks.

Who's on first cares not how it got to be this way,

it is this way and he who boats it brooks no chew,
hops no campfire and croaks.
Pulverized rubble wrecks the season's clatter as a
panda ghost sinks to the center of the world
and sits there and sings.

Special thanks: George Ferencz, Zivia Flomenhaft, Bob Jewett; Pam Berlin, Jerry Dempsey; Patty Lynch, John Richardson, Brass Tacks Theatre; Leo Shapiro, The Shaliko Company; Yusef Bulos, Richard Caliban, Reg E. Cathey, Elzbieta Czyzewska, Nora Dunfee, Anne Hamburger, Mollie O'Mara, Cordelia Richards, Glen Santiago, Omar Shapli, David Van Tieghem, Douglas Durst, En Garde Arts; Scott Feldsher, Jim Simpson, Julian Webber, Sledgehammer Theater; Stephen Mellor, Michael Roth, Mark Russell, PS 122, Peg Santvoord Foundation; New Dramatists, Elana Greenfield, Kyle Chepulis, Greta Gundersen, Jan Leslie Harding, John Seitz, Eric Overmyer, Connie Congdon, Jeff Jones, Len Jenkin, and Yolanda.

For rights to: *Harm's Way, The Self-Begotten, The Bad Infinity,* and *Dracula,* contact: Helen Merrill, 435 West Twenty-third Street, #1A, New York, NY 10011; for rights to *Whirligig, Crowbar, 7 Blowjobs,* and *Terminal Hip,* contact: Brad Kalos, International Creative Management, 40 West Fifty-seventh Street, New York, NY 10019.